THE POLITICS OF INDUSTRIAL CLOSURE

Also by Tony Dickson

SCOTTISH CAPITALISM (*editor*)
CAPITAL AND CLASS IN SCOTLAND (*editor*)

Also by David Judge

BACKBENCH SPECIALISATION IN THE HOUSE OF COMMONS
THE POLITICS OF PARLIAMENTARY REFORM (*editor*)

The Politics of Industrial Closure

Edited by
Tony Dickson
Head of the Department of Sociology
Glasgow College of Technology

and
David Judge

Lecturer in Politics
Paisley College

MACMILLAN
PRESS

First published 1987

Published by
THE MACMILLAN PRESS LTD
Houndmills, Basingstoke, Hampshire RG21 2XS
and London
Companies and representatives
throughout the world

Typeset by Vine & Gorfin Ltd
Exmouth, Devon

Printed in Hong Kong

British Library Cataloguing in Publication Data
The Politics of industrial closure.
1. Plant shutdowns—Political aspects
— Great Britain
I. Dickson, Tony   II. Judge, David
338.4′767′0941   HD5708.55.G7
ISBN 0-333-40492-0 (hardcase)
ISBN 0-333-40493-9 (paperback)

Contents

Notes on the Contributors

Lesley Baddon is research assistant, Centre for Research into Industrial Democracy and Participation, Glasgow University.

Huw Beynon is reader, Department of Sociology and Social Anthropology, University of Durham.

Tony Dickson is head of Department of Sociology, Glasgow College of Technology

Patricia Findlay is research student, Nuffield College, Oxford University.

Nigel Haworth is lecturer in industrial relations, Department of Industrial Relations, University of Strathclyde.

David Judge is lecturer in politics, Department of Applied Social Studies, Paisley College of Technology.

Cliff Lockyer is senior lecturer, Department of Industrial Relations, University of Strathclyde.

Des McNulty is lecturer, Department of Sociology, Glasgow College of Technology.

Harvie Ramsay is lecturer, Department of Industrial Relations, University of Strathclyde.

Introduction

Plant closure has become a depressingly commonplace feature of industrial life in Britain in the 1980s. Millions of people, especially those in the regions away from the south-east corner of England, have experienced directly or indirectly the consequences of closure upon their own lives or upon those of friends, relatives or communities. Admittedly, the experience of closure is not new, and has been a recurrent feature of capitalist development as new technologies and new investment patterns led to closure of outdated and less profitable plants. What is new is that whereas in the past old plants closed to be replaced by new factories, production methods and new jobs, in the 1980s closure and job loss are no longer counteracted by plant openings and job gains. To talk of the 'collapse of manufacturing', therefore, is not mere hyperbole, but is stark reality.

This volume has at its heart the chronicle of industrial failure. We do not seek to absolve any section of British society of this failure, nor to offer monocausal explanations of manufacturing decline and its contribution to closure. The very complexity of this decline and the processes culminating in closure prevent both simple explanations and simple solutions. What we offer instead is an analysis of the *political* dimensions of closure. By political we mean the extent to which closure and its consequences involve choice, decision-making and the conscious exercise of power. This contrasts with the view that closure results from some set of immutable economic forces over which the participants have little or no control. Whilst recourse to economic rationality is invariably invoked by governments and managers alike to legitimise closure, this very rationality has an inherent political dimension.

Chapter 1 outlines the role of successive governments in Britain's protracted industrial decline. The decimation of manufacturing since 1979 and the contribution of Thatcherism to closure is identified as a consequence of established class relationships and the perverse culmination of extant state policies. The real significance of the Thatcher government rests, therefore, in its attempts to depoliticise the issue of closure and to acclimatise labour, specifically, and the public, more generally, to the 'inevitability' of closure. Indeed, the inculcation of a sense of futility in the face of closure has been one of Thatcherism's more notable 'achievements'. The rhetoric of TINA ('there is no alternative') has become the 'common sense' of many workers confronted by closure. The choices made by the state, government and capital have served in turn to foreclose choice for labour.

On the basis of the macro-analysis of chapter 1, the contributions to this book are arranged to develop sequential and widening levels of analysis. The first 'tier' of analysis is thus the community and the impact of closure and political responses at that level. In chapter 2, Des McNulty identifies the constraints which frustrate community responses to closure, and, more positively, discusses the 'pro-active' policies designed to counter job loss and plant closure at the local/regional level.

Chapter 3 examines workers' resistance to closure through the sit-in, and extends the level of analysis by examining the effects of industrial action upon the political consciousness of women workers. Patricia Findlay highlights the sense of solidarity engendered by common interests of women – as workers, as members of a community and as women – and points to the importance of women in developing the organisational capacities of labour to counter closure.

Huw Beynon's contribution (chapter 4) extends the analysis more explicitly on to the international plane through his discussion of the international restructuring of industry and the increased powers of management over national workforces in these conditions. Using the examples of coal and cars, he develops the concept of the 'frightened workforce', where fear is a key element in limiting worker resistance to closure. But fear and a sense of threat are not infallible guides to action; they can be inverted to galvanise workers into defensive action – as the miners' strike of 1984–85 so visibly illustrated. Beynon's chapter raises the wider question of the international frame within which both management and labour now have to develop their respective strategies.

The question of management strategy is addressed in chapter 5 by Cliff Lockyer and Lesley Baddon. Using the case study of the closure of the Linwood car plant, they examine both the general conditioning factors and the operational policy of closure. Whilst the legitimation of closure within the wider frame of international corporate strategy is crucial to management's strategy, internal political struggles within management in multinational corporations (MNCs) also have to be considered in explaining the specific choices involved in closure.

Chapter 6 provides a theoretical overview of management and labour strategies in the process of the restructuring of international production. Through a comparison of orthodox and radical approaches to MNCs, Howarth and Ramsay reveal the complexities of the decision-making processes within such organisations. They illuminate both the coherence and the potential divisions and fragmentation within management decision-making. If labour is to contest the processes of restructuring and closure, then the labour movement has to understand the system of management decision-making, systematise its own institutional structures and develop its informal and formal political organisation at local, state and international levels. Yet for workers to extend their organisational horizons beyond their immediate place of work is in itself a political step.

It is that step which is examined in chapter 7. Identified there are the crucial variables and contradictions that need to be resolved in the construction of alternative strategies. To overcome the present deficiencies of counter-closure strategies, an alternative 'political economy of labour' has to be constructed, based upon the understanding that the needs of people should be placed before the requirements of impersonal market criteria in industrial and economic decision-making. Whether the proposed strategy has any realistic chance of success will be for the reader to decide. However, we hope that this volume will contribute to the debate on closure and better inform that debate of the political dimensions of closure.

Finally, we wish to record our thanks to the untiring and (relatively) uncomplaining efforts of Maureen Alexander and Margaret Bright in typing, retyping and re-retyping the many different versions of the chapters that appear in this book.

TONY DICKSON
DAVID JUDGE

Paisley, April 1986

1 The British State, Governments and Manufacturing Decline
David Judge and Tony Dickson

The collapse of manufacturing in Britain since 1979 is the culmination of a more protracted decline. Most sectors of the economy have been hit by the post-1979 recession, but it is manufacturing industry which has been most severely affected. Indeed, the process of 'de-industrialisation' is peculiarly, some would say almost uniquely, a British problem (see Smith, 1984, p. 34). No other advanced industrialised nation has experienced the contraction in manufacturing employment and the falls in output that have afflicted the United Kingdom. Whilst most OECD countries have suffered a setback in industrial production in the 1980s, they have, none the less, maintained production levels well above those of the UK.

So, why has manufacturing industry in Britain fared so badly? If the question is simple, the answer is complex. In fact, various competing answers abound. These range from economic explanations – the failure of investment policies (Pollard, 1984), the inability to maintain world trading shares in manufactures (Singh, 1977), the erosion of the industrial base through the expansion of the public sector (Bacon and Eltis, 1978), the dominance of finance capital (Longstreth, 1979); through social causes – an inappropriate educational system (Musgrave, 1967), an anti-entrepreneurial, anti-business culture (Nairn, 1982), the nature of British trade-unionism (Kilpatrick and Lawson, 1980); to political factors, such as the absence of coherent and lasting industrial policies (Smith, 1984), or the vagaries of adversarial politics (Chandler, 1984). In themselves, such monocausal explanations have proved to be incapable of adequately answering our initial question. A satisfactory answer can only be found through a comprehensive examination of the political, economic and social factors contributing to manufacturing decline in Britain. This chapter seeks to provide just such an examination and to use the state as the focusing point around which this analysis can be conducted; for the intermediation of the state in the relationships between the various fractions of capital, and between capital and labour, serves to define and explain the relative position of manufacturing in the British economy and its cumulative weakness.

The striking feature of the development of the British state since the 17th century has been its subordination to 'an independent sphere of private interests and private exchange' (Gamble, 1985, p. 72). As Stuart Hall (1984, p. 10) points out, 'the organisational principles which enabled commerce and trade to expand – free trade, the laws of the market and contract – were also the principles on which the new relationships between state and individual were modelled'. In the operationalisation of these principles, the economic interests of the propertied classes became conjoined with the political structure of the liberal state. This conjunction has subsequently been modified, but never fundamentally altered. Hence, the existing state structure proved flexible enough to accommodate the rise of manufacturing and the irrevocable changes wrought to the class system in the 19th century. The nature of the state, and its overarching concern with the preservation of the system of free exchange, certainly facilitated this accommodation, but so, too, did the nature of the dominant class. For the commercialised aristocracy in Britain had mutual interests with the emergent bourgeoisie – in profit, property, contract and trade; and these interests served to fuse a bourgeois–aristocratic alliance in England that was to be crucial to the development of the economy and the state in industrialised Britain.

The significance of this alliance for some Marxists such as Nairn (1982) and Anderson (1964) is that an old-style mercantilism, a limited and old-bourgeois form of capitalism, underpinned British industrialisation in the 19th century. In this sense, the seeds of Britain's long-term economic decline were endemic within its initial industrial success. The emphasis of this old-style capitalism was upon short-term profit maximisation, small enterprises, trade, and finance-oriented investment. In turn, this emphasis reflected the values of the established commercial and financial classes; and according to this interpretation, industrialism was unable to challenge the hegemony of the aristocratic classes. The essence of the Nairn–Anderson thesis, therefore, is that traditional values, an aristocratic ethos which was anti-industrial, prevailed throughout the 19th century and subverted the establishment of a separate identity on the part of the emergent industrial bourgeoisie. This value system simultaneously denigrated the worth of entrepreneurial endeavour and industrialism whilst emphasising the importance of financial and commercial endeavour in the world market. Hence, the very nature of the dominant class alliance as it developed in the 18th century, an alliance which germinated the industrial revolution and propagated the liberal state, ultimately served to frustrate a second industrial revolution required to maintain Britain's economic pre-eminence in the late 19th century.

The Nairn–Anderson thesis of unbroken aristocratic hegemony has not gone unchallenged. Most recently, Paul Warwick (1985) has demonstrated the discontinuities in this aristocratic cultural ascendancy. He argues that by the early 19th century the values of entrepreneurial endeavour and material enrichment outweighed aristocratic pretensions. However, the very success of 'bourgeois ideological production', and the propagation of the values of egalitarian openness, meritocracy and social mobility inherent within liberalism, came to pose its own threat to the newly ascendant class. Consequently, the very class which had gained from the openness of 18th century aristocratic society sought to restrict working class access to economic, social and political power. Social exclusiveness came rigidly to demarcate the upper levels of the social hierarchy. Thus, although members of the working class gained selective admission to the franchise in return for their quiescence and 'responsibility', they were simultaneously excluded from key social and state positions. The invention by the Victorian bourgeoisie of the role of the naturally privileged and superior 'gentleman' played a vital role in this strategy of exclusion. As part of this invention, an educational system was 'deliberately constructed to create class barriers and inhibit mobility across them' (Warwick, 1985, p. 123), a civil service was developed whose upper ranks constituted a 'sort of (bourgeois) free masonry' (see Leys, 1983, p. 234), and a military system was established wherein the commanding officers were recruited almost exclusively from public schools. In this process, the relatively fluid structure of late 18th century society was transformed into a static and class-divided society by the beginning of the 20th century. The significance of this cultural inversion for our analysis is that: 'if the price for creating this new society was the loss of technological and industrial leadership . . . it was, apparently, a price influential Victorians thought worth paying' (Warwick, 1985, p. 123).

This cultural revolution was, however, only the most apparent manifestation of the complex economic, social and political changes taking place in late 19th century Britain. The acquisition of an imperialist mentality by the British ruling class was another, and a natural response to the expansion of industrial capitalism on a world scale in the last decades of the 19th century. The manner in which British capitalists chose to respond to the industrial competition of Germany and the United States in this period set the pattern for manufacturing for most of the following century. Indeed, the imperial legacy helps to explain the industrial decline of Britain almost a century later.

FREE TRADE IMPERIALISM: THE FRACTURING OF CAPITAL'S INTERESTS

The decades at the end of the 19th century and the beginning of the 20th century were crucial in the development of the British economy and the British state. In this period, British pre-eminence in the world economy continued; with British supremacy contingent upon the internationalism of the world economy. Not surprisingly, therefore, the state sought to promote, and even enforce, this internationalism through free trade and imperial preference policies. Both industrial and finance capital in Britain derived benefits from the pursuit of free trade imperialism. On the one hand, industrial capital could still secure manufacturing growth and increased output through exports to an informal and formal empire. By retreating into empire markets, significant sectors of British industry therefore escaped the need to compete against the new industrial powers of Germany and the United States in the developed markets. Moreover, exports to the undeveloped world secured high levels of employment in the staple industries in Britain.

Finance capital, on the other hand, had a more universal interest in internationalism. British investments overseas were seen to be one of the most powerful means of integrating the international economy. Simply, British investments fuelled world trade. Increasingly, as all the major financial networks came to be routed via the City of London, so an integrated monetary system came to be centred on the British Central Bank. Whilst the Bank of England was nominally a private company, it acted, nevertheless, to promote national financial interests. It did this through maintaining the stability of the pound, ensuring the operation of the gold standard, and by using the bank rate to influence the international flow of capital in Britain's favour. In these circumstances, free trade and the international role of sterling were believed to be the preconditions of Britain's economic pre-eminence and prosperity. Britain's financial interests came to be treated synonymously with Britain's national interest. State policies came to reflect the 'universal' interests of finance capital. Indeed, the 'City's dominance has been so complete that its position has often been taken as the quintessence of responsible financial policy' (Longstreth, 1979, pp. 161–2).

That the parameters of economic policy have been largely set by finance capital since the late 19th century has arisen in large part because industrial capital has been unwilling, or unable, to assert its requirements as *national* requirements for the well-being of the whole economy. For long periods in the 19th century, industrial capital was not required to assert its requirements given the compatibility of its interests with those of finance capital over the freedom of international trade, the need for a strong currency and the availability of short-term loans. What British industrialists never systematically sought, nor gained, was state recognition of their interests as being synonymous with the wider national economic interest. This contrasted sharply with the position in the newly industrialised states. In Germany and Japan, for instance, the state and industrial capital combined resources not only to protect and subsidise domestic industry but also to foster close links between the banks and heavy industry; to provide and manage a basic infrastructure; to encourage cartels; and to mobilise strong nationalist ideologies. In Britain, however, industrialists were unable or unwilling to influence the state to protect the national economy via tariffs, or to intervene, institutionally, to promote industrial development. Paradoxically, therefore, the commitment of industrialists in the first industrial nation to the icons of *laissez-faire* principles and the market inhibited their ability to utilise the state to further their interests long after changing international conditions required such intervention to compete effectively with their main rivals in the USA and Germany. The hegemony of finance capital thus served to insulate state policies from such pressure as was occasionally exerted by industrial capital.

The dominance of finance capital over state policy is most clearly visible at those times of rapid change and increased competition in the international economy. At such times the respective interests of the two fractions of capital tend to segment and become differentiated. This was apparent at the turn of the 19th century over the issues of protection and foreign investment. On the question of Tariff Reform:

> When ... Joseph Chamberlain tried to rally the manufacturing interest in the Conservative Party behind the cause of protection for domestic industry, in the hope of launching a manufacturing revival, he was bitterly opposed by the financial interests. He and the manufacturers were decisively defeated. (Eatwell, 1982, pp. 65–6).

Similarly, on the issue of investment overseas, the interests of finance capital and domestic industry were fractured by the end of the 19th century. In the second half of the 19th century foreign investment multiplied rapidly; to the extent that by 1875 the cumulative net total of British assets abroad passed £1 billion, doubled to over £2 billion in 1900 and doubled again to £4 billion by 1914 (Crouzet, 1982, p. 365). A case can be made, however, that the export of capital neither directly nor detrimentally affected domestic investment in British manufacturing, as the latter was traditionally based upon reinvestment of profit by individual firms, or by short-term bank loans, which were readily available, or by raising finance within an entrepreneur's family. However, as foreign competition increased at the end of the century, and as the need to invest in new plant and technologies became necessary to enter the second phase of industrialisation – as, in other words, investment needed to be long-term and extensive – so investment overseas restricted the opportunities for growth and structural change in domestic industry. At this stage the interests of finance and industrial capital diverged. This divergence was reinforced institutionally in the divorce between the banking system and industry. Unlike the German banking system, which provided not only long-term finance, but also actively participated in industrial decision-making, the English banks played a passive and restrictive role. They did not conceive of an active industrial role – to encourage technological development, to stimulate industrial concentration or to promote effective organisation of the productive process. Generally, banks were reluctant to provide risk capital or long-term loans to British industry. The safety of capital investment, the defence of the free movement of capital, and the maintenance of the value of sterling were the basic preoccupations of the financial institutions. These preoccupations, which had tied industrial capital to the financial sector for much of the 19th century, now separated the two sectors by the end of the century. And this separation has underpinned the decline of manufacturing industry throughout the 20th century.

Not only was the policy of free trade imperialism crucial in the development of the relationships within British capital at the end of the 19th century, but it was also of significance in determining the relations between labour and industrial capital. In fact, by the last quarter of the 19th century, the state in Britain, partly in response to increasing democratisation and to a growing working class electorate, had legalised the status of trade unions and acknowledged some of the collective rights of workers. In this context, New Unions of unskilled workers developed alongside the older craft unions and for the most part the new organisations adopted craft union practices and sought to defend past gains and acquired customs (see Clarke, 1973, p. 12). Significantly, the customs and norms defended were those which predated mass production techniques. Thus a peculiarly British dimension to the organisation of labour in manufacturing was propagated – one which combined a defensive orientation with decentralised and unco-ordinated union structures. The impact of this dimension was considerable, for, although reorganisation of production was a continuous process in the 19th century, the strength of the trade unions and their willingness to resist changes on the grounds of past practice meant that concessions on work practices by British manufacturers were more common than in the newly industrialised countries. Indeed, as Kilpatrick and Lawson (1980, p. 90) argue, 'frequently these concessions provided the basis for further resistance so that one way or another industrial change proceeded more slowly than it would have done in the absence of resistance, and proceeded much more slowly than in other countries'. One consequence of such resistance was that British industrialists tended to avoid confrontations over the restructuring of production processes when other alternatives existed. British entrepreneurs, therefore, largely sidestepped conflict over the introduction of those new production techniques required to compete with German and US industries by directing their attention to the markets of the empire and the undeveloped world. Industrial capital and labour alike thus had a vested interest in imperialism and in insulating themselves from the effects of increased competition in the European markets.

INDUSTRIAL DEVELOPMENT BETWEEN THE WARS

The striking thing about economic development in Britain in the interwar years is how the legacies of 19th century economic pre-eminence continued to bind policy-makers to attitudes unsuited to the vastly different conditions pertaining in the new international economy and political order. Economic policy continued to be guided by the City's conception of 'sound financial principles'. Generally, the internationalist perspective of finance capital was undiminished, as the return to the Gold Standard in 1925 demonstrated. This move was seen 'as an expression of London's rightful place in the world financial system, as the only basis for the revival of British capitalism and for the imposition of a world monetary order' (Longstreth, 1979, p. 166). Few industrialists were willing to question such assertions. And only the most percipient industrialists sought assurances that the re-establishment of the Gold Standard would not curtail domestic credit. Only with hindsight did industry see the cost of this financial policy to be a depressed domestic market, increased unemployment and further damage to its international competitiveness through an over-valued exchange rate.

The irony of the international orientation of British finance capital was that its external aspirations for free trade and sterling were finally checked by the operations of the international financial markets themselves. The Wall Street Crash of 1929 and the general turmoil of banking and financial transactions led to pressure on sterling and the eventual decision to float the pound in 1931. Even in taking this decision the Bank of England's stated priority was to 'conserve the international utility of the London money market' (W. A. Brown quoted in Pollard, 1983, p. 145). Nonetheless, the ending of the Gold Standard marked a significant retreat by finance capital, a position compounded by the introduction of imperial tariff policy in 1932. Yet this retreat was enforced by external pressures. Within Britain, finance capital still maintained its hegemony over the state's policy-makers. This was demonstrated in the commitment of successive governments to balanced budgets and their refusal to intervene in the capital market through national investment banks or industrial development corporations.

When the state did intervene in the inter-war years it was not part of a coherent or developed industrial policy. A series of *ad hoc* interventions facilitated company mergers and the extension of monopolies, but invariably for defensive or protectionist reasons rather than on strategic grounds. By 1939, therefore, the British state was more interventionist and more protectionist than at any stage in its previous industrial history. Yet the state lacked, because its policy-makers did not conceive, nor were required by industry to conceive of, coherent industrial policy. Successive governments presided over a complex mixture of advances and retreats in industry. Advances were made in the modernisation and expansion of 'second phase' industries – in chemicals and motor manufactures, for example. At the same time, however, the old staple industries continued to decline, with the subsequent loss of employment. More generally, the retreat from free competition effectively meant in Hobsbawm's (1968, p. 183) graphic phrase that 'Britain became a non-competing country at home as well as abroad'. The changes made in the inter-war period thus did not constitute a fundamental restructuring of the relations between the state and industry in Britain. The legacy of the 19th century was still to fix governments' attention upon external policy, even though the ending of free trade and the liberal world economy redirected their activities towards domestic policy. But in the arena of internal economic policy, British governments were ill at ease and ill-prepared to take action. Only with the recovery of an international role for sterling and the revitalisation of City financial institutions after the Second World War was the mismatch resolved between governments' external orientations and their immediate policy concerns.

1945 AND AFTER: THE RESILIENCE OF FINANCE CAPITAL

The end of the Second World War heralded a phase of reconstruction in the major economies ravaged by war. In comparison with the crippled economies of Germany and Japan, British industry was better placed to recapture its export markets. This was despite its inheritance of underinvestment, labour-intensive production processes and inefficiencies. In fact, within a year pre-war production levels had been achieved, and increased by 30 per cent up to 1950. Correspondingly, exports reached their pre-war levels in 1946 and rose a further 70 per cent in the next four years (Smith, 1984, p. 76). Britain thus made a head start on its competitors. However, once more British industry was to be rapidly overtaken as its historical legacies came to prevail over the short-term innovations of the war period.

The resilience of financial capital and the gradual reassertion of its political strength was one major legacy. After the war Britain was allowed to act as a junior partner in the new open international order imposed by the US. Sterling retained its position as a major international currency, both because it was the unit of exchange for the sterling area and also because of its role in international trade (see Pollard, 1983, pp. 362–4; Coakley and Harris, 1983, pp. 33–5). The City's provision of financial services for the world and its traditional pattern of trading thus locked Britain more firmly into the new economic order than most of its major competitors; and the defence of sterling in this order was a major priority. As a result, British governments had little option but to maintain the sterling area, and, given the City's pre-eminence, to adopt policies favourable to the free flow of capital for portfolio and industrial investment overseas. For most of the first quarter of a century after the war, therefore, British governments were preoccupied with the 'problem of the Sterling Balances'. Successive administrations either sought to force overseas holders of sterling to hang on to the currency, or after 1958 and the convertibility of these balances, to persuade them to continue holding sterling. Maintaining confidence in sterling was of paramount importance for British governments.

Confidence in sterling was directly correlated with the British balance of payments. It is no coincidence, therefore, that the 'balance of payments was the focus of the one really determined effort of planning in which the [1945–51] Labour government engaged' (Cairncross, 1985, p. 503). Nor was it by chance that the stabilisation policy of successive Chancellors for over twenty years was determined by the external balance. A preoccupation with the balance of payments has been the continuous thread of British post-war economic policy (Gamble and Walkland, 1984, pp. 88–9). Throughout, British economic policy-makers looked at the world with 'traders' and bankers' eyes' (Pollard, 1984, p. 35) with their gaze firmly fixed on the fluctuations and uncertainties of the international financial and currency markets.

It was, and is, this international focus of British policy-makers which has proved to be so detrimental to industrial regeneration in Britain. Yet, the influence of internationally-oriented finance capital upon manufacturing decline is not direct. There is no simple correlation between the outflow of capital and the level of investment in domestic industry. Instead, there is a complex of forces leading to investment failure. It cannot be assumed that financial investment overseas could, or would, have been invested in British industry. Rather, it can be argued that 'the policies intended to maintain the position of sterling discouraged and distorted industrial investment through high interest rates to attract foreign funds and prevent the flight of "hot money", . . . and recurrent bouts of deflation to restrain home demand and "free" resources for export production' (Jessop, 1980, p. 32). In other words, the needs of the domestic economy tended to be subordinated to the maintenance of Britain's international financial networks. This subordination was apparent in the 'stop–go' cycle of the 1950s and 1960s when what was effectively stopped was domestic investment and the 'will to invest' (Pollard, 1984, p. 49). After every crisis, the ability of British industry to 'go' for growth was impaired by the restriction of investment. The problem was simply that 'whenever something went wrong with the balance of payments, domestic investment was hit on the head' (Eatwell, 1982, p. 129). But in taking a smack at investment in this manner manufacturing productivity was undermined, and this in turn contributed to a progressive deterioration in the balance of payments to which governments then had to react. Government reaction invariably aimed at sustaining foreign confidence in sterling and the integrity of British financial institutions.

It should not be assumed, however, that there is always a direct and explicit contradiction between the interests and requirements of finance capital and industrial capital. Such conflict is dependent upon both fractions acting consistently as homogeneous and discrete entities. This, however, is not the case. Within the industrial sector, for instance, there are significant differences between small and large firms, between multinational and national conglomerates and between export- and domestic-oriented manufacturers. Indeed, the growth of the monopoly sector, particularly after 1960, has witnessed the largest British manufacturing firms increasingly engaged in transnational operations. In the twenty year period 1950–70 the proportion of British firms operating six or more foreign subsidiaries increased from one-fifth to one-half, and by 1970 all of the top 100 manufacturing companies had become multinational (Gamble, 1985, p. 110). Britain is now second only to the US in the number of multinational corporations. The importance of this fact is that multinational corporations' investment decisions are based on long-term plans and a global outlook. The domestic manufacturing base and market is thus not the single, nor even major, consideration for these companies. Their dependence upon the viability of production within the UK is much reduced. In consequence, something resembling an 'overseas alliance' between the internationally-oriented manufacturing and financial sectors has operated for much of the post-war period. This has left nationally-based industrial capital in the same political position it had occupied all century 'namely that of junior partner to financial interests that were not directly geared to national economic reconstruction' (Coates, 1985, p. 48).

If the term 'overseas alliance' is therefore to have any meaning, it must also encompass the role of the state alongside the international perspectives of British finance and multinational capital. The success of internationally-oriented capital in defining the economic interests of the state as its own was noted earlier. But not only has Britain's economic policy been imbued with an external perspective, British defence and foreign policies have also, as a corollary, been conceived on a global scale.

The consequences of British governments' fixation with international status have been profound for manufacturing industry. Successive governments have been ensnared in an imperialist mentality, directly expressed through the maintenance of the empire in the immediate post-war period and cruelly exposed in the Suez debacle; or indirectly observed in support of US imperialist excursions. Moreover, British fears of militarist expansion by the Soviet Union, and the consequences of this for its alliance with the USA, served to sustain a world military role long after Britain's industrial performance warranted, or could afford, such a role. The very cost of the military budget itself impeded the competitive growth of British industry. Investment in key sections of British manufacturing was effectively crippled, and the momentum of the export drive was slowed, by the British rearmament programme at the crucial time of reconstruction in the early 1950s (see Cairncross, 1985, p. 231; Aaronovitch, 1981, p. 70). Thereafter, the level of defence expenditure has detrimentally affected the balance of payments (Calvocoressi, 1979, p. 217), skewed the Research and Development effort in Britain (see below p. 15) and has been maintained at higher levels than for any other OECD country other than the US.

THE STATE, MANUFACTURING AND THE WORKING CLASS

A further legacy contributing to Britain's industrial malaise has been the particular operation of the defensive power of organised labour. The inheritance of British trade unions was a resistance to change and decentralised structures. Unlike their major European and Japanese counterparts, they had neither been destroyed by the state in the 1930s nor fragmented by internal divisions. If anything, the British trade union movement emerged from the Second World War intact and strengthened. Indeed, the tentative incorporationist strategy pursued by the state in the decade before the outbreak of war culminated in the effective working partnership between the government and the General Council of the TUC in the 1940s. The major achievement of labour in this period was to secure the commitment that governments had 'as one of their primary responsibilities the maintenance of a high and stable level of employment' (Cmnd 6527, 1974). This commitment shaped the direction of state policy for a whole generation after 1945.

Full employment effectively undermined the disciplinary sanction of industrialists against labour, so strengthening the bargaining power of trade unions. Simultaneously, the decentralised system of collective bargaining was enhanced, with shop-floor institutions increasingly replacing the formal, national union machinery. These informal institutions, of shop steward and joint shop steward committees, establised close control over many key aspects of the production process – not least the terms on which reorganisation would, or would not, occur. Workplace collective bargaining in the context of full employment, therefore, served to slow the pace of the technological restructuring of British industry. Throughout the post-war period this defensive power of workers was demonstrated in 'restrictive practices concerning demarcation, apprenticeships, manning levels, work rates, overtime, etc., and in shop-floor resistance to reorganisation of the labour process' (Jessop, 1980, p. 35). In turn, this resistance reinforced the reluctance of significant sectors of industry to re-equip or restructure their British plants. In particular, British multinationals looked overseas to areas where labour was cheap, unorganised and compliant, and where the rate of exploitation was higher than in Britain.

In contradistinction to the international perspective of multinational industrial capital, finance capital and successive economic policy-makers, the primary focus of labour in Britain has been domestic, introspective and limited. The horizons of labour interests have been drawn at plant, or at best company, level. The defence of working conditions, customs and wages within these horizons has been the paramount objective of trade unions. The ramifications of this posture beyond these horizons has not preoccupied the participants in the decentralised bargaining process. Even if a 'national' interest has been articulated (and successive governments have attempted just this in their various incomes policies) the very decentralisation of the bargaining process in industry has militated against consistent action in pursuit of this interest. Paradoxically, the very activities and policies of governments in promoting the 'national' interest have merely reinforced the defensive and parochial orientation of British trade unions. Equally paradoxically, the very strength of trade union defensiveness designed to maintain employment stability has inherent within it the prospect of long-term destabilisation of employment. It has been argued, for example, that in major recessions the inflexibilities in work organisation may contribute to higher unemployment by ensuring that significant readjustments of labour take place through the closure of plants (Bowers, Deaton and Turk, 1982, p. 146).

INDUSTRIAL POLICY: 1945–79

Post-war Britain has not had a settled industrial policy. At best there has been a series of policies or overlapping approaches each having its 'own period of prominence, (and) each relying less than it might have on what went before' (Morris and Stout, 1985, p. 862). In part this discontinuity stems from the free-market legacy of the 19th century, with industrial firms retaining a predilection to keep government at 'arm's length' from their own operations. Equally significantly, governments have been unable to develop a consensual base upon which coherent industrial policies could be founded. The inability of the industrial sector to assert its interest as a hegemonic interest has itself frustrated the development of the foundations of an extensive state policy towards industry. As noted above, governments have largely attempted to influence industry through macro-economic policy. However, by the 1950s the unsophisticated techniques of macro-economic management convinced policymakers of the need to supplement demand management with microeconomic, supply-side policies to regulate manufacturing output. But, if governments could not fail to appreciate the linkage of macro- and micro-economic policies, they, nevertheless, remained unclear as to how they were linked and related to each other. This confusion was only increased by the divergent pressures arising from industry, and by the atomised and subordinate status of manufacturing within the state itself. As a consequence, industrial policy has remained unstable, incoherent and basically reactive. Policies have ebbed and flowed with the return of successive governments, leaving only the thinnest sedimentary strata of consistent policy upon which industry has been able to build.

The basic sediment of industrial policy has formed around regional policy. With its origins in the Special Area legislation of the 1930s, post-war regional policy up to 1979 was designed to alleviate regional unemployment problems. Its initial focus after 1945 was to safeguard and create new jobs in the assisted areas. Later in this period, however, priority was afforded in practice, if not in principle, to modernisation, rationalisation and the fostering of investment in industry *irrespective* of the employment consequences (Martin and Hodge, 1983, p. 136). A second sedimentary stratum washed over by successive government policies is selective support for ailing industries. Labour and Conservative governments alike have committed vast sums of public money to support declining industries. Amongst the most celebrated recipients of such aid have been Rolls-Royce, Upper Clyde Shipbuilders, British Leyland, Chrysler (UK), and International Computers Limited. A large part of this *ad hoc* approach to government aid to such industries was, of course, itself a legacy of the previous bargain on full employment implicitly struck between post-war governments and unions. A fear of the electoral consequences of being seen to depart from this bargain thus conditioned the actions of successive governments. Nonetheless, whilst governmental assistance matched labour's defensive approach to jobs, industrial capital remained ambivalent to such aid – pragmatically accepting *ad hoc* interventions on the one hand, yet, on the other, proclaiming a general ideological antipathy to such 'encroachments'.

A third stratum of industrial policy, more continuous and strategic than the first two, can be categorised as 'innovative policy'. Its main component has been the stimulation of new products and processes through Research and Development (R & D). As early as 1916 the state recognised the importance of R & D by encouraging industry to develop its own research associations and by directly financing research in universities through the Department of Scientific and Industrial Research. In 1948 the National Research Development Corporation (NRDC) was established to stimulate inventions deemed to be in the national interest. More recently, the Labour government in 1977 introduced the Product and Process Development Scheme (PPDS), and the Microprocessor Application Project (MAP) in 1978. Both schemes were designed in part to finance and stimulate innovation.

There has thus been no shortage of agencies and finance for R & D. Britain in fact devotes around the same proportion of its industrial output to R & D as other major industrialised nations. But, significantly, British governments have chosen to direct state R & D expenditure in different directions to those of her European and Japanese competitors. Over fifty per cent of British R & D resources has been devoted to military projects – primarily aviation and military electronics. This is yet more evidence of the legacy of Britain's imperial past and the fixation of the state's policy-makers with military and defence matters. The consequence of this R & D strategy has been that relatively few resources have been devoted to the dynamic civil industrial growth sectors of the economy. As Smith (1984, p. 93) concludes, the result of this 'research and development disaster was that British industry was progressively outstripped in technological terms by rival producers'.

A fourth, and intermittent, stratum of post-war policy has developed around the concepts of 'industrial strategy' and 'indicative planning'. Although this is not the place to dwell upon the details of planning since 1945, it is worth noting the reasons why a fully fledged industrial strategy has never developed. The success of 'planning' overseas in industrially innovative countries such as Japan and France – particularly France – attracted the attention of both major political parties in Britain. At various stages, up to 1979, all governments acknowledged the need for a forum within which consensus around these strategies could be built. Equally, since the late 1950s and the experience of 'stop-go', all governments have recognised that macro- and micro-economic policies are mutually dependent and that the specific problems of manufacturing industry could not be dealt with by macro-economic policies alone. In addition, the Labour party, in its more radical phases, has been attracted to the idea of planning, to facilitate a transition to 'democratic socialism', or more generally out of a recognition that market forces alone have signally failed to regenerate British industry.

This commitment to planning on the part of the Labour party has undoubtedly cooled the enthusiasm of the Conservative party for such policies. Nonetheless, both parties in office have utilised a range of 'planning' structures – though admittedly with different levels of enthusiasm and official commitment. Thus the Attlee government engaged in a limited attempt to initiate an industrial strategy through the introduction of Development Councils; the Macmillan government dabbled with indicative planning in the early 1960s with the establishment of the National Economic Development Council and its 'assessment of possibilities' for economic growth; the Wilson government after 1964 devised not only a coherent, ambitious, but flawed National Plan, but also the corresponding institutional arrangement of the Department of Economic Affairs. Even the Heath administration, after its initial flirtation with neo-liberalism, was, by 1972 and the Industry Act of that year, back within the fold of administrative planning for aid to industry and an interventionist strategy. Indeed, it was within the framework of the 1972 Act that much of the 1974–79 Labour government's industrial strategy was implemented (see Grant, 1982, p. 50). But this government more strongly and explicitly espoused a long-term industrial strategy and sought to develop an institutional framework, around the Sector Working Parties of the NEDC and the newly established National Enterprise Board, within which the strategy could be effected. Yet, for all that successive governments have accepted the need for some form of planning, the results have been modest. Either the institutional structures have been stunted, as in the case of the NEDC, or short-lived, as in the case of the Development Councils (1947–53), the DEA (1965–69), the IRC (1966–70), and the NEB (1975–81).

One reason for the discontinuities in 'planning' in Britain has been the antipathy of industrial capital both to the concept itself and its associated institutional structures. The opposition has reached its peak in periods of Labour governments and 'socialist' planning; but even Conservative flirtations with indicative planning in the early 1960s, or in Heath's industrial 'strategy' after 1972, were respectively greeted with little, or no, enthusiasm. The most powerful explanation, however, circles back to a constant theme of this chapter, namely, the preoccupation of all British governments with the balance of payments and the exchange rate. Put at its simplest: the micro-economic policies of successive governments have been undermined by their preoccupation with macro-economic policies. It is significant, for example, that the distinction between macro- and micro-economic policies was reinforced in the 1960s in the institutional separation of the Treasury from the DEA. The Treasury's overriding concern with the value of sterling ultimately buried the National Plan. Similarly, the industrial strategy of the Labour government between 1974–79 was neutralised, and on the question of unemployment significantly reversed, through its subordination to the economic imperatives of macro-economic policies. When confronted by the speculative movements of foreign currency and the unwillingness of foreign holders of sterling to leave short-term funds in London (particularly after the Treasury-inspired fall in the value of the pound in March 1976) the Labour government accorded priority to restoring international confidence in sterling. In this process its industrial strategy was effectively sacrificed. Planning was thus undermined by the very inability of government to control the macro-economic universe in which domestic industry had to operate.

In the absence of consistent, coherent and continuous industrial policies, or even a consensual basis for the development of such policies, post-war governments have sought remedies to British industry's competitive weakness primarily by attempting to increase the rate of exploitation of labour – through wage cuts, incomes policies, industrial relations legislation, etc. Yet for these remedies to work, it required the compliance, or at least the acquiescence, of organised labour. British trade unions had to be either co-opted or coerced into renouncing their voluntarist predilections. Each successive post-war government consequently has sought to restrain incomes and increase labour productivity through a variety of statutory and 'voluntary' programmes. In doing so, they have confronted a series of paradoxes. The first of these is simply that the state employs, directly or indirectly, a significant proportion of the workforce, and so has considerable potential control over labour. Although governmental control of incomes may, in principle, be easier to impose in the public sector, governments face in return the prospect of more overt political resistance from their workforce, since responsibility for wage levels cannot be ascribed to the market or some other outside 'impersonal' force or agency. A second paradox, more generally, is that incomes policies depend upon the co-operation of the workforce, yet the implementation of these policies generates disillusionment with the very political and institutional framework within which such income restraint is enacted. The history of post-war incomes policies has been characterised, therefore, by the transient nature of these policies and their propensity to generate industrial militancy (see Crouch, 1977; Panitch, 1976). A third paradox is that there has been a mismatch between the requirements for a centralised structure for tripartite and state control of wages and the decentralised structure and outlook of most British trade unions. In this sense, the resistance of industrial capital to state intervention, on the grounds of an attachment to the need to allow 'the market' to operate, has been echoed by the determination of organised labour not to depart from the principle of 'free collective bargaining'. The strength of this outlook has been reflected in the way that the power of shop-floor work-groups has normally counteracted the bargains which have been struck at the national level – as the 'Winter of Discontent' of 1978–79 so vividly demonstrated.

In response, governments have attempted to undermine the strength of organised labour from two directions. On one side, a direct, statutory challenge has been launched through industrial relations legislation. The 1969 White Paper, *In Place of Strife*, has been attributed to the Labour government's failure to continue a tough incomes policy and its need to 'restrict the power of labour in order to placate overseas holders of sterling' (Crouch, 1979, p. 70). This intention was translated into the 1971 Industrial Relations Act. In attempting to curb unofficial strikes and prescribe a pattern of 'legitimate' industrial action, the Conservative government clearly sought to alter the balance of power decisively in favour of employers. In the face of massive union opposition, the provisions of the 1971 Act increasingly became inoperable and the Heath government was forced, unsuccessfully, to attempt the containment of trade unions through tripartite agreements. Ultimately, and disastrously for the Conservative government, a comprehensive statutory wages policy was introduced.

By 1974 and their return to power, the leadership of the Labour party had been persuaded, by the failure of industrial relations legislation and statutory wages policies, to reconstruct controls on trade unions within the wider framework of the Social Contract and 'socialist planning'. Thus, for all that the original Labour party–TUC Liaison Committee agreement did not explicitly feature an incomes policy, by July 1975 such a policy had become the centrepiece of the Social Contract. The Labour leadership secured the self-denial and diminution of real living standards of workers through maintaining the form, if not the substance, of the Social Contract. Whatever short-term industrial gains were secured under the Contract were secured at the expense of the greater exploitation of labour and the avoidance of radical restructuring of the economy. The economic crisis inherited by Labour did not prove to be 'the occasion for fundamental change and not the excuse for postponing it', as predicted by Tony Benn (Labour Party, 1973, p. 187). Rather, as Leo Panitch (1979, p. 61) observes, 'the crisis became the basis for maintaining the existing balance of wealth and power in British society by increasing the exploitation of the working class'.

THATCHERISM: LESSONS FROM THE PAST

Incoming governments are confronted with the inheritance of the past. The novelty of Mrs Thatcher's 1979 administration is that upon securing office it dismissed most of the post-war orthodoxies of economic and industrial policy. Preceding Labour and Conservative governments alike (with the exception of Mr Heath's limited neo-liberal experiment) were seen, through their perversion of the market order under Keynesian orthodoxies, to have contributed directly to economic decline and the erosion of Britain's industrial base. In Mrs Thatcher's eyes, her predecessors had intervened too much and conceded too much to labour. The results of the social democratic consensus were manifest: on the one side, a bloated, bureaucratic state supervised a large, 'unproductive', public sector and required a massive debt to fund its services. This state structure had been actively promoted and supported by an aggressive and self-interested labour movement. On the other side was an over-burdened private sector, with industry sapped of efficiency and enterprise, and with a diminished reputation on the world stage. If the problem was obvious then so, too, for Mrs Thatcher and her acolytes, were the solutions. These were based as much upon the petty bourgeois experience of the Conservative leader, upon her prejudices and 'feelings', as upon their intellectual sugar-coating by the works of Hayek and Friedman. Moreover, the solutions were simple – to do what her post-war predecessors had not done, and not to do what most had in fact done.

At the heart of the Thatcherite strategy has been the re-alignment between internal and external policy (Gamble, 1985, pp. 142–5). Whilst external policy had remained essentially liberal, free trade and market-oriented since the 19th century, domestic policy was geared to matching British industry to the requirements of international capitalist competition. These requirements were couched in an internationalist perspective derived from finance capital and its dominance of, and competitiveness in, world markets. Thus, for Thatcherism, the international market provided not only the context within which British industry had to operate, but also its salvation. Through the operation of the market, the rigidities and inefficiencies of domestic industry would be shaken out, so leaving a more competitive corporate sector to prosper on the world stage. Central to both the prejudice and ideology of Thatcherism, therefore, is this predisposition in favour of the market.

In conformity with its market philosophy, one of the initial acts of the Thatcher government in the autumn of 1979 was to abolish exchange controls. A substantial outflow of investment followed. Whereas only 8.7 per cent of the total investments of pension funds had been invested overseas in 1979, by 1982 this proportion had risen to 28.5 per cent. Similarly, the overseas investments of insurance companies rose from six per cent of total investment in 1979 to twenty-two per cent in 1982. In terms of net external assets the abolition of exchange control produced a spectacular growth from some £10 billion in 1978 to over £70 billion in 1984 (*The Times*, 16 August 1985).

The impact of the international market was equally apparent on the exchange rate. Unlike those governments between 1945 and 1971 which tried to stabilise exchange and interest rates in accordance with Keynesian techniques, the government after 1979 chose to let the market primarily determine the exchange rate. Mrs Thatcher enthusiastically accepted what the Labour government in 1976 had reluctantly been forced to accept: that the sheer weight, size and mobility of currency transactions negated effective government action. Indeed, according to William Keegan (1984, p. 44), one of the major 'milestones on the road to the Thatcher administration's monetarism' was the Labour government's decision to allow the pound to float to protect its published monetary targets. In this manner, monetarism and the *laissez-faire* operation of the international monetary markets become inextricably linked. Market confidence in sterling subsequently is seen to reflect the belief of international traders in the sanctity of the money supply and government borrowing figures as the major indicators of economic vibrancy. Of necessity, governments have to react to this belief by controlling both sets of figures. In a real sense, therefore, 'the *laissez-faire* element of monetarism was the policy of the City, the result of the way the City markets operated' (Coakley and Harris, 1983, p. 213). The very operation of the international markets, the model for the Thatcher strategy, led logically to the Conservative government's open embrace of monetarism.

In the search for 'monetary conditions that will . . . bring down inflation' (N. Lawson quoted in *The Times*, 22 June 1985) interest rates have become an essential ingredient in the policy mix of Chancellors since 1979. From August 1981 until January 1985 the government had no official interest rate policy. The suspension of the Minimum Lending Rate ended the Bank of England's discretionary control of interest rates. Thereafter, market mechanisms were supposed to determine short-term rates. In practice, however, the Treasury and the Bank of England still guided interest rates and came to do so with increasing sensitivity to exchange rates. Nevertheless, the freedom of the credit market was greater and more volatile than at any stage in the post-war period. This volatility is in itself a reflection of the impact of world markets upon the domestic economy. Modern British governments have been unable to escape the international constraints within which the domestic economy has to operate. As we noted above, the last Labour government adopted monetary targets and public expenditure reductions as a direct result of the priorities it accorded to sustaining Britain's international financial standing. Yet its pragmatic monetarism fitted uneasily with its domestic policies – its interventionist pretensions, its industrial strategy and its Social Contract. The mismatch between its micro-economic policies and its internationally focused macro-economic policies became ever more apparent and contradictory.

The true significance of the Thatcher government is that it has brought a unity to economic and industrial policy. There are now few pretences that the two can be separated or that British industrial capital can escape the full rigour of international competition. The achievement, if that is the right word, of Mrs Thatcher has been to integrate the British economy more firmly into the world economy. The need to re-align domestic policy to the liberal foreign economic policy has been one of the main themes of the present government. Monetary and financial policies, as we noted above, have been attuned to this aim. More specifically, an industrial 'strategy' has been designed to undermine those forces which seek to insulate industry from international competition, or to mitigate its effects. British industry is to be made to compete, whether it likes it or not. Hence, the problem of modernising and restructuring manufacturing industry has been set unambiguously within an international context. Those industries which were already internationally competitive and those with transnational operations were lauded by the Prime Minister. Those industries which were not competitive in world markets were largely left to feel the full effects of international competition. The logic of the Thatcherite strategy was, as Andrew Gamble (1985, p. 195) has cogently argued, that 'the attempt to secure prosperity for the whole national economy was implicitly abandoned'. The government has accepted a massive contraction in Britain's manufacturing base as the price of economic salvation. Thus, under Mrs Thatcher's administration, domestic manufacturing weakness has not been rectified, whilst multinational and internationally oriented firms have been strengthened. The result is, again in Gamble's words (1985, p. 226), 'a lopsided pattern of British integration in the world economy . . . there is a declining national economy and a thriving multinational economy side by side'. A logical consequence of this pattern is domestic 'de-industrialisation'. For the first time in its industrial history, Britain has a government ready to accept the logic of this position and to resign itself, and its people, to the destruction of much of its manufacturing base.

The essence of Thatcherism's negative approach to industry was set out in the 1979 Manifesto in the section on 'Industry, Commerce and Jobs'. There a general responsibility was claimed for government to establish the conditions in which industrial modernisation could occur, but primary responsibility for success or failure was seen to rest with individual firms themselves. In the words of the Manifesto, 'government cannot do industry's job for it'; 'government strategies and plans cannot produce revival nor can subsidies'. Nationalisation and interference by governments had only served to curb entrepreneurial spirit by placing too much emphasis on attempts to preserve existing jobs and placing too little emphasis upon creating new jobs in small businesses. Explicit within the Manifesto, therefore, was an outright rejection of Labour's industrial strategy. Indeed, Sir Keith Joseph came to the Department of Industry in 1979 boasting of not having an industrial policy and astounded his officials by asking 'Why [do] we need a Department of Industry?' (quoted in Holmes, 1985, p. 155). Although Sir Keith and his successors rediscovered the 'need' for the department over time, none the less the underpinning philosophy remained essentially negative. State disengagement from industry and the reversal of the interventionist role of the state has remained a consistent preoccupation of Conservative Secretaries of State for Industry since 1979.

That this preoccupation has not reached its full objective is revealed in the increased public expenditure devoted to industry between 1978–9 and 1984–5. In this period, public expenditure on industry increased by 1.2 per cent in real terms (*Guardian*, 4 July 1985). Throughout, the Thatcher government has displayed a contradictory stance towards selective intervention in industry. Nowhere are these contradictions better epitomised than in the granting of financial assistance to British Leyland. Support was granted to BL in December 1979 and renewed in January 1981, even though, as Wilks (1983, p. 146) points out, 'this subsidy was clearly in total contravention of Conservative ideology'. The social and industrial ramifications of BL's demise upon the West Midlands, and the short-term costs which would be incurred by the Treasury persuaded the Cabinet to intervene. At this stage in the Thatcher adminstration the possible electoral consequences of its economic policy still weighed fairly heavily with the government. Nevertheless, Sir Keith actually counselled the Cabinet to reject his own department's case for intervention (see Keegan, 1984, p. 176). Similarly, in Sir Keith's eyes, support for Harland & Wolff, BSC, NCB, ICL and Meriden all pointed to the undoubted failure of the non-interventionist strategy of the Conservative government in its early years. However, a condition of government aid was invariably the restoration of profitability on the part of assisted firms. Short-term concessions were made by the government in the prospect of the longer-term restructuring of the industries concerned. Initial subsidies were thus to be paid for in the long run by 'rationalisation' and job-loss. Hence, the corporate plans for BSC, NCB and BL, for example, all entailed the mutilation of the corporations and their workforces. Clearly, jobs were no longer a priority of the Thatcher government.

This negative approach is echoed throughout other areas of interaction between government and industry. Regional policy, for long a mainstay of governments' attempts to reduce unemployment in the depressed regions, has been severely pruned. In June 1979 the scope of assisted area status was reduced from forty-four to twenty-seven per cent of the population. In November 1984 the designation of the areas eligible for aid was redefined and a further £300 million was cut from the financial aid available to the remaining areas. Regional policy as a form of 'spatial Keynesianism' became a casualty of Thatcherism's wider rejection of Keynesianism. Correspondingly, the present government has sought to dismantle the institutional structure of its predecessor's planning and industrial strategy. Although the NEB, unlike the IRC in 1970, was not immediately abolished, it was none the less instructed to restore some £130 million of its assets to the private sector, to abandon its responsibility for extending public ownership, and to hand over its control of BL and Rolls-Royce to the Department of Industry. Eventually, in 1981, the NEB merged with the National Research Development Corporation to form the British Technology Group with a focus upon securing innovation and investment in the 'sunrise' industries. After the 1983 election, the Conservative government went still further and terminated the NEB-type functions of the BTG.

The NEDC escaped the onslaught upon the instruments of 'socialist planning'. It was retained, but has come to symbolise the Conservative's rejection of economic planning and their determination to reduce organised labour's contribution to the formulation of state policy. Some senior representatives of industry have, for instance, openly acknowledged that 'the NEDC structure, composition and aims . . . are incompatible with the present government's approach to the development of a social market economy' (G. Mather quoted in *The Times*, 2 March 1984). From the trade union's perspective, membership of the NEDC has increasingly taken on the appearance of 'loitering without intent in the corridors of power' (K. Gill quoted in *The Times*, 6 September 1984). In effect, therefore, the necessary consensus for the operation of the tripartite structure of the NEDC was an early victim of Mrs Thatcher's style of commitment politics.

This style of politics openly disavowed the interventionist philosophy and procedures of the Social Contract. In particular, incomes policies were denounced for their tendency to enable unions 'to demand and obtain policies in exchange for restraint which either damage the national interest as a whole . . . or which they hope will further their own interests at the expense of the rest of the community. The basic bargain is likely to mean that the government promises to do things that ought not to be done . . .' (The Right Approach, 1976, pp. 37–8). Even when these promises were unfulfilled, as between 1974–79, they were sufficient to alarm capital. Industrialists began to express openly a belief that 'Mrs Thatcher's government is all that stands between us and a rapid slide into a down-market version of the German Democratic Republic' (see Leys, 1985, p. 17). The control by capital over the production process, and more generally its abilities to influence state policy, were perceived to have been threatened by the corporatist structures developed under the Labour government. Defusing this threat has been a major priority of the Thatcher administration.

The tripartism and planning systems of Labour's social democratic modernisation strategy have been countered by the emphasis placed upon free markets and disengagement in the neo-liberal modernisation strategy. Indeed, a significant achievement of the Thatcher strategy has been to elevate the impersonal market mechanism to the status of a 'commonsense' proposition. Popular perceptions of Britain's economic and industrial problems have subsequently come to be framed more within a market philosophy; a key element of which has been the government's abrogation of its responsibility for unemployment. Hence, the Thatcher government has been the first post-war administration that has not explicitly committed itself to the preservation of manufacturing jobs. This has been because the philosophy of the social market economy maintains that jobs cannot be preserved while trade unions price their members out of work. Higher wages lead to higher prices, and, in the *laissez-faire* operations of international markets, customers are driven 'to buy from other countries, forcing thousands of employers out of business and hundreds of thousands of workers out of jobs' (The Conservative Manifesto, 1983, p. 13). The trend towards unemployment has also been exacerbated further by the activities of politicised trade unions 'associated with Luddism' (Sir Keith Joseph quoted in Holmes, 1985, p. 37). Unemployment, in this view, is thus no more than an 'inevitable' result of the monopolistic power of trade unions in the labour market and their capacity to obstruct changes in the process of production.

In apportioning blame to the trade unions in this manner, the government has sought to legitimise its attack upon the fundamental rights of organised labour in terms of removing the 'rigidities' of the labour market. Undoubtedly, widespread unemployment and its demoralising consequences for the workforce has assisted this attack: fear has been a consistent element of the Conservatives' 'commonsense' stance on unemployment. Indeed, fear has eased the acceptance of policies designed to remedy unemployment but which in practice have served only to exacerbate job loss. The paradoxes of the government's strategy on unemployment are all too depressingly self-evident. Yet, its strategy has been successful in gaining a widespread acceptance that the market, not governments, carries the responsibility for employment. The recession and unemployment have often been presented as 'acts of God', as world forces beyond the control of government. If opinion polls are to be believed, a majority of the electorate by 1983 also seemingly subscribed to the same view. Importantly, at the level of public perceptions and ideology, Thatcherism has successfully attained the goal of linking external and internal policy – of linking the operation of the domestic labour market to the vagaries of the international trading markets.

THATCHERISM AND MANUFACTURING: CLOSURE AND RESISTANCE

It has been argued that the economic rationale of the Thatcher government is 'extremely simple: it amounts to crashing the economy' (Harrison, 1982, p. 19). However, such kamikaze intent is not the basis of the Thatcher strategy. Rather, the analogy to be drawn is with a pilot trained on bi-planes attempting to fly Concorde. In true early-Biggles style, Mrs Thatcher has assumed control of the flight deck only to declare that the sophisticated instruments so far developed to steer, monitor and control the economy have proved defective in the past. Therefore, they should be ignored. In their place old skills and techniques are to be utilised, with only the guiding light of M3 money supply figures needed to illuminate the control-panel. Flying by the seat of one's pants, with the speed and direction of economic progress determined by the winds of international market conditions, is the new style. To press the analogy still further; to ensure that the working-class passengers aboard the state airline do not seek to disturb this exhilarating experience, the crew have sought to strap them firmly into their seats – either through the restraint of industrial relations legislation or through invoking the fear of being sucked out of the economic cabin in the rapid depressurisation of recession. Should labour venture to object, then increased stewarding of the aisles (albeit with riot gear if necessary!) has been provided by the governmental air crew. If Thatcherism has not sought to crash the economy, it has certainly put it into a steep dive.

Undoubtedly, the actions of the Thatcher government have exacerbated Britain's industrial position, but many of its policies have only added a short-term recession onto the underlying long-term decline of manufacturing. 'Thatcherism' alone cannot provide a simple explanation of Britain's industrial malaise in the 1980s. In many ways the Thatcher strategy is as much a consequence as a cause of industrial decline. This is not to absolve Mrs Thatcher's government of blame, for the economic effects of its decisions have been truly disastrous, but only to argue that its policies are a logical, if perverse, culmination of some of the long-run tendencies within state-industry relations in Britain.

To set what has happened since 1979 in context, it is necessary to appreciate both the extent of Britain's comparative industrial weakness and also the domestic weakness of manufacturing within the British economy over time. In comparative terms, Britain's industrial malaise has been apparent for some considerable time. In terms of annual growth rates in industrial production and the overall share of trade in manufactures, Britain has increasingly lagged behind her major competitors (see Tables 1.1, 1.2).

Table 1.1   Growth of industrial production 1957–76

	Annual growth of industrial production %	Total growth of industrial production %
UK	2.27	57.8
France	5.03	151.2
West Germany	4.93	146.6
Italy	6.41	219.6
EEC (the Six)	5.32	160.4

Source: *National Institute Economic Review*, No. 77, August 1976, p. 80.

Table 1.2   Shares in the value of world exports of manufactures (%)

	1950	1960	1970	1975	1979	1980	1981	1982	1983	1984	1985
UK	25.5	16.5	10.8	9.3	9.7	10.2	8.8	8.4	7.8	7.6	7.8
France	9.9	9.6	8.7	10.2	10.4	9.9	9.0	9.0	8.9	8.5	8.5
W Germany	7.3	19.3	19.8	20.3	20.7	19.8	18.3	19.6	19.0	18.0	18.6
Japan	3.4	6.9	11.7	13.6	13.6	14.7	17.8	17.2	18.4	20.0	19.7
USA	27.3	21.6	18.5	17.7	15.9	17.1	18.8	18.0	17.2	17.4	16.8

Sources: A Gamble, *Britain in Decline*, 2nd edn, 1985, p. 17; *National Institute Economic Review* 118, 1986, NIESR, p. 102.

The domestic weakness of British manufacturing was less apparent until the 1970s. Until then, manufacturing output had increased by about thirty per cent per decade since the 1930s. By the mid-1960s, however, the rate of industrial growth began to lag behind the general growth in economic output. In the period 1966–79, although GDP increased by twenty nine per cent, the growth in manufacturing output was only eleven per cent. Indeed, industrial production peaked in 1973; thereafter there was a significant downturn. Industrial output had, therefore, begun to decline absolutely before 1979 (see Table 1.3).

Table 1.3   Index of output in British manufacturing industries (1980 = 100)

1950	56.8	1975	105.0	1981	94.0
1960	77.2	1976	106.9	1982	94.2
1965	90.1	1977	109.0	1983	96.8
1970	103.4	1978	109.7	1984	100.6
1973	114.2	1979	109.5	1985	103.9
1974	112.7	1980	100.0		

Source: CSO, Economic Trends, Annual Supplement, 1986 edn, HMSO.

Similarly, employment in manufacturing had shown a steady decline well before the return of the Conservative government in 1979. In 1970 employment in manufacturing stood at 97 per cent of its 1966 level (the highest level of manufacturing employment). In 1973 this figure was down to 91 per cent and declined to 84 per cent in 1979. Between 1979 and 1982 manufacturing employment fell from 7 197 000 to 5 776 000, a 20 per cent drop in three years, so that employment in manufacturing stood at 67 per cent of the 1966 total. Yet, the effects of the Thatcher-induced recession were more keenly felt by manufacturing employees than those in other sectors of the economy (see Table 1.4).

Table 1.4   Wage earners by activity 1979–84 (%)

	1979	1980	1981	1982	1983	1984
Agriculture	1.6	1.6	1.6	1.7	1.7	1.6
Mining and quarrying	1.5	1.6	1.6	1.6	1.5	1.4
Manufacturing	31.4	30.2	28.4	27.5	26.6	26.0
Electricity, gas, water	1.5	1.5	1.6	1.6	1.6	1.5
Construction	5.4	5.5	5.2	4.9	4.8	4.6
Trade: wholesale, retail, catering	17.6	18.0	18.2	18.6	19.0	19.6
Transport, storage and communication	6.4	6.5	6.5	6.4	6.3	6.2
Finance, insurance, business services, etc.	7.0	7.3	7.8	8.2	8.5	8.8
Community, social and personal services	27.6	28.0	29.0	29.5	30.1	30.3
Total	100.0	100.0	100.0	100.0	100.0	100.0

Source: OECD, Labour Force Statistics 1964–1984, OECD, 1986, pp. 452–3.

If industrial output and employment were in decline before 1979, the recession after 1979 certainly steepened the trajectory of decline. In the first year of the Thatcher government, manufacturing output fell by fifteen per cent. Rowthorn (1983, p. 73) compares this slump with a fall in output of 5.5 per cent in the worst year of the Great Depression between 1878 and 1879 and a fall of 6.9 per cent in 1930–31. In this context even the industrial giants, such as ICI, took a pounding. So great was the downturn that in the third quarter of 1980, ICI announced a loss. The shock within the company led to the unprecedented step of the chairman going to Downing Street to inform the Prime Minister personally of the effects of her government's policies upon manufacturing industry (see Keegan, 1984, p. 155). As ICI floundered, other smaller and less competitive manufacturers capsized, sinking their entire labour forces in the trough of the recession. Significant sectors of manufacturing industry were submerged, particularly in the traditionally depressed regions. Thus, in the Merseyside Special Development Area, 384 plants, with more than ten employees, closed between 1979–82. 25 511 jobs were subsequently lost (HC Debates, 14 November, 1983, Vol. 48, col. 316). In Scotland, between June 1979 and June 1984, 613 closures of manufacturing firms were notified to the Manpower Services Commission (HC Debates, 5 December 1984, Vol. 49, col. 206). 164 000 jobs were lost as a result. In Wales, 576 manufacturing plants closed in the period 1978–84 (HC Debates, 1 March 1984, Vol. 55, col. 294). More generally, 577 foreign-owned plants closed in the period January 1979–June 1984, with a loss of 106 510 jobs in the UK (HC Debates, 2 May 1984, Vol. 59, col. 178; 6 June 1984, Vol. 61, col. 179).

With closure on this scale, and with one-third of total job losses since 1979 resulting from closure, the politics of plant closure was forced on to the public agenda. What needs to be explained is how the state attempted to foreclose, pre-empt and depoliticise this issue; for, within the space of a decade, the state has systematically, and largely successfully, undermined resistance to closure. One observable change in this period has been the response of governments to unemployment. Even the precursor of the Thatcher government, the Conservative administration of the early 1970s, was firmly locked into the social democratic consensus and had a major and 'emotional' concern with the problem of unemployment (Holmes, 1982, pp. 44–8). Indeed, the rise in unemployment to one million in 1972 triggered the famous 'u-turns' in Heath's neo-liberal strategy.

One of the most famous of Heath's 'u-turns' came with the granting of state aid to Upper Clyde Shipbuilders. Whereas in June 1971 the government had declared its intention of liquidating UCS as the basis for restructuring the company, by February 1972 this decision had been reversed and £35 million was injected into the newly formed Govan Shipbuilders (see Young, 1974, pp. 155–63). The importance of the UCS work-in for our purposes is that the Heath government was unable to counter the arguments of the UCS shop-stewards concerning the catastrophic employment prospects of closure in an area where there was already considerable unemployment. The work-in underscored the legitimacy of the *right* to work: a right that had been secured in the post-war consensus. So entrenched was this right that support for the UCS workforce galvanised 100 000 people to stop work and 50 000 to join a demonstration in Glasgow on 24 June 1971; two months later, on 18 August, 200 000 strikers and 80 000 marchers demonstrated in support of UCS (Hardy, 1985, p. 17). Indeed, the very scale of local support for the UCS workforce and real fears of widespread public disorder in Glasgow contributed to the u-turn (Holmes, 1982, p. 44). In the early 1970s, therefore, the state was thus both ideologically and institutionally unprepared to deal with workforce resistance to its modernisation strategy. Political leaders were psychologically unprepared to contemplate mass unemployment and the forces of law and order were operationally unprepared to deal with widespread industrial resistance. By the return of the Conservative government in 1979, however, the state apparatus had been geared for confrontation (see Jeffrey and Hennessy, 1983) and the new political leadership was ideologically predisposed to accept high levels of unemployment.

Staying for the moment with the effects of the UCS work-in, it ushered in a brief period, between 1970 and 1975, when factory occupations became a fairly common way for groups of workers to resist closure. These 'sit-ins' or 'work-ins' appeared to many in the labour movement to be a more effective weapon against closure than the strike, since they prevented the disposal of the assets concerned and demonstrated the commitment of the employees to the plant concerned. In this period there were around 200 factory occupations involving 150 000 workers (see Clarke, 1979). However, as Hardy (1985, p. 17) has noted, this phase of opposition to closure lasted only until around 1975 and, thereafter, the factory occupation became a far less common tactic – with occasional notable exceptions, such as the struggle of women workers at the Lee Jeans factory in Greenock in 1981 and at Plessey in Bathgate in 1982 (see chapter 3).

The resistance to closure has been eroded by structural failings within the trade union movement; by the attrition of management strategies and by the actions of the state itself. The problems of labour solidarity, the local focus and segmented perceptions of workers, especially in multi-plant and multi-national organisations, will be examined later in this volume. Similarly, the strategies of management, in their attempts to redefine the legitimacy of closure and to justify closure in the technocratic and impersonal language of markets and technological change, form a major part of the analysis of chapter 5. Our concern here, however, is to monitor how the state has sought to acclimatise the workforce to manufacturing closure.

The state was directly confronted with this need for acclimatisation after the 1973–74 oil-generated world recession spotlighted the weakness of British manufacturing industry. After this date the contradictions of the post-war social democratic consensus were apparent in the simple fact that the time at which state intervention and expenditure was needed marked the very time that the state appeared unable to afford such expenditure. Callaghan's statement to the 1976 Labour party conference revealed the extent to which even a Labour government had abandoned the Keynesian consensus: 'We used to think you could spend your way out of recession, and increase employment by cutting taxes and boosting government spending. I tell you in all candour that that option no longer exists' (Labour Party, 1976, p. 188).

In jettisoning Keynesian demand-management, as explained earlier, Callaghan's government demonstrated the dominance of external policy and the inescapability of monetarism in the face of the operation of the international financial markets. Increasingly, ministers fitted the intractability of Britain's economic and industrial problems within this world frame. Shirley Williams, for example, admitted the government's helplessness in a speech in February 1977: 'We are seeing the increase in unemployment throughout the industrial world, and it is a problem for which we still have no real answer' (quoted in Coates, 1980, p. 71). Similarly, Jim Callaghan, in his 'Foreword' to the 1979 Manifesto, attempted to set Labour's record within the context of the 'worldwide unemployment crisis'. The Manifesto proceeded to declare Labour's commitment for employment protection within a 'healthy and expanding economy'. Although Callaghan was pressed by the left within his party to resolve the mismatch between internal and external policies, through the adoption of the Alternative Economic Strategy and its insulation of British industry from the international order, he chose to define a 'healthy' economy in terms of its internationally competitive position. Given this emphasis, unemployment was portrayed as inescapable, as but an intrinsic part of the new international industrial order. From this basis the rhetoric of Thatcherism merely completed a logical circle: if unemployment was the product of international forces, there was little that British governments could achieve. Unemployment was thus deemed to be a 'natural' consequence of Britain's manufacturing international competitive weakness.

Resistance to closure in the early 1970s was also facilitated by the fact that no government could be said to have developed a coherent, or explicitly stated, policy on closure. The Heath government hinted at such a policy in its Selsdon phase but failed to enact the necessary measures when confronted by their consequences. Increased public expenditure was ultimately preferred to higher levels of unemployment by the 1970–74 government. Similarly, the Labour government came to office in 1974 committed to maintaining jobs. Indeed, under the direction of Tony Benn at the Department of Industry, a structure within which closure could be fought was developed in the assistance provided to three workers' co-operatives, at Meriden (Triumph Motor Cycles), Kirkby (Fisher-Bendix), and Glasgow (Scottish Daily Express). Significantly, even though the sums of public money provided were relatively small, some £10 million, the response from the Treasury and the 'establishment' was determinedly obstructive (see Benn, 1980, pp. 158–9). More generally, the antipathy of the Treasury and financiers towards Labour's industrial programme perverted its original aims of job enhancement and creation into state-sponsored rationalisation and job destruction. By the end of their term in office, Labour ministers had been obliged 'to add their own voices to those of management, in the call to subordinate industrial policy to the dictates of the world market, and transformed even radical ministers into the most adamant proponents of industrial competitiveness' (Coates, 1980, p. 131). Thus, even before Mrs Thatcher came into office in 1979, the foundations of a 'Thatcherite' industrial strategy were embedded within state policies!

Nevertheless, it is important to stress the particular contribution made by Thatcherism to the legitimation of closure and unemployment. Although the logic of its economic policy was inevitably to abandon the attempt to preserve jobs, the 1979 administration, as noted above, was sufficiently wary of the electoral implications to continue, in selected cases, the policy of government assistance to declining industries. However, as the policy consequences inevitably began to work through and the rate of closures (and unemployment) rose, the government was forced to underpin its strategy with a consistent legitimation explaining such factors in terms of, on the one hand, the necessity of short-term suffering for long-term gain and, on the other, the impact of world-wide recession. Thus unemployment was presented as a universal phenomenon amongst western nations and hence unavoidable.

But the post-war consensus on full employment, established over many years, could not be discarded quite so easily. The volatility of voting behaviour over the last twenty years, which has been the subject of considerable debate (see Alt, 1978; Crewe and Sarlvik, 1983), can, at least partly, be ascribed to the failure of successive governments to manage the economy successfully. The rapid rise in unemployment after 1979 seemed to have a similar effect on the Thatcher administration as opinion polls showed its ratings in 1981 to be amongst the lowest for a post-war government. The supreme irony was that the issue which decisively swung public opinion behind Thatcherism – the Falklands War – illustrated so clearly the imperialist legacy which has been so destructive in economic terms. The popular sentiment and jingoism aroused by a military victory over a foreign nation disputing Britain's claim to territory half-way across the world was to underpin Thatcherism's relentless pursuit of the destruction of jobs in manufacturing.

Thus the Conservative electoral triumph of 1983 was taken as the signal for full steam ahead. Unemployment continued to rise inexorably (see Table 1.5 below). This massive and unrelenting increase meant that a greater proportion of public expenditure had to be devoted to unemployment and social security benefits. For example, between 1979 and 1984, government expenditure on unemployment benefits rose by 163 per cent in real terms (*Guardian*, 4 July 1985). In consequence, public expenditure was skewed still further towards welfare benefits and away from capital investment. In particular, under central direction, local authority spending on construction, especially on housing, plummeted. Indeed, the deterioration of Britain's infrastructure so worried the CBI (1985) that it issued a warning in November 1985 that the inadequacy and continued degeneration of basic infrastructure was a contributory factor in maintaining British industry's high production costs. Another twist to the spiral of under-investment and the declining competitiveness of manufacturing industry was thus added by the Thatcherite public expenditure policies.

Table 1.5   Unemployment rate (% of total labour force)

1970	2.2	1980	6.6
1972	3.2	1981	9.8
1974	2.2	1982	11.7
1976	5.2	1983	12.1
1978	5.5	1984	12.1
1979	5.1	1985	12.3

Source: OECD, *Labour Force Statistics 1964–84*, OECD, 1986, pp. 496–7.

Resistance to closure in this climate seemed futile. It is in this context that the miners' strike of 1984–85 assumed such symbolic importance.

The claim of the NUM that jobs in the industry were as much the property of those who worked in it as of their employer struck at the heart of Thatcherism. In particular, it challenged three basic tenets of the strategy – the social market philosophy which declared that only the market should determine profitability and employment levels, the position of the government as the employer, and its ability to remove the influence of unions as a market distortion. The centrality of this challenge explains the significance of the chancellor's claim that, whatever the price of the miners' strike, it was a price worth paying. If Thatcherism was to remain intact, it was a conflict the government could not afford to lose.

CLOSURE AND POLITICAL ACTION

Thatcherism, then, can be seen in both its domestic and external dimensions, as but an extreme development of some of the policy options used by British capital and the state throughout Britain's industrial development. Our immediate concern in this study is to focus on one important outcome of these policies – the collapse of British manufacturing and its impact in terms of the number and scale of plant closures. The rest of this volume is devoted to examining in more detail different aspects of the process of closure and its effects. In particular, through a better understanding of the phenomenon, we wish to raise some questions about the prospect for the future. The defeat of the most explicit challenge to the legitimacy of closures – the miners' strike of 1984–85 – makes these questions especially pertinent. How, for example, if at all, may the general processes leading to particular closures be addressed and countered? In what ways can those individuals, groups and communities directly affected by plant closures resist the process? Are such closures more effectively fought on an individual plant basis, or does the labour movement need to develop a wider strategy? Indeed, is there a need for groups of workers to forge wider international alliances? In the concluding chapter of the study we will return to these issues.

2 Local Dimensions of Closure
Des McNulty

In recent years the gap between levels of unemployment in the North and South of Great Britain has widened very considerably. Not all of the South is prosperous; the London conurbation contains many areas that are desperately deprived and there are pockets of high unemployment outside the capital as well as in it. Equally, not all of the North is poor; some places, most notably market towns in the better off agricultural and tourist areas have flourished economically over the last decade. In part, this unevenness within regions is a product of a second related trend, whereby unemployment has increased much more rapidly in the larger towns and cities than it has in predominantly rural areas. These two processes together have led to a growing geographical and social polarisation between north and south on the one hand, and between the larger towns and cities and the rest of the country on the other.

A major contributory factor to these increased regional and urban–rural disparities has been the volume and distribution of job loss in manufacturing industry. As the recession of the late 1970s and early 1980s bit more deeply into manufacturing than other sectors of the economy, almost inevitably those regions most dependent on manufacturing were among the most badly affected. The North of England, Scotland and Wales, where the older traditional industries were mainly based, suffered substantial job loss. The biggest proportional job loss, however, was experienced in the West Midlands, where sixteen per cent of manufacturing jobs were lost between January 1980 and June 1983, plunging the region down the league table of regional unemployment. The extent of job loss in the various UK regions during this period is shown in Table 2.1.

Measuring the extent to which job loss is 'responsible' for unemployment either at a regional or a national level is extremely difficult, not least because of problems arising out of the way in which the relevant statistics are collected and presented. (Statistics for redundancies and for unemployment are gathered by different means and the geographical areas to which the statistics refer do not always

Table 2.1 Employment decline by region: January 1980–June 1983

	No. of jobs lost	% loss
West Midlands	358 000	16.0
North	190 000	15.2
Wales	145 000	14.1
North West	357 000	13.3
Yorkshire and Humberside	259 000	12.9
East Midlands	161 000	10.3
Scotland	206 000	9.9
South East	636 000	8.5
East Anglia	47 000	6.6
South West	103 000	6.5
Great Britain	2 463 000	10.9

Source: *Department of Employment Gazette.*

coincide). The unemployment statistics normally used for such comparisons are for 'Travel To Work Areas' (hence TTWAs), on the basis that the smallest area for which such statistics are useful as economic rather than as social indicators is the area which constitutes a single labour market. Further disaggregation would show up local variations at the expense of general trends. In the case of large-scale closures this creates no undue difficulty, since the closure is usually easily identifiable as the main factor in raising levels of unemployment.

In other situations, however, the connection between closure and unemployment growth is obscured. Where smaller closures occur, the number of jobs lost may be tiny in comparison with the overall numbers of people employed in a TTWA. Unless there is a spate of closures all taking place at the same time in the same area, it can be almost impossible to disentangle the contribution that closure has made to movements in the unemployment statistics from that of other factors. Job loss is also by no means always a consequence of closure. In many plants, sizeable redundancies have occurred without the plant actually closing, and in others contraction has taken the form of piecemeal redundancies in which small groups of workers are laid off successively over a period of time. The cumulative effect of job losses of these various types, smaller closures, lay-offs and labour shedding, taken together with larger closures, can be considerable. In Doncaster, for example, the town's top ten manufacturing companies shed nearly half their workforces between 1975 and 1985, from almost 40 000 to 22 000 jobs. This pattern has been repeated all over the north and in the major cities.

Even where closures have led to a particularly heavy loss of jobs, it can, depending on the circumstances, be almost impossible to demonstrate conclusively that job loss is the prime cause of unemployment. At a national level, job loss is only one of the factors which have contributed to higher levels of unemployment. Other factors that would need to be considered if we were to attempt to account fully for rising unemployment are growing participation rates among women and increases in the overall size of the workforce consequent on the fact that many fewer people are reaching retirement age and withdrawing from the workforce than are joining it for the first time. Job loss itself can be a product of high interest rates, low levels of past investment, management inefficiency and poor productivity, and any one of these may well be seen as a more fundamental cause of high unemployment than closure.

In many parts of the country however, and especially in those areas where manufacturing has historically been concentrated, there has been a dramatic and possibly irreversible collapse of the manufacturing base, which has triggered a sudden escalation in levels of unemployment, even if it is not the sole cause. The timing and the trajectory of decline vary from place to place. In some areas, the collapse has taken place over a protracted period, punctuated by phases of rapid deterioration. In others, while the process of decline may have been evident for a decade or more, it accelerated sharply with the onset of recession.

The most graphic illustrations of the profound effects which the collapse of manufacturing has had are to be found in those areas which have experienced large-scale closure or contraction in the older 'smoke stack' industries. In a study carried out by a group at Newcastle University (Champion and Green, 1985), covering the period 1971–81, Britain was divided into 280 local labour market areas. A prosperity index was then constructed which linked together unemployment and consumption, and of the twenty least prosperous areas, seven were shipbuilding centres, including Wearside, Birkenhead and the Lower Clyde; four were coalfield areas; and a further seven were steelmaking centres, including Corby, Consett and Port Talbot. The coal, steel and shipbuilding industries have dominated the labour market in most of the places where pits or factories have been sited, employing hundreds, and sometimes thousands, of people. When closure or a major contraction occurs in a plant on which the local economy is dependent to this extent, the effects are shattering.

Quite apart from the numbers of people who are made unemployed, closure unleashes two types of multiplier effect on the locality. On the one hand, there is the linkage multiplier whereby firms supplying equipment and materials, together with those parts of the public sector responsible for services such as fuel, water, transport and maintenance of the infrastructure, find that the local market for their product has disappeared. On the other hand, the income multiplier effect involves the reduction of the purchasing power of consumers and the revenue base of local authorities as consequences of closure. The result of the operation of these two effects is to put at risk the jobs of those in related industries and in the service sector. The consequence of closure is to force everyone to cut back: from small shopkeepers to the larger firms operating in the area and local government. Hence, the local economy is significantly undermined.

The full effects of large scale closure are experienced, therefore, by localities and communities rather than by regions. Focusing on the effects on the community is not to ignore the effects on regions. Some large-scale closures and contractions, like the partial shutdown of the steelworks at Port Talbot in 1980, or the closure of strategic plants like the Gartcosh steel mill in Scotland in 1986, may have massive repercussions for an entire region, let alone the immediate community. The recession may have more damaging effects in other parts of the region than large scale closure has in a particular locality (Fevre, 1983). In addition, knock-on effects of major closure, such as the breaking of trading links or the switching of resources to meet the immediate crisis, can undoubtedly spread the effects out to other communities.

Within every region in Britain, however, there are extremes of both unemployment and prosperity (Thomas, 1983), and the incidence of closure has had a major impact on their distribution. Both large scale closures and smaller closures fall most heavily on those communities which were dependent on the plant(s) concerned. Closure selectively destroys the economic and social fabric of those communities in which it strikes hardest. In many cases the damage is such that the community is then condemned to a slow and lingering decline. The principal victims of closure therefore, besides individual workers and their families, are local communities, and it is to the effects which closure has on communities that we wish to pay particular attention in this chapter.

In a large town or city it would be very unusual for a single closure to have anything like the impact which the closure of its steel plant had on Shotton in North Wales. The size of the plant at Shotton and the degree to which the local economy was based on a single industry finds no ready parallel in larger towns and cities where closures are likely to be smaller and the greater size of population and diversity of economic activity diminishes the overall effects of closures that do take place. However, although no single closure by itself is the cause of an economic breakdown, the attrition which has been taking place in manufacturing has had a devastating effect. From the late 1970s onwards the pace of job loss has increased dramatically in most of the major conurbations as the decline of manufacturing generally has quickened.

It is the accumulation of closures, large and small, rather than any 'big bang', which is significant. The effects have perhaps not been so obvious, since cities like London, Manchester or Coventry are too big to be considered as single communities in the sense that steel towns or colliery villages are. Also the resilience of the retail and financial sectors have offset the effects of the decline in manufacturing to some extent (although we have yet to see the full impact of developments such as out of town superstore shopping and computerised financial services). But the decline of manufacturing has been especially acute in the cities and has contributed a great deal to the problems which they presently face.

Job loss in manufacturing need not, of course, necessarily lead to rising unemployment. Employment in manufacturing in Britain has been declining since 1966 (Massey and Meegan, 1982). Yet the bulk of the increase in the level of unemployment did not come about until the late 1970s. In favourable circumstances, particular industries can achieve substantial increases in output with a much reduced workforce, thanks to improvements in productivity. Provided those people who are released can be re-absorbed into employment in the service sector or in new industries, there need to be no net effect on unemployment levels.

In some parts of the country this seems to be working. Harlow in Essex, for example, suffered the highest percentage of job losses between 1975 and 1985, but the unemployment rate remained at under ten per cent. New starts, relocations and switching from the manufacturing to the service sector created just about enough new jobs to make up for those that were lost. Outside the South of England, however, precisely in those areas where new jobs were most needed as a result of closure, there has typically been much less spontaneous economic regeneration and diversification.

In these areas closure is not a temporary setback, which will rectify itself once the market has got to work, but a part of a fundamental change with long-term consequences. Industrial restructuring, the movement of capital from one sector to another, is taking place at the expense of communities in the north and in the cities. The decline in the number of jobs in manufacturing has been accompanied by a major shift in its location (Fothergill and Vincent, 1985). What growth there is in the manufacturing sector itself is generally taking place in those parts of the country with below average unemployment. Meanwhile, in the service sector, the relative position of the north and many of the metropolitan areas, apart from London, has deteriorated. Growth in the service sector, which some people have argued should compensate for job loss in manufacturing, has taken place at a much slower rate in the north than in the south.

The very fact of high unemployment contributes further to the problems in that it affects the market for new products and services. Large-scale closure, in particular, threatens not only the position of existing manufacturing and service industries in a given locality, but also the prospects for new jobs. Low levels of demand, which are a consequence of high unemployment, diminish the market for new services, which tends to be very heavily influenced by marginal shifts in disposable income. Areas like the North East of England, which have lost a large number of jobs in manufacturing, are, therefore, highly unlikely to benefit greatly from growth in the service sector.

The reasons why existing firms and new enterprises are locating in the south rather than elsewhere are complex. One key factor is undoubtedly communication and transport links, which focus on the capital. Another factor may well be access and proximity to markets. The high levels of disposable income among consumers and the buoyancy of the service sector in London and the South East, taken together with the population size, make it the most profitable internal market in the UK. Locating production near to major markets cuts distribution costs and eases transportation problems. The very considerable amounts of public investment which have been pumped into building motorway links, such as the new M25 orbital road, and improving the rest of the motorway system in the South East, have contributed substantially to the attractiveness of the South East from the point of view of the industrialist.

A further factor is the changing character of manufacturing itself. There is a shift away from mass production in enormous factories towards small batch production of goods, carefully tailored to consumer demand, in which monitoring by computer of both demand and production plays an increasingly important role. This has a number of implications. On the one hand, labour costs are a less pressing consideration in making location decisions within Britain and, given the fact that unemployment levels are fairly high throughout the country, labour shortages are unlikely to propel firms towards areas of high unemployment.

On the other hand, it creates a separation between the production process, which can take place practically anywhere in the world, and design, planning, marketing and other functions, which are being located increasingly in the South East, or even in other European countries. Associated with the relocation of manufacturing, therefore, has been the internationalisation of production. Over the last few years, Britain has been importing an increasing percentage of manufactured goods from abroad, either from Europe, Japan and the USA, or from developing countries such as Hong Kong and Taiwan. For the first time since the Industrial Revolution, Britain had become by the mid-1980s a net importer of manufactured goods.

It is the manufacturing heartlands of Britain that have been squeezed in this process, having neither the very low labour costs of third world economies, nor the locational advantages of the South East. Those individuals within society best able, in terms of management experience, business contacts, and access to capital, to take advantage of gaps in the market are predominantly located in the South. As a result, the more dynamic companies are disproportionately likely to emerge and take root in the already more prosperous regions. This dual process, the centralisation of control in conjunction with worldwide dispersion of production, adds a qualitative dimension to the quantitative transference of employment. Management élites located in economically advantaged areas make critical decisions about the economic fate, not only of groups of workers but, effectively, also of communities in less advantaged parts of the country. Insofar as jobs are created in the less advantaged areas, they tend to be low status jobs, which include few functions of control (Massey, 1984).

A good example of this is provided by the high technology based industries, which, it has been claimed, are the key to Britain's future economic prospects. A high percentage of the headquarters of firms in the computing and information technology sector are to be found along the so-called M4 corridor. One important reason for firms in the high technology industries huddling together is the unusual degree of mutual interdependence which exists. Firms are, in many instances, each other's main suppliers or customers and the technology is changing so rapidly that there is a particular need for managers and highly skilled personnel to maintain close contact for the exchange of ideas, skills and information about market opportunities. In this context, location decisions made by certain key firms have had a great influence on decisions by other enterprises.

We should not forget also the role which has been played by certain universities and research establishments in developing the knowledge base on which innovation has rested. Many high technology firms have been established by people who have been trained in these institutions, and there is a continued reliance on educational and other institutions to perform new research and to supply highly qualified personnel needed by the commercial sector. Whatever the reasons for locating in the South East of England, whether it is a gravitational pull peculiar to high technology industry which is exerted once a certain 'critical mass' is obtained, or whether it reflects the centralising tendency to which manufacturing in general is subject, the effect is that other regions have tended to benefit little from the growth of high technology industry. Apart from the central belt of Scotland, where a particular combination of circumstances has allowed high technology industries to develop, comparatively little high technology industry has established itself in Britain outside the South East, other than assembly plants.

The end result of the restructuring process has thus been the de-industrialisation of many parts of Britain, with many communities affected by closure or contraction having little hope of new investment and replacement jobs. De-industrialisation for these communities is not a return to some pre-industrial rural idyll. Nor is it a positive move into a post-industrial society in which individuals or the community itself will be able to determine its own destiny. The future prospects of communities caught in this limbo are bleak, especially where the community concerned is geographically isolated from major urban centres. Faced with no employment opportunities, many members of these communities will be forced to leave. The effects of emigration to other parts of the country or abroad can be extremely damaging to a community. It is generally the young, those with marketable skills and the ambitious who are likely to leave, while older people and the less skilled remain.

Not everyone who wishes to move away may be able to do so. More than anything else, the structure of housing provision and the housing market in Britain is a constraint on movement. The relatively much higher cost of housing in the South, the dearth of council housing, and the difficulties of transferring within the publicly owned rented sector from one housing authority area to another, make it extremely difficult for families to relocate themselves from areas without work into areas where work might be available. The residual population tends to consist largely, therefore, of those who are trapped.

COMMUNITY RESPONSES TO CLOSURE

Given the impact which job loss, especially following closure, has had on communities, it might be expected that at least some of the communities concerned would respond vigorously to the threat of closure. In practice, however, there have been very few effective community campaigns against closure mounted since 1979. By effective, we do not necessarily mean campaigns that are successful in preventing closure. An effective campaign would be one that manages to mobilise a considerable cross-section of the community in protest either at closure itself or its likely consequences. For a whole series of reasons, most closures, including major closures, have met with little sustained resistance even from the workforces concerned and frequently only limited protest from representatives of the community.

This is not to suggest that there are no instances of communities becoming involved in campaigns against closure. The major industrial struggle of the post-1979 period in Britain, the 1984–85 miners' strike, had an especially powerful community dimension and, as we shall see later in the chapter, pressures from the community have been a crucial stimulus in the emergence of local economic and employment initiatives by local authorities, many of which are aimed at preventing closure or mitigating its effects. But, in the light of the profound problems which result from closure, it is remarkable that community voices have not been heard more in protest against closure and that there has not been a greater involvement on the part of communities in attempts by workers to save their jobs.

The likelihood of an effective community response is governed by a number of factors. The most obvious immediate factors are the size of the closure and the impact it is likely to have on the community. The greater the number of jobs to be lost, and the bigger the proportion that jobs lost would represent of the total quantity of jobs available to a community, the more likely it is that a community will be driven to respond. This goes some way to explaining why many of the anti-closure campaigns in which communities have been most involved over the last fifteen years have been in areas where traditional heavy industries such as coal, steel and shipbuilding predominated and where, given the size of production units, there was a high degree of dependency on the industry locally. (Examples include campaigns to save steel plants, especially in Scotland and Wales; campaigns to retain specific pits like the Bates colliery in Northumberland; and the campaigns to save shipyards on Clydeside, Tyneside and Wearside.)

Additional factors in the case of heavy industry are what sociologists have called 'occupational identity' and 'occupational community'. According to Eldridge (1968, p. 93) writing about skilled workers in the shipbuilding industry:

> membership of such an occupational group was of central importance in the life experience of the group member. Not only did his craft training implant in him a sense of his exclusive competence in relation to a particular range of techniques, which members of the trade could undertake, but his work expectations were geared to that particular craft. To this extent he was captive by his occupation and, upon the fortunes of his occupation in the labour market, hinged his own personal and familial security.

Workers in these industries not only share a strong sense of common identity and a high degree of job involvement, but they are also typically concentrated together in solidary communities insulated from the influences of the wider society (see Lockwood, 1966).

Occupational identity and occupational community provide an organisational and, in many ways, an ideological foundation for campaigning against closure both in the workplace and in the community. In other industries, such as textiles, vehicle production or engineering, there are frequently some similarities with coal, steel and shipbuilding industries, but there are also important differences, whether in size of plant, the extent to which communities are dependent on a single plant, the gender and occupational structure of the workforce or, significantly, political and social attitudes.

These differences do not prevent workers in these industries from winning community support for action against closure. The seven months long occupation by women workers at the Lee Jeans factory in Greenock in 1981 attracted massive support both from the local community and from community and trade union organisations in Scotland. As Patricia Findlay shows in chapter 3, women workers may be able to draw on community support in ways which are not open to male workers, because women's struggles frequently involve community as well as industrial issues and because many community groups and organisations are well disposed towards supporting women workers.

Yet there is not the same immediate and automatic identification of the interests of the community with those of the workforce in these industries as exists in the smoke stack industries. If members of an occupationally mixed community are to become involved in a campaign to protect someone else's job, then they must be persuaded to do so, either by the workforce or its representatives or by organisations, institutions and leaders within the community.

This raises the question of leadership of the anti-closure campaign and the extent to which the community can be mobilised in support of the objective of preventing closure. In most instances, it is only after an initial response to the threat of closure has been made by a workforce that an appeal to the community is likely to be made. The terms of community involvement are thus largely set by the response of the workforce. There are exceptions to this, for example in situations where closure has been threatened before or where there is a continuing threat, and local authorities, community organisations and assorted community 'representatives' have been involved over a period of time. Under such circumstances, community support can be called on immediately in support of the workforce when the plant appears to be under a fresh threat, (for example, the recent campaign to retain the Ravenscraig steel plant in Scotland built upon a previous campaign of the 1970s). Even in these circumstances, it is almost always the workforce, trade union representatives or full time trade union officials who make most of the key decisions about the conduct of a campaign against closure.

Community involvement is, therefore, doubly dependent, first of all on whether the workforce is ready to mount a campaign to fight closure and, secondly, on whether those responsible for the campaign take the view that community participation is a priority and are able to gather community support. A key factor in determining the will to fight closure on the part of both workforces and communities has been the attitude of government. Since 1979, as indicated in chapter 1, the antipathy of the Conservative government towards intervention and public subsidy has significantly affected the readiness of both trade unionists and community members towards mounting anti-closure campaigns. Previous Labour and Conservative governments were susceptible, in particular circumstances, to political pressure regarding the social and economic consequences of closure. In many instances, the concessions won from government were largely symbolic, with factories being kept open with the help of public money, but the workforce itself dramatically reduced.

In certain cases, opposition to closure on the part of unions and communities either overcame the reluctance of government to intervene, or forced the government to revise its strategy towards a particular sector of industry. Much has been made of the role of the miners' strikes in 1972 and 1974 in contributing to the demise of the Conservative government. In many respects, however, the combination of a work-in and community involvement in the campaign to save Upper Clyde Shipbuilders was equally significant in forcing a major reversal in government policy and this marked a turning point between two distinct phases of economic and industrial policy on the part of the Heath government (see chapter 1).

But the Thatcher government has remained obdurate when faced with industrial and political action against the threat of closure. In some parts of the nationalised industries, especially the steel and coal industries, it enforced closure by the criteria it laid down for the performance of the industry and carefully prepared itself to resist economic and political challenges. Given the rigidity of this stance and the political and economic climate in which many closures have been taking place, the trade unions have discovered in many instances that neither their members nor communities were willing to fight for a lost cause.

Even the National Union of Mineworkers, operating in an industry where the consequences of closure for miners and mining communities were likely to be especially profound, had a great deal of difficulty in the lead-up to the 1984 strike. The source of this difficulty in organising a collective response revolved largely around the internal divisions between those insisting that it was necessary to contest the run-down of the industry and those who wanted to negotiate the basis on which further pit closures would take place.

The closures which took place in the steel industry in the first two years of the Thatcher government set the pattern for much that followed. The steel unions took strike action for thirteen weeks from the beginning of January 1980 in what was a set piece confrontation with the government over a pay claim. The eventual settlement at sixteen per cent, in comparison with an initial offer of two per cent, at first sight might appear to represent a victory. However, the strike revealed substantial divisions in the Iron and Steel Trades Confederation: it was unsuccessful in preventing steel being supplied from abroad; the strike effectively collapsed in the private sector; and, rather than making the steel workers battle-hardened, it made them battle-weary. Although the government was defeated, in the sense that the settlement exceeded pay norms, it maintained its non-interventionist stance. At the same time, it laid down the first of the parliamentary bills to outlaw mass picketing and substantially weaken the ability of unions to exert their industrial muscle.

When the British Steel Corporation subsequently announced its programme of closures and massive cutbacks, the willingness of the workforce to resist had been drained. In steel, as in other industries, individual workers resigned themselves to the fact that there seemed little prospect of overturning the closure decisions and this pessimism led the workforce into accepting the relatively large sums being offered as redundancy payments by the Corporation. Under these circumstances, even though communities had responded on previous occasions to calls to defend steel plants, with workforces and communities campaigning together, the community was forced to accept the decision of the workforce. The weakness of the leadership of the steel unions, and the confusion that existed as a result of wrangles over the conduct of the pay strike, had sapped the strength of the steel workers and undermined the chances of an effective community response.

During the 1979–83 period, the trade union movement as a whole adopted a strategy of building up a national campaign for changes in government policy, rather than focusing on the effects of particular closures. Even during the steel strike and its aftermath, when the steel industry was sustaining massive closures, the main thrust of TUC activity was opposition to the government's new employment legislation and the mounting of a national crusade for jobs. Whether this policy was correct in the circumstances is difficult to judge even with hindsight, but the result was that attention was focused on the broad effects of government policy rather than on the particular consequences of closure for communities. Although the trade union movement tried to obtain support from community leaders and community organisations such as the Churches, this was normally not in the context of mobilising a community-based campaign to fight closure in particular localities, but in order to generate opposition to government policy nationally.

The issues involved here are complex and are considered more fully in later chapters. Anti-closure struggles are fundamentally limited in that they are almost always geared towards either getting an employer to change his decision to close a plant or getting government to intervene. Even if in a particular instance the campaign is successful in preventing closure, it generally succeeds only in gaining a temporary reprieve, sometimes at a considerable cost in jobs. Employers have used the opportunity presented by economic conditions and the lack of any interference on the part of government to rationalise production and shed labour, using the threat of closure to obtain the agreement of the workforce. A broad-based political campaign might not have the disadvantage of having such a limited objective but at the same time may not strike the same chord within specific communities.

In most cases, however, trade union leaders at both national and local levels have preferred to use trade union and Labour Party networks, or political channels such as MPs or local authorities, whatever their political complexion, rather than take the issue out into the community. Using only the former means of gathering support may constrict the forms of support that may be available; if communities are potential reservoirs of support, then trade unionists have generally failed to tap them properly. One area where there has sometimes been particular deficiencies is in the activation of public opinion through the media. Even in circumstances where there is some sympathy for the campaign against closure, union officials have frequently failed to make effective use of the press and local radio in getting their arguments across to members of the community.

There is·some evidence to show that unions are becoming more sophisticated in handling both the media and public opinion and that experience of anti-closure campaigns is being passed on and assimilated (many of the larger trade unions, for example, now run training courses to help officials and shop stewards present their case to the press and on television). There is, on the other hand, a risk that constantly stressing the effects that closure will have, or is having, on communities will lead to the exhaustion of public sympathy and indifference. Part of that risk is dissipated by the fact that anti-closure campaigns are essentially temporary; if they succeed in averting closure, the campaign is over, at least until the next attempt at rationalisation; whereas, if they fail, then to continue the campaign against closure would be pointless and some other avenue of response to the after-effects of closure must be found.

To combat major closures, unions have increasingly used sympathetic academics, professional consultants and specialist research staff of their own to vet management plans and make alternative proposals. In most instances, the purpose of the proposals put forward on behalf of the unions is to contest the rationality of the decision to implement a closure in industrial and commercial terms. Increasingly, however, research into closures has taken the social consequences of closure into account and social audits have been drawn up, both by unions and by local authorities, to try to identify the overall costs of closure. Besides illustrating the fact that the cost to the community of closure may be considerably more than the amounts of money required to keep the plant in operation, one of the purposes of such audits is to provide information of the effects on communities in order to convince as many people within the community as possible of the need for a community response.

Social audits are a particularly effective way of pointing up the shortcomings of the economic logic that leads to closure. The justification produced for closure by managements is normally related to the balance sheet; the losses that are being sustained in a particular plant or the inadequacy of the return which is being obtained on capital, relative to profits obtainable elsewhere. Under the capitalist economic system, the only really absolute right is the right of the individual to maximise his return; the capitalist, whether individual or collective, owes no obligation to the community.

Following this logic through, an individual or company is entitled to shut down a factory in an area whatever the cost to the community in unemployment, to the local authority in loss of revenue and to the government in tax, national insurance contributions, the cost of benefit, etc., if it is felt that this is in the best interests of the individual or company. (In the USA there have been attempts, which proved ultimately unsuccessful, by union and community organisations to contest this right in law – see Lynd, 1982. These attempts perhaps reflect a greater faith in the courts to protect the rights of communities or workers than exists among most community organisations or trade unions in Britain). Very little of the true cost of closure, other than statutory obligations such as redundancy payments, are borne by the capitalist. The balance sheet argument is particularly absurd when the plant or industry concerned is run by the government which must absorb the biggest part of the cost in financial terms. This was illustrated in February 1980 when Derwentside and Durham District Councils presented figures at a meeting to discuss the potential consequences of closure at Consett, which showed that the cost to the government of saving an estimated £7 million a year by the closure of the Consett steel mill, would be £14.6 million a year under other headings.

The involvement of local authorities in making a case for the retention of plants in the locality is a particularly important development as it allows anti-closure campaigns to move from being a holding operation, towards becoming part of a broader campaign to contain the process of restructuring in its impact of the local community. Workforces and unions get access to much needed additional resources to make their case and, as we shall see later in this chapter, some local authorities have established mechanisms through which capital can be made available to safeguard jobs by keeping factories open and, where possible, creating new jobs.

Before we move on to look at local authority economic initiatives and the different strands of government policy towards restructuring, however, attention must be turned to the 1984–85 miners' strike which raised a whole series of questions about the role of the community in relation to closure. The political background to the strike has been dealt with fully elsewhere (see for example Beynon, 1985; Lloyd, 1985). In its initial phases, the strike was fought on traditional industrial lines; the objective of the NUM was to block coal production and delivery, to involve all the miners and the coalfields in the action and to call support from other unions like the steelworkers and the railwaymen who were traditional allies of the miners. As the strike progressed, however, communities became increasingly involved not only in coping with the financial hardship and social tensions which were a consequence of the strike, but also in aspects of the day-to-day strike related activities.

The community support the miners enjoyed was based on history and tradition as well as on the dependence of many mining communities on the mining industry. The struggles that had been fought in the past, from the 1920s and 1930s to the 1970s, had a major influence not only on the level of solidarity within the community, but also on the extent to which communities were ready to mobilise in support of the strikers. Miners' welfare clubs were used to feed strikers and their families, and arrangements were made to look after those who were debarred from receiving welfare payments. The determination of the strikers to win through to victory was shared by most members of mining communities.

The extent to which mining communities were united in support of the NUM should not be exaggerated; the strike opened up bitter divisions between coalfields and within communities. Towards the end of the strike, the drift back to work opened up fresh wounds which may take a long time to heal. But it was support from the local communities which allowed the strike to carry on for almost a year, despite the hardship that was entailed. This local support was supplemented by support from trade unions and from community organisations, including miners' support committees up and down the country, which collected hundreds of thousands of pounds by workplace and street corner collections, benefits and donations. Local authorities in particular provided funds to assist miners unable to obtain welfare benefits and also made resources available to local strike committees. Food, as well as money, was collected and through this activity, and speakers from the mining communities coming to explain developments in the strike, non-mining communities began to have an involvement in the strike.

Women played a major role in the strike, not just in running the canteens and soup kitchens, but on the picket lines and in building support both within the pit communities and outside. The establishment of a separate women's organisation, Women Against Pit Closures, was an expression of women's changed role within the community as a result of the strike and became the vehicle for women's participation in the strike itself. In many respects the involvement of women was the bond which knitted together the strikers and the community as a whole. Instead of men fighting closure and women remaining passive, the strike saw a wholesale mobilisation of communities which, as the strike wore on, brought about significant changes in notions of what the strike was about.

The strike's most significant aspect, however, was the way in which the justification for the strike switched from saving jobs and the mining industry towards saving communities. Miners' leaders claimed that the struggle was not just to save their own jobs, but to preserve the chance of employment for miners' children. The threat which was being confronted was economic dereliction and the social dissolution of communities where pits were shut down. The survival of mining communities thus became the central issue in the strike. Community groups and organisations, local authorities, even local shopkeepers and representatives of the clergy were drawn in, not necessarily to support the strike, but to make appeals on behalf of the communities involved.

In the end, the miners were defeated, chiefly because of the enormous cost which the government was prepared to accept in order to win what it saw as a crucial victory. Industrially the strike marks a watershed. After the defeat of the miners, traditionally the most powerful industrial group, other trade unions have had to re-assess their tactics and there has been a move away from reliance on the all-out strike as an industrial weapon. In terms of community politics, on the other hand, the experience and outcome of the miners' strike opened out the question of whether communities should accept the decisions of management or government, or the logic of the market as determining their future in a very stark fashion.

Elsewhere it might be impossible to achieve the community mobilisation behind a workforce that occurred in the miners' strike. The nature of mining communities, the character of the mining industry and the special status that miners enjoy in the labour movement are all factors in making the miners a unique case. The activities of other community based bodies in combating the effects of industrial restructuring, however, especially those of local authorities under Labour control, raise similar issues and have been another avenue of community response. In the next section of the chapter we turn to look at the economic and employment policies of these authorities which, we argue, have to be examined in conjunction with those policies of central government aimed at alleviating the consequences of industrial restructuring on communities.

CENTRAL AND LOCAL GOVERNMENT RESPONSES TO RESTRUCTURING

Given the continued existence of regional policies and the introduction of other measures aimed at assisting disadvantaged communities, it cannot be claimed that the post-1979 Thatcher government wholly ignored the plight of communities affected by industrial restructuring. Limited though they may be in scope and funding, measures aimed at alleviating hardship and sparking economic regeneration have helped communities to deal with the immediate problems they face. Local authorities have participated in many central government initiatives designed to deal with the problems caused by restructuring. Many local authorities' policies have also been designed to maximise the resources which can be extracted from central government and the EEC under various schemes. The economic deterioration of many areas and its attendant social problems have prompted a considerable number of local authorities to introduce additional measures of their own designed to combat the decline.

There are a number of possible ways to analyse central and local government policies aimed at assisting communities affected by restructuring. One obvious method is to categorise them on an institutional basis; separating out central and local government and further subdividing into separate government departments (for example, Department of Trade and Industry, Department of the Environment, Industry Department for Scotland etc.), quasi-bodies (for example, Scottish Development Agency, Welsh Development Agency etc.) and the various types of local authorities (Metropolitan, Shire County, District and Borough Councils in England and Wales, Regional and District Councils in Scotland). A second method would involve classifying policies by functional area. Divisions could be made between locational policies (such as regional policies, industrial promotion, enterprise zones, etc.) aimed at encouraging firms to create new jobs in a specific area; training and technology transfer policies, aimed at updating the skills of workers; and environmental policies aimed at making the area more attractive both for those who live there and for prospective employers.

Both these models are perfectly valid approaches and a case can be made for using either of them. Their disadvantage is that it is very difficult using such systems of classification to separate out the appropriateness or inappropriateness of particular policies as responses to the problems caused by restructuring and their relevance to the needs of communities. In particular, it might give a false picture of the activities of central and local government if we were to separate the two; many policies overlap or are embarked on in co-operation, while some policies are formulated by either central or local government partly in response to the activity or inactivity of the other.

Although our argument is that there is a growing antithesis between the respective approaches of central and local government to the problems posed by restructuring; to draw distinctions between policies, based simply on the institutional source of those policies, would ultimately be unhelpful. To obtain a firmer analytical grasp of the issues involved, we propose the categorisation of policies into the following groupings: 'non-specific', 'reactive' and 'pro-active'.

'Non-specific' policies are those which have been developed and implemented without reference to the effects of job loss in a particular locality. Job loss, or rather the consequences of job loss in the form of high unemployment, may play a role in determining whether or not a locality is eligible to become a beneficiary of a non-specific policy, but the policy itself is not primarily a response to job loss. Examples of non-specific policies would include UK regional policy, small business and community business policies and many of the local economic development measures adopted by local authorities.

'Reactive' policies are those which are put into effect by central or local government, or by private sector bodies, in the aftermath of closure. The distinction between 'reactive' and 'non-specific' policies lies in the fact that the former are implemented explicitly in response to major contractions or closures. The boundaries between 'reactive' and 'non-specific' policies are not always clear-cut, but 'reactive' policies would include the activities of BSC Industry and NCB (Enterprises) Ltd; the task forces which have been set up, for example by the Scottish Development Agency to work in Clydebank and the Garnock Valley; and initiatives taken by local authorities explicitly to deal with the consequences of closures.

'Pro-active' policies are defined as those which attempt to counteract or control pressures which might lead to job loss in a particular region or locality, including the creation of new employment locally. Clearly, this is the most radical of the three approaches. The analysis of the policies of

Local Dimensions of Closure

the post-1979 Conservative government in chapter 1 clearly indicates that the government had a strong antipathy towards any sort of pro-active policy. The development of pro-active policies has therefore been mainly carried out by local authorities. This should not blind us to the fact that central government could, with a different political programme, carry out pro-active policies; indeed, only central government at present has the resources which would be needed to develop a comprehensive and coherent package of pro-active policies, and central government alone is pre-notified of impending closures and redundancies.

Moreover those departments of government with territorial responsibilities such as the Scottish Office, the Welsh Office and the Northern Ireland Office, have in the past been pioneers of pro-active policies. Through the Development Agencies which they sponsor, these departments have continued, even since 1979, to attempt to influence restructuring in particular directions. The policies of central government have not been applied altogether consistently, especially where government departments are pleading on behalf of special interests – either regional or sectoral. The local and regional dimensions are central, however, to our definition; 'pro-active' policies are those which aim to secure the future of existing regional and/or local industry and the workforce on behalf of the community.

i) **Non-specific policies**

Regional policy is spatially targeted on assisted areas (special development areas, development areas, and intermediate areas) which normally do not coincide with economic planning regions. Assisted areas are delineated on the basis of above average unemployment rates. To the extent, therefore, that job loss gives rise to very high levels of unemployment, the classification of assisted areas may reflect the impact of job loss on localities. Even before the flow of job losses became a flood, successive UK governments adopted a blanket approach to assisting problem areas; conferring assisted area status so widely that by 1979, forty-four per cent of the UK population was resident in the assisted areas. This led to criticisms being levelled at regional policy because of its ineffectiveness and because it was increasingly being overtaken by rising levels of unemployment.

This failure to discriminate effectively between localities and the dilution of the assistance available in resource terms was one of the key factors in diminishing the impact of regional policy before 1979. Since

1976–77, governments have taken some steps to make regional policy more selective and also to reduce the extent to which firms in the assisted areas were simply using it as a state subsidy for capital investment, rather than an incentive to create employment. But whereas the original justification for regional policy was to provide a compensatory and redistributive mechanism to balance growth between the various regions and to assist the modernisation and restructuring of British industry, the rationale for regional policies under the Thatcher government has been essentially social and political, rather than economic. Latterly the effects of the policy have been largely neutralised as a result of drastic cuts imposed on expenditure on it.

Ineffective though it may have been, regional policy offered some support to firms in areas of above average unemployment and played a significant role in job creation. It has been suggested that between 1971 and 1981, 268 000 jobs were created in the depressed areas as a result of regional policy and that the policy was continuing to create jobs into the early 1980s (*Guardian*, 26 March 1986). From the standpoint of communities, however, regional policy is unlikely to be the decisive factor in keeping plants open or shutting them down. It is insufficiently oriented to meet the particular needs of firms and local industries in general to be a bulwark protecting the community from the possibility of closure. The deficiencies of the policy as a means of preventing job loss are clearly illustrated by the case of the West Midlands, which was ineligible for regional aid during the 1979–83 period at a time when the region lost proportionally many more jobs than were lost in the development areas. Thus while regional assistance may have tempered the effect of the recession in the historically disadvantaged areas, it may actually have contributed to a worsening of the situation in the West Midlands, where employers could not count on the support from government that they would have been entitled to elsewhere. Certainly, the absence of regional support and the slowness of the government in responding to the rapid deterioration in the relative position of the West Midlands was a source of many complaints from both sides of industry and from local politicians in the area.

Among other 'non-specific' policies which impact on communities are small business policies, local authority land and buildings policies and industrial promotion. Both local authorities and central government are involved in these activities, the latter generally through quasi-governmental agencies whose activities are monitored by government. Small business policies have a particular attraction for the Thatcher administration, given its concern with the nurturing of an 'enterprise culture'. Special emphasis was placed by the government on the need for more unemployed people to consider the possibility of starting up a business. The forms of assistance offered included information and advice on setting up businesses, the loan guarantee scheme, the business expansion scheme and sundry other incentives. In terms of reducing unemployment, there is little evidence to suggest that small business policy has had any significant impact. The worst affected communities are often the worst environments in which to set up small businesses. Even though there may be a surfeit of available skilled and unskilled labour, closures and contractions, as we have already seen, have a series of knock-on effects which affect demand. Unless the product can rapidly reach a market where there is sufficient demand, then the prospects for success of small businesses are limited. Small business policy is more likely to bear fruit in the more prosperous areas than in areas where high unemployment exists as a result of substantial job loss.

Both local government and quasi-governmental bodies have also been involved in land and buildings policies and industrial promotion. Land and premises policies have been used as a way of providing incoming industry with ready-made production facilities, often at below market rates, and cleaning up the environment so that industry can be attracted to locate in a particular area. Industrial promotion involves advertising in the press, sponsoring special press reports, promoting and sponsoring trade fairs and exhibitions and overseas promotion and marketing. More recently, local authorities have established trade, capacity and supplier registers and have increasingly moved towards providing business advice and information on assistance to industry. A recent survey found, for example, that 77 per cent of authorities participated in promotion and marketing and 89 per cent engaged in business development. The problem authorities face in trying to promote their areas, however, is that the pool of available mobile industry is limited and, given the number of bodies engaged in it, promotional activity has become increasingly competitive. Not only do authorities face the prospect of diminishing returns on their outlay as the pool becomes exhausted, but success is often achieved only at the expense of other areas in difficulty.

ii)　Reactive policies

Reactive policies, policies produced directly in response to redundancies and job losses arising out of closure or severe contraction, are implemented in most cases as a response to a particular large-scale closure. The clearest examples of reactive policies are re-industrialisation strategies put into effect by local authorities, private sector firms and the outgoing public sector corporations in the steel and coal industries. These are aimed at job creation, rather than maintaining existing industries. This may mean that the jobs which are created are not matched to the needs of those who have been made redundant, although in some cases there is an attempt to use the existing skills of a workforce by creating 'pheonix' industries.

In Consett, for example, an organisation called 'Derwentside Industrial Development Centre' was set up in 1980 to spearhead the generation of new jobs and this organisation subsequently evolved into Derwentside Industrial Development Agency (DIDA), an enterprise trust financially supported by British Steel Corporation (Industry) Limited, Derwentside District Council and private sector firms. The purpose of this organisation, according to its own literature, was to identify and bring to maturity any project capable of creating long-term employment in Derwentside. DIDA was a 'one-stop' facility, offering advice and assistance which would enable existing and incoming firms to obtain a very favourable package of incentives primarily funded out of money given for that purpose by the government to BSC(I).

This co-ordination of measures to combat the effects of a very large and damaging closure has enjoyed considerable success. By 1984, 1800 jobs had been created. The achievements have to be put into perspective, however, by the fact that over half the 3500 people who were made redundant in 1980 when the steelworks closed were still employed in 1984. In addition, a further 2000 jobs had been lost since 1980 at the two other major plants in the area (RHP and Ever Ready). Although the strategy has not compensated for jobs lost in the collapse of 1980–81, it has more or less managed to compensate for jobs lost since 1982. As Robinson and Sadler (1984, p. 38) point out, however:

> Derwentside is losing its prominent position as the economic disaster area as other places in this and other regions find themselves in the same league in terms of unemployment rates. . . . and as Consett/Derwentside loses its prominence, so it may lose some of the commitment from which it has benefited in the form of 'generous' treatment by Government departments, special funding for factory building and reclamation and so on.

Despite its anti-interventionist stance, even the government was prepared to countenance exceptional measures aimed at job creation, given the depth of the crisis facing Consett after the closure. It is political rather than economic considerations, however, which dominate in the allocation of resources to assist communities like Consett. Once Consett ceases to stand out as the major economic disaster area and the undertaking to assist in the transition following closure lapses, additional support is likely to be withdrawn. Even if it were to continue, the future for the community looks bleak, with unemployment continuing in excess of twenty per cent.

The market philosophy of the Thatcher government in fact began to surface in some of the reactive policies which the government implemented. The Scottish and Welsh Development Agencies shifted the emphasis of their activities from alleviating the consequences of closure in particularly badly affected areas towards initiatives where the agencies acted to promote self-help projects. The SDA for example, which previously had established seven area initiatives mainly in areas where closure and contraction had resulted in massive job loss, creating or providing jobs for over 12 000 people (SDA, 1985), has recently been moving away from gearing initiatives in response to major closures. Thus, even though political considerations made the government fight shy of abolishing the Agency, the SDA has been brought increasingly into line with the main thrust of government policy.

More radical developments in this direction are the creation of enterprise zones, freeports, and urban development corporations. The intention behind enterprise zones, according to the then chancellor, Sir Geoffrey Howe, was that they should 'achieve a significant impact by way of new development, improvement of existing property or increased economic activity within a reasonable scale' (Budget speech, 1980). The means by which these benefits were to be achieved was by the removal of certain fiscal burdens and statutory or administrative controls; taking the form of rates exemptions, exemptions from development land tax, 100 per cent allowances against corporation tax, relaxation of planning controls, exemption from industrial training levies, customs facilities and freedom from requests from government for information. Enterprise zones were initially established in twelve locations in 1980. In 1982 a further ten were added and the total number of zones in 1986 stands at twenty eight. In addition, freeports have been established at Southampton, Brighton, Belfast, Cardiff, Prestwick and Liverpool, and two urban development corporations have been created to bring the dynamism of a Hong Kong type economy to particular areas in the UK.

These initiatives were introduced by the Thatcher government as measures to generate economic activity and create jobs by promoting enterprise. Despite supply side rhetoric, it is clear from the timing of their introduction and the siting of most enterprise zones and freeports that these measures were introduced principally as a political response to unemployment and industrial closure. The zones were created mainly in areas that had suffered particularly badly, rather than in places where there might have been a more logical case on purely economic grounds for situating them. Enterprise zones have enjoyed mixed success, some have patently failed while others have attracted a considerable volume of new industry (Catalano, 1984). In many instances, however, enterprise zones have simply acted as a magnet for firms already located in the vicinity of the zone, adding little to the stock of jobs in the area or region.

Among other policies aimed at alleviating unemployment within specific communities was the Community Programme. The intention behind the Community Programme was to give the long-term unemployed fresh work experience in order to improve their employment prospects. In 1985, over 140 000 people were on Community Projects in the UK. The problem with the Community Programme and other training schemes in localities where high levels of unemployment are prevalent is that if there are few available jobs, the improvement of the employment prospects of one group is achieved only at the expense of another group, with no net effect on the overall numbers unemployed. The effect is cosmetic rather than a serious attempt to deal with the unemployment problems of badly affected areas.

iii) Pro-active policies

Most local authorities are realistic enough to recognise that they will not be able to achieve the regeneration of the local economy. Even arresting the decline may be beyond their capabilities, given the limited resources they can bring to bear and the constraints under which they operate. None the less, local authorities have been forced to become increasingly involved in economic development, not just by the gravity of the situation for the local economy, but also as a consequence of the vacuum created by the non-interventionist policies adopted by central government. The object of local authority initiatives is therefore limited; it is not to halt the restructuring process, but to exercise some sort of control over it, and to deflect some of the consequences it might otherwise have, especially in terms of increased demand for some of the welfare services provided by local authorities.

The most significant responses to the effects of restructuring on communities and localities have been the economic and employment initiatives. Traditionally, local authorities have not concerned themselves with the practical functioning of the local economy. Their involvement was in most cases restricted before the mid-1970s to land and buildings policies. These policies involved making provision for factory space and essential services for existing and incoming industry, and industrial promotion aimed at attracting inward investment. Economic development was not a statutory responsibility of local authorities and tended to have a low priority among councillors when set against the administration of mainstream local authority services.

Given their overall responsibility for the well-being of the areas they cover, many local authorities felt obliged to intervene once economic conditions worsened in order to prevent further damage and to sustain local industry. The initial reason for local authority involvement with the economic structure of their areas was therefore defensive; it was to protect areas from the consequences of restructuring. Early initiatives included the establishment of a co-ordinating Employment and Economic Development sub-committee by West Yorkshire County Council to assist in the production of a structure plan for the area. The plan was to form the basis on which the authority could orchestrate its activities (Mawson et al., 1983).

The fact that this sub-committee survived the transfer of power to a Conservative adminstration in 1977 indicates that at a local level the need for local authority initiatives was recognised by both major parties. Even though Conservative councillors in West Yorkshire and in other badly affected parts of the country were less inclined than their Labour counterparts to support local authority intervention in the affairs of particular firms, they none the less accepted the need for local authorities to develop their own economic policies if industrial regeneration was to take place and if public resources were to be used effectively as a means of achieving this.

This acceptance was reinforced by the attitude of central government. There seemed to be no point in local authorities lobbying central government for assistance once the policies of the post-1979 government became clear. If something was to be done, then local authorities would have to take action themselves. One important step in this direction was the establishment by Sheffield City Council of an Employment Department with its own chief officer. Sheffield had lost 15 500 jobs in the steel industry between 1978 and 1981, and many more jobs were lost in related industries such as engineering.

According to a document entitled *An Initial Outline* (City of Sheffield Employment Department, 1982):

The immediate reason for setting up an Employment Department is ... the rapid rise in unemployment and the crisis facing Sheffield's traditional industries. However, the longer term aim is to try to gain more direct, local, democratic control over employment, and to try to impose a greater degree of social planning on the structural and technological changes taking place in Sheffield, along with many other manufacturing communities.

The more positive approach intimated in the document is highly significant. The authority was seeking to intervene not just to protect jobs but actively to influence the restructuring process. Central government policy provided a further stimulus to this with the imposition of expenditure controls which induced many local authorities to set up development corporations and enterprise boards as a means of avoiding controls and conserving resources. Finally, the accession to power of the Labour party in some of the larger local authorities triggered off the launching of a range of local economic initiatives.

In many ways, the most significant of these initiatives was the establishment of enterprise boards. The lead in setting up enterprise boards was taken by the Greater London Council and the West Midlands County Council, and by 1985 approximately twenty local authorities had set up enterprise boards or development corporations taking on similar tasks. The prime intention of enterprise boards was to provide a mechanism through which local authorities could invest in local industry and, through this, influence companies' response to restructuring in a preferred direction. To do this more effectively, local enterprise boards have recruited specialist staff whose job it is to analyse trends in the local economy, identify key sectors, evaluate company prospects and investment needs and monitor the activities of client companies over the longer term.

Not all authorities have felt that the creation of enterprise boards is necessary in order for local authorities to carry out this sort of activity. In Sheffield for example, the City Council has taken the view that it is preferable for the Council to exercise direct control over these activities through the Employment Department. In most cases, however, it was felt that creating a separate board would be more acceptable both to central government and to the private sector, and would insulate the board from the likelihood of sudden policy shifts consequent on any change in political control over the parent authority.

The initial source of finance for local government economic initiatives has been grants or loans made available by local authorities under Section 137 of the 1972 Local Government Act, which allows authorities to raise funds up to a 2p rate for use 'in the interests of their area'. This source of funding has been consolidated under the 1982 Local Government Act, which allows authorities to provide financial assistance to individuals and companies. Funding has been supplemented by money obtained from private and other public sources. The success of enterprise boards has been based to a considerable extent on their ability to attract private sector funds, either on a partnership basis between the board and banks, insurance companies and pension funds or, alternatively, where the enterprise board acts as an agent for other institutions, managing an investment.

The firms which approach enterprise boards do so when facing financial and other problems. Not all investments are in firms in need of capital to get started or ensure survival; some funding is given to finance merger, demerger, expansion or corporate restructuring. Once a firm does approach an enterprise board, a thorough investigation is carried out. This is to see whether the management of the firm is sound, whether there is a realistic business plan, whether the product which the firm produces has reasonable prospects in the marketplace and whether investment in the firm would fit in with the overall strategic programme developed by the local authority. If the business concerned meets these criteria the enterprise board may provide grants or loans, or may take an equity share in the business.

In most instances, conditions are attached to funding, generally in the form of a planning agreement between the firm and the board. The desire to monitor closely the operation of these agreements has been an important factor in leading many enterprise boards to take equity in companies rather than offer grants or loans. Another factor has been the desire on the part of those running enterprise boards to exercise influence over a longer term on assisted firms. Planning agreements might typically involve restrictions on the movement of plant or jobs to another area; compliance with employment legislation and desirable employment practices such as equal opportunities; conferring full trade union rights on employees and allowing union participation in the decision making process. In addition to these requirements, enterprise boards have demanded on occasion that the investment is accompanied by managerial changes, either in personnel or strategy in order to maximise the chances of success. This combination of commercial and broader social and economic considerations in the drawing up of planning agreements is a distinctive feature of the work of the enterprise boards.

Many local authorities have set up early warning systems whereby companies likely to experience difficulties are identified at an early stage. Local trade union organisations and the specialist staff recruited by local authorities play a key role in gathering information. The research activities of enterprise boards and local authority departments have themselves added a very significant dimension to the authorities' involvement in the local economy. Councillors have been made much more aware about the state of local industry and the knowledge and experience which has been gained has frequently been used to develop and direct policies.

Although the activities of enterprise boards have been tailored to local requirements, there are different needs in different parts of the country and a wide diversity of approaches have been adopted. West Midlands Enterprise Board, for example, has concentrated on medium-sized companies in strategically important sectors, which are viable as industrial units, but have encountered difficulties as a result of shortage of capital or company restructuring. The West Yorkshire Enterprise Board, on the other hand, has invested in smaller companies and concentrated on locations within the region, rather than on sectors, even though the economy of the region has been hit by the decline of a leading sector.

Both enterprise boards have seen their major contribution in connecting local firms with sources of medium- and long-term capital. Financial institutions, it is argued, typically prefer to invest on a short-term basis or where there are few risks. If an enterprise board, using local authority funding, is prepared to cover part of a risk and also has a good track record at managing investments, then major financial institutions will be inclined to be sympathetic towards making joint investments. There is a risk in this that enterprise boards might end up simply playing the role of a specialist merchant bank. Enterprise boards would have little validity as local authority responses to restructuring if they were simply to act as surrogate suppliers of development capital from the private sector. The critical dimension that separates out enterprise boards from financial institutions is the fact that their strategic and operational objectives have been established by the parent local authorities and control continues to be exercised over them by local councillors.

The problems which exist in the London economy are obviously different from those which exist in the West Midlands or West

Yorkshire. According to the Greater London Enterprise Board, the major problems arose out of changing markets and the development of new methods of production. In contrast to the West Midlands policy of providing conditional support for manufacturing in strategic sectors, the Greater London Enterprise Board emphasised the importance of influencing restructuring by advantaging labour in the form of better conditions, more jobs and improving the employment prospects of disadvantaged sections of the community, including women and the ethnic minorities. The West Midlands County Council and its Enterprise Board also prioritised the acquisition of skill and co-operatives. But the differences between the policies of the West Midlands Enterprise Board and the Greater London Enterprise Board were not just a consequence of the differences that existed between the economic situation in the two places. They reflected contrasting approaches within a single broad political framework which informed the diagnoses of the problems of the respective areas.

In the case of GLEB, the survival of existing industry was seen as secondary to the need for local authorities to help labour adapt and create new employment possibilities. This type of approach, which favoured particularly worker controlled production, co-operatives and community businesses, fitted in closely with the general policy orientation of the Labour controlled Greater London Council. Besides providing investment funding for employment projects, the GLC set up a Popular Planning Unit to promote and communicate its strategy to the wider community in London and to specific groups. The aim was to bring about a broad popular political mobilisation by targeting particular segments of the community and providing active support and assistance to community groups. In *The London Industrial Strategy*, published by the GLC in June 1985, the role of trade unions, consumer groups and other community organisations was heavily emphasised and the document has been used as a framework for campaigning among these groups by the Labour party in London.

Other enterprise boards have implemented strategies based on either one or other of these models, some combination of the two or with some policies peculiar to the particular authority. The approaches of the WMEB and the GLEB were very influential and were widely copied. Since 1983 there has been a growing dissatisfaction within some labour authorities at having to perform a fire-fighting role in coming to the assistance of firms about to go into liquidation. Authorities came to recognise that with limited resources and small staffs they were unable to provide a comprehensive service for the whole local economy and that they should therefore specialise. This led some authorities such as Sheffield and Leeds City Councils to concentrate on initiatives linked to existing local authority functions where the authority already had staff and could use its other resources in support of initiatives.

The approach pioneered by the enterprise boards and economic development and employment departments of the local authorities has spread to the running of the affairs of the authorities themselves. Local councils are major employers and exert a great influence on the local economy, especially in those areas where manufacturing has been devastated and few new jobs have been created. One of the ways that local authorities have found to protect jobs in local industry has been to divert their purchasing and contracts towards firms in the locality. Whilst there are legal limitations on authorities' ability to exclude outside firms from tendering for contracts, there has undoubtedly been a move by local authorities towards using their control over expenditure to achieve social and economic objectives. Local authorities have also come to examine their own employment practices as a result of concern with this issue in the local economy generally, often making significant modifications both in terms of employment practices and in terms of trying to maximise the resources available to create new jobs.

Typically, therefore, authorities have come to see enterprise boards and employment and development initiatives as one element in a range of interventionist measures designed to meet particular political objectives. Concern with the broad restructuring process, rather than simply job loss and unemployment, has led some local authorities to invest in new forms of training provision. Leeds City Council, for example, has established workshop schemes geared towards cultivating skills in micro-electronic engineering and computer programming among unemployed teenagers. These initiatives have to some extent been undermined by a reduction in central government funding for ITECs, the inner city training centres, of five per cent for 1987. Despite government spending restrictions, however, local authorities are attempting both to create a skilled workforce which might attract potential employers and to provide training which gives disadvantaged people some chance of gaining employment connected with the use of new technology.

The impact of new technology and the need to modernise local industry and attract new employment has led several local authorities into collaboration with universities and polytechnics. Examples of this collaboration are the establishment of science parks and the sponsoring of research aimed at making new technology available to local people and local firms. One of the main factors which stimulated the latter was the example set by the Lucas Aerospace Alternative plan drawn up by shop stewards at the Lucas plant in response to redundancy proposals from the company's management (Wainwright and Elliot, 1982). The Lucas stewards advocated the switching of resources and investment from 'socially destructive' purposes towards making 'socially useful' products such as energy saving vehicles and equipment for use by the disabled. A number of the larger local authorities have subsequently set up units aimed at developing new products either within the authority itself or in higher educational institutions. A good example of an authority involving itself in the development of useful products is the involvement of Sheffield City Council in commissioning work on producing a de-humidifier to prevent dampness in houses which could potentially be sold to local authorities in other areas.

This concern with new technology symbolises the innovative and positive side of local authority initiatives. Obviously the initiatives have only had a small impact on the economic situation in those areas where they have been put into effect. The financial restrictions imposed by central government on local authority expenditure, and the scale of the problems which other departments of the local authorities have to deal with, have ruled out anything other than limited intervention. These limits on the extent to which local authorities and enterprise boards have been able to act should not be allowed to disguise either the positive effects which intervention has had, or the significance of local economic initiatives as both experiment and propaganda.

CONCLUSION

In the course of this chapter we have seen the ways in which industrial restructuring has disproportionately affected particular communities, and examined the responses which communities have made both to the threat of closure and to the consequences of the restructuring process. The policies of central government have played a crucial role in this. The refusal of government to make resources available to protect communities from the effects of restructuring inhibited some sorts of responses and resulted in others. The Conservative government's determination to enforce the logic of the market and to resist political challenges to market domination (noted in chapter 1) has had a major influence on the nature and effectiveness of different responses that have been made. Finally, the antipathy of central government towards those local authorities that mounted the most effective responses to restructuring on behalf of communities culminated, in 1986, in the abolition of the metropolitan counties – the parent bodies of many of the more successful enterprise boards.

Enterprise boards will, in many cases, survive in the former metropolitan counties, albeit in altered form, administered conjointly by the district councils which will take over the functions of the metropolitan authorities. In some places, consideration has been given to floating the boards as private sector companies, using the existing capital base and with former councillors retaining control as board members. It is not the survival of enterprise boards as institutions, however, but the ideas that they embodied which may have ultimately the greater effect.

There is, in Britain, an intense conflict between different economic philosophies, between a 'left' and a 'right' approach to restructuring. The Conservatives take the view that restructuring is an essential and natural process of renewal within capitalism which government should foster rather than curtail in the long term interests of the economy. This economic approach of central government is in many ways blind to the consequences of economic change for communities. It implicitly denies that consideration should be given to the position of communities in arriving at policy. In the context of restructuring, what this means is that if the market cannot create new employment, either with government assistance or without it, then logically the human resources of the community should disperse in search of employment elsewhere. The imperatives of the market take precedence over the integrity and survival of communities.

Labour local authorities, on the other hand, have argued that the costs of market-led restructuring are unacceptable and that it is the responsibility of local and central governments to intervene both to alleviate the consequences of restructuring and to influence the process of economic change in ways that benefit the community. This disagreement is not purely academic. As David Blunkett (*Guardian*, 17 June 1983), leader of Sheffield City Council, has suggested:

> Local government is threatened so severely by Thatcher because it offers a genuine and legitimate defence against the encroachment of a new order. It is a living example of community as opposed to private endeavour. In key areas it offers a coherent socialist alternative which genuinely wins popular support.

The crucial element is the focus on the community and community needs. What local authorities have been doing is showing that there can be an alternative. Each successful economic initiative is in a sense a demonstration that local and regional economies can be revived through the actions of public sector bodies. The limited resources with which enterprise boards and local authorities have had to work, especially given the ever tightening restrictions which have been placed on authorities by central government, have restricted the scope of what can be achieved. One thing that perhaps has been demonstrated is the need for large local authorities, covering entire regions, metropolitan areas or very sizeable areas within regions, if authorities are to function effectively in the economic sphere. Such authorities would be much better able than smaller authorities to identify and assist strategic sectors of industry and to direct resources on the scale which might be required.

The bringing into being of mega- local authorities of this sort, or the devolution of some economic decision-making powers to regional assemblies, are possible methods of creating the required tier of government. The creation of such bodies would, however, fundamentally alter the character of local government. Although the Labour party, amongst others, is committed to devolution for Scotland and Wales as well as regional decentralisation, there is as yet no detailed working out of the implications of this for local authorities. With regard to economic policy, Labour politicians do not seem to have decided amongst themselves on the balance to be sought between local or regional and national control. While John Smith, as shadow industry minister, has indicated his intention of giving greater decision-making powers to local authorities and has taken a strong interest in the activities of enterprise boards, Roy Hattersley, as shadow chancellor, has emphasised the need for a National Investment Bank and the policies which could be pursued nationally.

The entry into parliament of individuals such as Ken Livingstone and David Blunkett, who have been powerful influences on the development of 'municipal socialism', may have an impact on Labour party policy. One indication of the effect that local socialism may already have had is the use both by Neil Kinnock, and Robin Murray of the Greater London Enterprise Board, of the idea of the 'enabling' as opposed to the 'providing' state. One reason for developing the idea of the enabling state is to dissociate the Labour party from its own past reliance on the central state and the imposition of social programmes from above. Neil Kinnock has gone out of his way to emphasise the concern with liberty as part of Labour's appeal. The enabling state has also been a crucial notion in developing policies that involve the participation of the community rather than policies developed 'for' the community. The importance of the experiments with local economic initiatives may not be fully recognised until and unless the Labour party returns to government.

There are limits to what can be achieved by either local or central government within a capitalist economy. Cochrane (1983) has described local economic initiatives as trying to drain an ocean with a teaspoon, and it may well be that both local and national economic policies are inadequate to turn the tide in the context of an international capitalist economy. Local economic policies should not, however, be rejected because they do not provide complete solutions. In many ways, their most important function may be to raise specific issues in the context of an economic system which, by its very nature, takes no cognisance of the needs of communities. In so far as these policies may ease the plight of particular communities and help to maintain at least some sort of employment within local economies, they are valuable in themselves.

3 Resistance, Restructuring and Gender: The Plessey Occupation
Patricia Findlay

INTRODUCTION

The first years of the 1980s have been characterised by a resurgence in the use of the factory occupation in industrial disputes. Various occupations have attracted large amounts of media coverage, much of it sympathetic, and have obtained overwhelming public support in the communities in which the occupations have taken place. The sit-ins at Lee Jeans in Greenock and at Lovable in Cumbernauld are just two examples from this period.

The present analysis will focus on the occupation of the Bathgate plant of Plessey Capacitors which took place in 1982. The Plessey occupation is interesting in several respects: first, it occurred at a time when unemployment was rising rapidly in Bathgate; secondly, it occurred in the electronics industry, a growth sector of the economy – not a declining traditional industry; thirdly, the workers at Bathgate were not known for their militancy – most were middle aged female workers, many taking industrial action for the first time in their lives, despite aggressive employer tactics against them; and finally, the legal aspects of the Plessey sit-in are of particular importance.

This chapter will, therefore, examine the reasons for the adoption of the sit-in strategy to confront closure; the degree of success of this strategy, and, following from this, will look at the particular role of gender and its impact upon the conduct of this dispute. The material presented here is based on a series of interviews carried out in the period August to November 1983. Time constraints prevented interviewing the workforce on a large scale. However, attempts were made to interview representatives of the various categories of workers involved in the dispute: that is, shop stewards, both male and female; ordinary workers involved in the occupation, including workers who had been re-employed after the occupation as well as workers who had been made

70

redundant; full time union officials; and members of a group which acted as a support to the Plessey workers. Attempts were made to interview a representative of the Plessey management and a representative of the Engineering Employers' Federation, of which Plessey is a member, but both refused to be interviewed. This case study attempts to bring together the views held by these workers, as well as the opinions expressed in publications concerning the occupation.

The workers of the Plessey plant chose to occupy their factory in response to its proposed closure, rather than to negotiate with the company over the closure through official trade union channels. Why was such a tactic chosen? This can be considered in terms of three main conditions which the chosen form of industrial action had to satisfy. First, the action had to generate the support and active involvement of the majority of workers threatened with redundancy. Secondly, it had to take account of the rationale behind the operation of multinational corporations like Plessey, and therefore had to have the potential of challenging directly that rationale. Thirdly, the form of action chosen had to be able to overcome the usual limitations of official trade union action with respect to closure. The Plessey workers' assessment of the sit-in as a strategy which could fulfil these three conditions will be looked at in more detail. Some evaluation will be made of the potential gains for workers in choosing direct action rather than negotiation in response to the policies of multinational corporations, as well as any limitations in doing so. Before this, however, the dispute must be set in context by looking at the main activities of the Plessey Company worldwide, particularly at its changing corporate strategies in recent years; as well as the setting up of the Plessey plant in Bathgate; the characteristics of its workforce; and its industrial relations.

THE PLESSEY COMPANY

Plessey began as a small jig and tool-making firm in East London in 1917. The company expanded steadily in the years up to the Second World War, and after the war, a series of mergers diversified the company into such areas as machine tool control, hydraulics and consumer electricals. Further mergers took place in the 1960s, bringing Plessey into the areas of telecommunications, numerical control, radar and semiconductors. Today Plessey's business activity is made up of three main divisions: telecommunications and office systems, electronics systems and engineering. The company operates in 130 countries, having research and development establishments in thirteen countries. This does not put Plessey, however, in the top league of multinational corporations by the standards of its international competitors like IBM. Plessey is the fourth largest UK electronics company (TURU Report, 1982), and ranks twenty-seventh in the league table of leading British manufacturing multinationals (Labour Research, 1978). Sales in the United Kingdom account for 51 per cent of Plessey's turnover, with its next largest market being the USA, with fourteen per cent of sales. Continental Europe and Asia follow closely behind. The group also has sales and subsidiaries in Africa, including South Africa, Australia and Latin America.

In terms of sales and profits, telecommunications and electronic systems and equipment are the mainstay of Plessey's business. Taken together, these areas provided Plessey with 76 per cent of its operating profit and 72 per cent of sales in 1981-82. Most of these sales figures stem from state contracts, with British Telecom and government departments (particularly the Ministry of Defence) being Plessey's major customers. State involvement in Plessey has also taken the form of government grants and finance to assist in the development of projects specific to the Plessey company (see Elder, 1982) and state finance in the general area of electronics, which recent governments have considered the growth industry of the future. Plessey clearly has need of the state and, it is logical to assume, will act in such a way as to ensure that the state is sympathetic to its interests. In particular, the Plessey company has nurtured contacts with the Conservative Party, contributing to the party's funds to the sum of £74 672 in 1970-71 (CSE, 1982), and to other organisations linked to the Tory Party (in 1970-81 the British United Industrialists received £133 000, while the Centre for Policy Studies received £4000 in the period 1976-80).

Finally, in this brief review of the Plessey company, in 1975 it employed approximately 55 180 workers in the UK. But by 1981, Plessey's UK workforce had fallen to 39 922 – a fall of around 35 per cent. The reasons behind such a massive fall in employment levels will be looked at in some depth later.

PLESSEY CAPACITORS, BATHGATE

Plessey Capacitors, a wholly owned subsidiary of Plessey Ltd., began its operations in Bathgate in 1965, after taking over the existing plant of the Telegraph Condenser Company. TCC had set up in Bathgate in 1947 to manufacture condensers for electrical and electronic machinery. Before this, the town had relied on the shale oil, coal, iron and steel industries for employment. TCC was, therefore, the first major employer in the area not dependent on the exploitation of natural resources. Further, its establishment linked the local economy to one of the post-war boom industries, and brought increased employment opportunities for women. This was of importance in an area dominated by traditional industries, where employment was almost wholly a male preserve. The takeover incorporated the Bathgate plant and its workforce into a major international manufacturing operation in the increasingly competitive electronics industry. The Bathgate factory consisted of four plants producing four lines of capacitors and some related products. Employment at the plant rose from 1400 in 1965 to around 2400 by 1973. Around 75 per cent of the employees at the plant were women involved in the production of capacitors.

In the years before the occupation, Plessey was considered by many of its workers at Bathgate to be a relatively good employer in terms of wages and conditions, comparing favourably with other plants in the area. In contrast to many of the electronics plants in Scotland, trade unions were accepted by the Plessey management at Bathgate, and the workforce was heavily unionised. The majority of assembly workers were members of the Amalgamated Union of Engineering Workers, while the staff employees were represented by TASS. A small number of workers were represented by the Electrical, Electronic, Telecommunications and Plumbing Union and the Association of Professional, Executive, Clerical and Computer Staff.

It appears that industrial relations at Plessey Bathgate were relatively peaceful up until the 1980s. Most workers could remember only one major stoppage in the period since the Plessey takeover, when the workforce took part in a national strike in pursuance of the thirty five hour working week. There had also been some short, unofficial strikes over the years, mainly among the staff members of TASS.

Plessey's decision to invest in the Bathgate plant in 1965 was, in some ways, the result of attempts made by local leaders from the late 1950s onwards to attract external capital to the town, to compensate for the continual decline of the town's two traditional industries (coal and shale oil), and the weakness of the local manufacturing base. This campaign coincided with the introduction of government measures to boost regional development. The campaign paid off, in January 1960, when the British Motor Corporation announced its intention to build an £11 million truck and tractor assembly plant on the outskirts of Bathgate.

This development, along with the October announcement that the Rootes Company was to build a £23 million car plant in Linwood, was seen as the first steps towards the establishment of an integrated Scottish vehicle industry. When the British Motor Corporation plant came into operation in 1961, the company announced a target labour force of 5600, with only a small number of these being recruited outside Scotland.

However, Bathgate's period of industrial prosperity, brought about by incoming firms such as BL and Plessey, was fairly short-lived. By the mid-1960s it was evident that the motor industry was especially vulnerable to the first throes of world recession and that BMC (later to become BL) was in difficulty. Indeed, in 1967 BMC's share of the world truck market was halved in a single year. Thereafter, 'rationalisation' became a consistent management strategy at Bathgate, with over 2000 jobs shed in BL by 1981. This strategy eventually culminated in the closure of the plant in 1986.

But BL was not the only casualty in Bathgate of Britain's continued economic decline. The town's local steel foundries and fire brick manufacturers also cut back on employment throughout the late 1970s and early 1980s. Contraction was also experienced in local public sector employment as a result of public expenditure cuts. A further blow to Bathgate came in the late 1970s with the transfer of some of its local public services – such as the district hospital and the head post office – to Livingston New Town. In addition, Livingston's clean environment, new roads and housing, and its particularly energetic development corporation meant that it attracted the bulk of overseas investment in the area.

In this general environment, the Plessey company itself was not immune from restructuring. In the late 1970s and early 1980s, the Bathgate plant became the victim of Plessey's changing corporate strategies. In the post-war period, Plessey had followed a policy of mergers, expansion and diversification, such that between 1962 and 1971 the company's turnover grew fivefold. Nevertheless, Plessey's profitability record was poor, with earnings per share in 1971 the same as they had been in 1963.

In response to this, Plessey began to pursue a policy of consolidation and 'strategic divestment' in the early 1970s. This involved the elimination of all those businesses considered to be outside the mainstream activities of the company, such as turntables, hydraulics, sheet metals and capacitors, in order to release resources for more lucrative areas of production, such as office systems and defence equipment. It was not considered important that in some cases these items were being produced profitably. As Elder (1982) points out, on the basis of an interview with a senior Plessey executive, the issue had to be looked at from a corporate standpoint, where the key issue was total corporate profit position, not individual plant profitability. Thus, the company appear to have based their decision to move into other areas of production on the expectation that a higher rate of profit could be secured.

As pointed out earlier, the employment consequences of the strategic divestment policy were immense, with UK employment falling by 35 per cent. The Bathgate plant did not escape rationalisation, and through both voluntary and compulsory redundancy, employment levels fell steadily from 1973, when 2400 workers were employed, until 1981, when only 330 workers were left at the plant. This was the size of the workforce at the time of the occupation.

In retrospect, it is surprising that there was little worker reaction against the redundancies, although many of the stewards had argued that redundancies should be resisted. As one of the women interviewed told me: 'there were big rows because we couldn't stop people volunteering for redundancy. The shop stewards wanted them to fight, and not sell their jobs, but they didn't take any notice . . . people could get jobs in Edinburgh then . . . it's different now'. It is interesting to speculate on why no worker action was taken in response to previous job losses. The women themselves argued that at the time of these redundancies the surrounding labour market was less depressed, and thus the effects of redundancies may not have been so severe. Further, there were hopes that cutbacks in production and job losses could be reversed at a later date when the effects of the world recession had lessened. The closure announcement destroyed any such hopes!

In December 1981, Plessey announced that the Bathgate capacitor division would close in March 1982, on the grounds that the capacitor market was flooded; that the plant itself was technologically obsolete; and that the factory was making losses of £500 000 per annum – despite a significant investment programme in recent years. This announcement set in motion an occupation by over 220 workers. The occupation lasted eight weeks, and ended with a takeover by Wedge International Holdings BV, the company to which the entire capacitor division of Plessey, both in the UK and abroad, was sold. The takeover retained sixty two jobs at the plant, while the rest of the workforce was made redundant.

THE DECISION TO OCCUPY

Most of the Bathgate workforce were totally stunned by the closure announcement. Although they had been on reduced working hours for some time, and had witnessed a gradual rundown in production and employment at the plant over the years, very few of the rank and file workers expected complete closure. Given the strength of feeling amongst the Plessey workforce at the time of the closure announcement, some worker action to resist closure was inevitable. Resistance was further strengthened by the knowledge that closure would inevitably lead to unemployment for most workers. In 1981 there were already 3350 men and 1685 women unemployed in the Bathgate area as a result of the continual decline of the area's traditional industries and major manufacturing establishments. Indeed, taking Bathgate and the nearby towns of Broxburn and Livingston together, male unemployment stood at twenty one per cent, while official female unemployment stood at nineteen per cent. As one Plessey worker commented: 'I was only 45, and I was thinking, where will I get another job at my age, with so many unemployed?'

Concern for the future of the local communities also increased the resolve to fight. Pervading the views of all the women interviewed was a concern for the relatively tight knit communities, and particularly the youth of Bathgate and its surrounding areas: 'We had watched the place go down through the years and there wasn't any other employment in the area. . . this was the major employer for women in the area . . . so the women had said, enough is enough'. 'We all thought the same – where are our kids going to work?' This concern was especially strong among the older women, many of whom were approaching retirement age, having worked in the plant for more than thirty years. For these women, it would have been in their own self-interest to have taken their redundancy payments, but they decided to support the sit-in for the sake of maintaining employment in the area, thus risking the loss of their redundancy entitlement.

However, the reasons put forward most strongly by the Plessey workforce to justify their resistance to the plant closure was a belief in their own profitability. The workers were very scathing of Plessey's claims of heavy losses and technological obsolescence of the equipment at Bathgate. These management claims were greeted with total disbelief. And this disbelief on the part of the workforce was a major contribution to the strength of feeling that the closure should be resisted.

The Plessey workers believed, and were eventually proved right, that the company's aim was to move out of capacitor manufacture altogether. It is plausible to argue that for some years Plessey had been interested in getting out of components production in the UK. The introduction, in recent years, of technologically advanced machinery at Plessey's Arco factory in Italy meant that the company was able to consider closing production at Bathgate. These developments had made the Arco production line, which produces many of the same products as the Bathgate plant, far more highly automated in comparison with the relatively labour intensive production process in the Scottish plant. Indeed, a report by the Edinburgh CSE group argued that Plessey's concentration of their research and development effort at Arco, and the neglect of Bathgate (that is, the failure to invest in the modernisation of the production line, or even to keep the factory building, granted free from the SDA, in good repair) indicated that a decision to concentrate capacitor production in a single plant in Arco had been taken at a far earlier stage than the Bathgate closure announcement. Such an argument would also explain the specific statement of the management at Bathgate that under no circumstances would they consider selling off machinery. To the workers this implied that the machinery would be relocated in another Plessey plant – most probably at Arco or at one of the company's German plants. Hence, the management statement simply cast further doubts in the mind of the workforce that the plant was obsolete.

The workforce's own assessment of the product lines at Bathgate was that they were far from the state of obsolescence as described by management. In fact, Plessey's 'minibox' automated production line was technologically advanced, and, the workers believed, had a reasonable lifetime ahead of it. The same capacitor was being mass produced at Plessey's highly profitable and expanding plant at Arco, in Italy. With regard to the metallised polypropylene capacitor line, Plessey had full order books, and was holding its own in the market for this product. Other lines, filters and suppressors, were special design jobs for customers, which required a highly skilled team of design engineers, whose knowledge clearly constituted a valuable asset to the firm. The manufacture of filters was a new line at Bathgate, which the workers and the CSE group believed had a long life ahead of it, and at the time of the closure announcement, the order books for this product were full. Only paper and high voltage capacitors, the oldest lines at Bathgate, were identified as being technologically obsolete; but even then it was believed that these lines would remain modestly profitable for some years to come.

The workforce's assessment was supported by a report on the plant's profitability by the Trade Union Research Unit of Glasgow College of Technology (TURU, 1982). This report pointed out that while there were two other capacitor manufacturing operations in Scotland, (Hughes Micro-Electronics in Glenrothes, and Sprague Electrical in Galashiels – both foreign owned), their product ranges were narrower than Bathgate's, and their combined sales only half of Bathgate's. Plessey Bathgate was therefore Scotland's major manufacturer of capacitors. The Report agreed with the workers' assessment that the machinery at Bathgate was not technologically obsolete. It was felt that the manufacturing equipment installed at Bathgate was comparable, in terms of efficiency, with that used by other manufacturers. Indeed, £200 000 worth of new machinery had been installed at Bathgate as recently as September 1981. The Report argued that Plessey's strategy of trying to build up defence contracts and communications systems and software, while at the same time phasing out its manufacture of microelectronics and components, including capacitors, was extremely risky. It also argued that to sell out the major British owned capacitor operation into foreign control, or cut back, or close, the major manufacturing base of that operation (Bathgate) made no sense for the electronics components industry or for the Scottish, or UK, economy.

At the time of the closure announcement, the order books of the Bathgate plant were full and growing. The annual accounts of Plessey Capacitors, Bathgate show sales of £6 575 000 in 1981, an increase of £128 000 on the previous year's figures. Yet the annual profit and loss statements for Plessey Capacitors for 1979, 1980 and 1981 reveal losses on sales in each year. The workforce, however, was able to demonstrate that these losses were deliberately engineered by the company. The accompanying notes to the annual reports were used to show that 'paper losses' were recorded; whereby in 1979, for instance, provision was made for 'product rationalisation, including redundancy and evacuation of building costs', so, effectively converting a profit on trade for that year into a substantial loss.

The true picture of the plant's profitability was further obscured, in the workforce's eyes, by Plessey's transfer pricing policy. Transfer prices between Plessey's plants were set at levels detrimental to Bathgate; with the result that some of Bathgate's actual profits were transferred to other plants. Moreover, there was a belief that the company was also diverting orders to other plants – again to the detriment of Bathgate. Certain long standing orders ceased to be placed at Bathgate:

this didn't ring true in the capacitor world. In the capacitor industry you have to keep ahead with new designs, but old designs keep on going – they trickle out – they don't dry up at once.

I just didn't believe them – there was a lot of our work going down to England, and Plessey were deliberately diverting orders.

This disbelief of the management case, and the workers' countervailing belief in the plant's profitability and efficiency, ultimately played a greater part in stimulating resistance than any abstract conception of a 'right' to employment.

One identifiable group of workers, however, was not convinced by the reasons put forward for resisting the closure of the plant. Out of a group of 80 skilled and semi-skilled men employed in the plant, only twelve agreed to stay and fight with the women workers. Two alternative views were put forward as to why this was the case: one steward argued that the skilled men at Plessey had 'a track record of weakness and lack of political clarity with respect to their situation . . . with very little trade union principles'; another explained the refusal of the skilled men to support their action as being a response to previous hostilities which had existed between the toolmakers and particular stewards, 'Skilled men are very petty, they always have been. They won't be dictated to by semi-skilled people'. Other workers argued that the skilled men thought it unlikely that their action would achieve any measure of success, and they may have believed that having a skill made it more likely that they would obtain alternative employment. Whatever their reasons, the failure of the male workers as a whole, skilled or semi-skilled, to support their fellow workers indicates the traditional problems of trying to build solidarity where internal divisions exist, based on skill, sex or some other factor, among the workforce.

The workers realised that some extraordinary action was needed if Plessey was to be forced to reconsider its decision. They considered that the factory's machinery and stocks were still valuable assets for Plessey. The building itself belonged to the Scottish Development Agency, therefore, occupying the factory provided the best method of keeping control over these two assets. It was felt that to try to negotiate with Plessey through traditional trade union channels, or to try to block the removal of equipment and stocks from outside the plant would have proved ineffective. As one worker exclaimed: 'we couldn't go on a strike and we couldn't go on a go slow – what was the point?'.

The period between the closure announcement and the start of the occupation was used by the Plessey stewards to debate the problems which could possibly arise once the factory was taken over, to make contacts with trade union bodies, local councils, other sit-in workers and the media. During this time, the workers were encouraged to produce as much output as possible. This was for two reasons: first, it enabled them to earn increased bonus payments, thus helping to ease the financial difficulties likely to occur when wages ceased to be paid. Secondly, by holding back work in the dispatch stage, the workers were increasing the value of the assets which they would control.

The decision on what action to take against Plessey was influenced by the workers' assessment of the most potentially effective ways of fighting multinational companies like Plessey. However, the decision was also conditioned by a belief on the part of some of the workers that conventional trade union tactics were of little use in dealing with multinational corporations. These issues have been dealt with elsewhere (Baldry et al., 1984). Such a choice may be more attractive to women workers, many of whom do not feel themselves to be wholly integrated into trade union practices and forms of struggle. Thus, it is necessary to assess how effective such a tactic was for the Plessey women.

EVALUATING THE OCCUPATION

The success of an occupation can be assessed essentially by looking at how far the occupation achieved its aims – in this case, whether or not the factory closed. Evidently, such an assessment is over-simplistic: one must also consider the number of jobs saved, the likely security of these jobs, and any changes which took place in terms and conditions of employment. Thus, the actual tangible outcome of the sit-in must be considered.

Elson and Pearson (1981) have argued, however, for a different method of assessing industrial action by groups of women workers. For them, industrial action by women workers at a factory level 'has to be judged not simply as an instrument for making economic gains, but as a way of developing the capacities of those involved in it, particularly the capacity for self-organisation'. Elson and Pearson see participation for women in collective action at a factory level as being much more important than purely formal membership of a trade union. This participation helps women workers understand the forces which shape their lives, since 'the forms that workers' organisations have traditionally taken have been inadequate from women's point of view because they have failed to recognise and build into their structure the specificity of gender . . . the failure to take account of gender means that in practice they have tended to represent male workers'. Thus, while it is important to look at the material outcome of the Plessey occupation, it is also necessary to consider the less tangible outcomes of the sit-in. In instrumental terms, it is difficult to assess whether the occupation was particularly successful or not. The occupation ended after eight weeks of very intense struggle, particularly during the court action, when Arcotronics, a subsidiary of Wedge Holdings, took over part of the plant and agreed to employ around 80 workers on the condition that the occupation be terminated immediately.

Talks between the unions involved in the Plessey occupation and the company management were first held at ACAS in Glasgow on 5th February 1982. Very little emerged from these talks. One week later the Plessey representatives informed unions of a possible management buy-out plan under which the Plessey Managing Director, Harold Jackson, with the company's approval, would take over part of the plant and employ around 80 workers. In the days which followed, the unions refused to consider any takeover plan until the company withdrew the threat of court action and the dismissal notices which had been issued.

The first real hint of any breakthrough came much later, however, on March 8th, when the union negotiating team attended talks at the London offices of the Arbitration and Conciliation Advisory Service on the invitation of the company. The talks were arranged to consider a proposed management buy-out plan, and also to discuss a possible take-over by Wedge International Holdings BV. At the end of these discussions, a plan was outlined in which Arcotronics proposed to take over part of the plant and employ around 80 workers on the condition that the occupation be terminated immediately. The 80 jobs were to be guaranteed for three months. However, at a mass meeting, the workers at Bathgate, on the recommendation of their stewards, voted overwhelmingly to reject the Arcotronics takeover bid. They were dissatisfied with the number of jobs on offer; they were not convinced that the takeover would prevent an asset stripping operation by Plessey; and they did not believe that they had enough information on Arcotronics to warrant accepting their offer. As one shop steward pointed out, 'It was like asking you to take a house with no roof'. Only seven days later, however, the Plessey workforce voted two to one to accept the Arcotronics takeover bid. The proposal had changed little since it had been on offer the previous week, except that Plessey had agreed to guarantee that the jobs would remain in existence for one year, by placing sufficient orders with Arcotronics.

Some of the Plessey workers have very strong views on why the takeover was finally accepted so soon after being overwhelmingly rejected. The Convener at the plant believed that in the week separating the two offers the trade union officials worked to undermine the sit-in. According to this steward, the officials were talking privately to key shop stewards, and winning them over to their position, 'they were really saying "that's all you're going to get; reject this and you'll lose everything".' Other rank and file workers argued that the unions, along with management, 'had an almost common objective to bring the occupation to a halt as quickly as possible':

> We felt they [the union officials] could have got more jobs than 80, but they said it was over. They weren't for us, they were for the firm . . . more on the management side than on our side.

> They wanted to get us off their back really – they were paying us strike pay and unions don't like to pay strike pay.

> They [the union officials] said they did their best, but you've just got their word for that.

For these workers, the sit-in was still going strong: the interim interdict and order for eviction against the workers had been recalled; the Italian factory had indicated some willingness to refuse to allow any of the Bathgate machinery into their plant; and financial contributions were flowing in at a rate of £6000–£7000 per week.

However, many of the occupying workers held opposing views to these, as indicated by the outcome of the vote. Many workers accepted the interpretation of the situation given by the union officials: 'they had taken us to the end of the road, and there was nowhere else they could take us', 'the unions were persuading us to accept the takeover – I listened to them and thought "80 jobs are better than none" '. As the sit-in progressed into its later stages, divisions appeared between the workers. Some became increasingly disaffected with the struggle, and were more vulnerable to mounting external pressures. To them, the sit-in was falling apart, and the workers were becoming depressed and anxious over the possible loss of redundancy payments. As one woman pointed out: 'You can fight as long as you have your troops, but when people want out, irrespective of what the union thinks, or what the people who have led that fight think, they're not going to stay and fight, and the majority of people in that hall had had enough'. It is difficult to assess which view of the sit-in was more realistic. On the one hand, the offer involved only 80 jobs, which meant that only one third of those workers who occupied would remain in employment; the offer included a management right to appoint the workers they wanted; and a wage freeze imposed for one year. Further, workers were to sign an agreement saying that they would not oppose the movement of any machinery out of the plant, in direct opposition to the aims of the sit-in. On the other hand, there is little concrete evidence to indicate that a more acceptable settlement could have been obtained. Moreover, there were obvious difficulties in sustaining the momentum of the industrial action over a long period of time, and the appearance of divisions among the occupying force augured badly for the continuance of the sit-in.

Coates (1981) has argued that the factory occupation is one further strategy in the struggle between labour and capital, a new strategy which is adopted as labour is confronted with new problems. In the early 1980s these problems were clearly identifiable; the effects of world recession, the lack of a government commitment to full employment and the relocation policies of multinational corporations had all contributed towards the increasing prevalence of mass redundancies. Redundancies generally lie outside the realm of union influence: the essential component of collective bargaining is the assumption of a continuing relationship between the two parties involved, with negotiations taking place within the limits set by the two parties. Thus, for example, on wage setting, an upper limit exists, beyond which employers would prefer a strike or closure rather than agree to further concessions. Similarly, a lower limit exists, below which unions would prefer to strike rather than reach an agreement. However, in the case of factory closure there is no assumption of a continuing bargaining relationship, hence the threat to strike loses most of its power. As the TUC (1974) pointed out in its debate on sit-ins and work-ins: 'The need for this form of defensive industrial action indicates the kinds of decisions that remain outside the collective bargaining process, and this pinpoints the limitations of collective bargaining'.

In the case of factory closures, occupations represent a more direct form of economic sanction than the strike, since they prevent the transfer of materials and machinery out of a workplace. Where the machinery is up-to-date and capable of operating profitably, as was the case at Plessey, the sit-in can prove to be a significant sanction. Sit-ins are also of tremendous importance as a demonstrative form of protest which elevates the problem of redundancy to the level of a public social issue, and which puts pressure on third parties (generally the state) to bring about a settlement more favourable to the workforce than otherwise would have occurred. The mobilisation of public opinion in favour of job retention has put pressure on employers to become, at least in appearance, more socially responsible.

However, it can be argued that occupations, at least temporarily, bring about changes in the relations of individuals to the means of production. By challenging the property rights of capital, workers no longer relate to the means of production at the behest of capital. While individual workers involved in occupations may not realise it, by its very nature the sit-in can be seen as a potentially radical course of action. As such, actions of this nature will encourage significant retaliation by capital. Therefore, when we assess the gains made by the Plessey workers, it must be remembered that these gains were made despite immense pressures being put on sit-in workers by employers.

PLESSEY'S TACTICS

In its attempts to end the occupation, the Plessey company used various tactics to put pressure on the workers occupying the factory. At an early stage in the occupation, the *Glasgow Herald* newspaper reported the workers' fears that Plessey might organise a raid on the plant to snatch £650 000 worth of components for electronic circuits. These fears were fuelled by the appearance, on several occasions, of a Plessey helicopter circling above the plant. In their defence, the workers had piled up barrels and wooden pallets in readiness for scattering to prevent any helicopter landing.

In a similar move to intimidate the workforce, Plessey management left dismissal notices at the gatehouse of the factory for all of the workers involved in the occupation, informing them that they had been dismissed without any entitlement to redundancy payments. At the same time, the company instructed telephone engineers to cut off all telephone lines at the factory, leaving the workers with only the payphone at their social club. Despite these mounting pressures, and even after the company had announced the dismissals on radio, and had intimated that the sit-in had cost the workers their redundancy payments, the workers unanimously reaffirmed their intention to continue the occupation.

It can be argued, however, that all these pressures had a far smaller effect on the workers than had the court action taken by Plessey against the occupying workers. For ordinary working people, the courts are an arena in which they have very little experience, and about which they appear to have great apprehension. The complex debate on the legal situation surrounding the Plessey occupation cannot be discussed here (for a detailed discussion, see Findlay, 1984). The attempts by Plessey to use the courts to evict the occupying workers, although ultimately unsuccessful, were significant in indicating that the owners of capital will resort to any tactics to defend their property rights against perceived challenges by workers.

THE PLESSEY JUDGEMENT

Perhaps the most significant aspect of the Plessey occupation was the legal action taken by the Plessey company against the workers involved in the sit-in. As Miller (1982) points out, 'It was this particular sit-in which for the first time tested the legitimacy of such action in Scotland'. Plessey applied to the Court of Session for an order against the occupying workers for interim interdict and eviction. Despite protestations from the workers' representatives that this was an industrial dispute and not a legal issue, and that the sit-in was being carried out in a responsible manner, solely to protect the jobs and future of the workforce, Lord Kincraig granted Plessey interim interdict and outlawed the occupation after only one week. In the court's view, the actions of the workforce constituted a trespass on the premises and were clearly unlawful. Lord Kincraig argued that the presence of the workers in the premises was not incidental to the carrying out of the duties of their employment, but was solely in furtherance of their demands, and if such actions persisted they were likely to cause very serious damage to the company.

The sit-in workers, while realising that they were breaking the law and were liable to fines or imprisonment for contempt of court, none the less voted unanimously to defy the interdict and remain in the plant. In reply to this, the Plessey management returned to the Court of Session in a second bid to end the occupation by informing the court that the interdict had not been obeyed.

In granting an interim interdict, or deciding whether one should be recalled, a judge must take two factors into consideration. First, the judge must decide where the 'balance of convenience' lies between making and not making an interim order. In weighing this balance, the judge must assess the likelihood of one or other of the parties winning if the case went to full proof. The weighing of this balance is particularly important in cases involving industrial action. Most of these cases do not proceed beyond the interim stage, as the dispute has usually been settled out of court. Secondly, the judge must take into account the extent of loss or inconvenience caused by the alleged wrongful act. Ross (1982) argues that in this part of the assessment it is rare for a judge to find that the balance comes down other than heavily in favour of the employer. Moreover, the extent of loss or inconvenience has frequently overshadowed the likelihood of one or other party winning if the case went to full proof.

In the Plessey case, however, Lord Kincraig did take into account the likelihood of either party winning the case at full proof. He argued that it was possible that at full proof the workers could successfully invoke the provision of Section 13(ii) of the Trade Union and Labour Relations Act of 1974, which made the activities of the workers non-actionable in law since they were taken 'in contemplation or furtherance of a trade dispute'. Thus, the interim interdict was lifted, because, as Lord Kincraig pointed out, 'to continue the interdict would be to prevent the respondents [i.e. the workers] acting in the way they consider appropriate to resolving the trade dispute, and would be tantamount to deciding the case in favour of the petitioners' (Kincraig, quoted in *Scots Law Times*, 1983a, p. 140).

One important element in Lord Kincraig's thinking, and in the thinking of the Appeal judges who subsequently upheld his decision, was his view that: 'The courts should be slow to interfere with the resolution of industrial disputes or attempt to resolve them by applying established rules of law germane to other contentious issues' (Kincraig, quoted in *Scots Law Times*, 1983a, p. 140). The significance of the Plessey ruling should not be underestimated. The Scottish TUC publicly welcomed the court's ruling as establishing the sit-in as a legitimate action on the part of workers facing redundancy. And, as expected, Scottish employers were horrified at the ruling.

The labour movement in Scotland did not have long to celebrate their victory. In July 1982, an Amendment to the Employment Bill was introduced at the Committee Stage in the House of Lords which amended Sections 13 and 30 of TULRA 1974, thus plugging the gap which made possible the Plessey ruling. In the discussion on the amendment, Lord Mackay pointed out that:

It has been suggested that the judgement in the Plessey case might in every case protect workers who occupy a factory to protest about its closure. As one can imagine, this has caused considerable concern in Scottish industry. Some people have suggested that it might provide an encouragement to occupy factories in Scotland without fear of the legal consequences of doing so (Mackay, *HL Debates*, 14 July 1982, Vol 433, col 296).

For such reasons, he argued that the subsection should be repealed, as it was felt that this was not the proper intention of the legislation. Thus, since the Employment Act came into effect in November 1982, there has existed no immunity from civil proceedings for workers involved in occupations in Scotland.

It would be wrong to argue, however, that had section 13(ii) not been repealed, workers could have relied on that particular section to provide them with immunity when occupying their factories. For instance, in the case of the occupation by the workers of the Phestos Shipping Company (*Scots Law Times*, 1983b), the court did not feel itself obliged to follow the Plessey judgement.

The 'Plessey Judgement' was without doubt of extreme importance for workers in Scotland. Contrary to the beliefs of the wider trade union movement, the occupation of the Plessey plant was legitimised by the courts. However, the speed with which the government took measures to prevent further legitimation of such actions indicates that the court ruling was both unexpected and unacceptable to the government and employers, and that similar court rulings favourable to workers are unlikely in the future.

ORGANISATION OF THE SIT-IN

One of the first tasks facing the 220 Plessey workers occupying the plant was to overcome the practical difficulties of providing an adequate environment for large numbers of people to live in whilst maintaining the factory, conducting an industrial dispute and organising support from other sections of the community. Not surprisingly, most workers described the first few days of the sit-in as extremely chaotic:

We had to cover the factory 24 hours a day, and we needed someone on the factory gates at all times. We also had to find transport and organise cooking and cleaning. But the effort put in by the workers was absolutely tremendous . . . people were willing to do shifts for the sit-in, but they never would have worked shifts for Plessey.

Since there were many tasks to be done, committees were set up to take charge of the workforce's finance, to establish contact with other workers and other trade unions; to speak at meetings in the surrounding communities; to cope with the large amount of correspondence which came in; and to collect funds from other organisations: 'Each member of the working committee took charge of a specific task. There had to be people to share responsibility with the stewards – that's where a lot of things fall, with big shots trying to do everything themselves, instead of drawing all the people together'. Inevitably, it took a few days for any order to be arrived at, but most of those involved give the impression that the organisation of the sit-in was very effective. Serious attempts were made to involve the whole workforce in decision making. Mass meetings were held regularly and all of the major decisions were taken when the entire occupying force was present; no matter what shift was in progress when a meeting was held, the workers from all other shifts were called to the factory to attend. Furthermore, in the views of the workers interviewed, most people were keen to make their opinions known, both during mass meetings and in the day to day conduct of the occupation. They were keen to become involved in the actual running of the sit-in, and this view is encapsulated in one worker's statement that: 'Everybody got their say. But the stewards did a good job and we were quite happy to follow their leadership'.

INDUSTRIAL ACTION AND CONSCIOUSNESS

The occupation secured very real gains for the Plessey women. Very simply, their consciousness was heightened. The Plessey workers generated high levels of morale, solidarity and collective consciousness. Workers dedicated a far greater proportion of their lives to the sit-in than would have been devoted to work, in most cases completely uprooting their domestic life in the process. Women, many of whom had never been involved in industrial action in their lives, were encouraged to go out and address public meetings, to visit other plants and ask for the support, both moral and financial of other workers. Thus, there were many positive aspects of the Plessey occupation, no matter what its eventual material outcome. This involvement was important for many of the women:

We all got really involved as we got to understand more . . . we were happy to get involved when we realised the degree of support we had, and we knew we were not fighting alone.

I know the sit-in was successful in getting people involved. There was a definite feeling of everybody working together.

It is paradoxical that women are willing to undertake a form of industrial struggle which more than other forms of action disrupts their domestic life. Sit-ins require a great deal of workers' time and commitment. Since many women have a double burden, wage work and unpaid domestic labour, one might expect them to be less attracted to forms of action which make extra demands on their time. Participation in the Plessey occupation did involve added burdens for many women. These were two-fold: first, working shift rotas in the sit-in and looking after children proved to be particularly difficult. Efforts were made to exclude women with children from the night shifts, since this may have led to problems of child care. There is, however, no indication that any collective child-care was organised. Secondly, for some women, the attitudes of their husbands proved to be a source of anxiety:

A few women left as it [the sit-in] was causing family problems . . . it was difficult to cope with families without a wage. Some got a lot of stick from their husbands and had to leave the sit-in to prevent domestic troubles. But there were many glowing examples of husbands changing their attitudes.

However, although the women workers did believe that their domestic situation made participation in the sit-in more difficult, many of them also believed that women in general possess greater determination and stamina than men when faced with an adverse situation: 'If women put their teeth into anything, and are really determined enough, they will exceed men at any time . . . women are more determined than men will ever be, and they'll take more knocks than men'. Informal discussions with a group of women involved in the occupation indicated that the solidarity they felt may well have been engendered by a sense of common interest as women: the belief that they shared a common work and life situation. The awareness of women workers of the similar situation of other women workers, most of whom share similar domestic responsibilities, may foster attitudes of co-operation and mutual assistance. This can obviously be a great advantage during industrial disputes. Whatever the explanation of the fact that recent prominent sit-ins in Scotland have been carried out by women workers, the women of Lee Jeans, Plessey and many others have clearly smashed the notion of women as passive workers (for further discussion of women's industrial 'passivity', see Elson and Pearson, 1981; and Purcell, 1979). As one woman pointed out: 'One of the achievements was that women were able to speak up for themselves, women that I would never have dreamt would have made a contribution at a union meeting, all had an opinion to give . . . it puts a backbone into people'.

SOLIDARITY FROM OTHER SECTIONS OF THE LABOUR MOVEMENT

Most of the occupations which have taken place have gained considerable support from other sections of the labour movement. The Plessey occupation was no exception. Stewards from other Plessey plants in Britain were asked to elicit the support of their members for the workers' struggle at Bathgate. According to the Bathgate stewards, the response was heartening. Regular financial contributions were made to the Bathgate strike fund, and representatives of the other workers were often present at the Bathgate plant to offer their moral support: 'The other Plessey workers gave us a tremendous amount of support . . . they showed great interest and levied their members to give us finance'. On another level, the workers at other Plessey plants in Britain took part in a one hour stoppage and then in one half-day stoppage to show their support for their fellow workers at Bathgate. They also demonstrated outside Plessey headquarters in London. The Bathgate stewards believed that these actions alarmed the Plessey management. Hence, before the half-day stoppage, management at the English plants printed and distributed thousands of leaflets to their own workers, telling them that they should not support the Bathgate struggle. The Bathgate workers felt that this was an indication that the management were feeling pressurised: 'In a way, the company must have realised that if we were getting support from other places, they might have the same problem on their hands later on'. Some of the workers had hoped that the company's employees outside Bathgate would call a full stoppage to support them. Others seemed more aware of the difficulties involved in such a course of action: 'Some of the Bathgate plant was being transferred down south, so it meant jobs for them . . . they weren't going to strike to put themselves out of a job'.

The dispute shows the contradictions involved in any attempt to co-ordinate protest between employees of the same company in different plants in different parts of the country, or across countries. While it may be in the workers' long-term interest to try to prevent the implementation of policies which involve mass redundancies, in the short term, the increased job security which the closure of one plant may mean for another plant can be a source of division among workers (see Haworth and Ramsay, 1984).

Despite the fact that the support of other Plessey workers was qualified, the Bathgate stewards argue that it was significant: 'It was the first time Plessey factories had ever helped each other, and it hasn't happened since. There have been other redundancies and closures, but none of them even fought'. However, the workers involved in the occupation, and those subsequently re-employed in the Plessey plant, do now show a great deal of solidarity with other workers' struggles. They actively make financial contributions to other strike funds and offer help and advice to other groups of workers. This appears to be in marked contrast to their behaviour prior to the occupation. It can be argued that, for some of the Plessey workers at least, experience of collective struggle did enhance their belief in the need for labour solidarity to fight multinational corporations, and their consciousness of the resources which workers possess. At the same time, it may also have increased their awareness of the contradictions involved in attempts to extend solidarity among workers!

An attempt was made to co-ordinate pressure on Plessey internationally, by making contacts with the Plessey plant at Arco in Italy, a sister plant to the one in Bathgate. Such contacts were made, however, towards the end of the occupation. Initially, Bathgate workers had encountered difficulties in getting information on their struggle to the Italian workforce (as the Italian management had provided their workforce with entirely false information on the dispute). Finally, the Bathgate workers had to resort to sending a representative to Italy to inform the Italian workers of the occupation.

Since the occupation ended shortly after the contact was made, it was impossible to test whether the Italian workers would have taken direct action in support of their Bathgate colleagues. Many of the workers and shop stewards at Bathgate believed that a basis was there for extending the struggle to an international level, with the Italian workers refusing to accept machinery and stocks from the Bathgate plant, and perhaps pressurising the Plessey management through stoppages. This hope appears to have been based on a verbal commitment from the Italian workers to take some action on Bathgate's behalf.

Had the dispute continued, the hopes of the Bathgate workers may have been disappointed. The divisions which exist among workers at one plant can have a detrimental effect on solidarity, and this is compounded by divisions which exist between workers at different plants, even where these workers are employed by the same company.

Such difficulties are magnified when attempts are made at international solidarity (see Haworth and Ramsay, 1983). This is not to say that international labour solidarity is unachievable. All it means is that such solidarity cannot be assumed to exist automatically.

Support in the United Kingdom for the Plessey women was not confined to Plessey employees. According to one worker: 'We caught the imagination of the trade union and labour movement in Scotland'. This certainly appears to be true. The Plessey workers received massive financial contributions. Ship workers, miners and others paid a levy from their wages each week into a strike fund, and many other workplaces carried out collections at regular intervals. Towards the end of the sit-in, the workers were receiving between £5000 and £6000 per week. Clearly, this was a crucial component in the ability of the workforce to continue with the sit-in. More importantly, however, the Plessey workers emphasised that support from other workers, mobilised in the main through informal shop steward networks, provided a tremendous boost to their morale: 'This is what gave the women the will to fight on . . . they felt that to stop fighting wasn't only letting themselves down, it was letting down the whole labour movement as well'. 'If we'd been left on our own, I don't know if we would have lasted eight weeks'.

The dispute does show that the labour movement can generate solidarity and support. However, there are constraints on such support: it will be forthcoming to the extent that other workers do not feel they are putting their jobs in jeopardy by offering support. Financial contributions and participation in demonstrations are unlikely to jeopardise jobs. However, by striking, other Plessey employees may indeed have put their own jobs at risk, and this may explain why such action was not taken.

COMMUNITY BASED SUPPORT

The sit-in not only won the support of workers in other areas, but it also won the commitment of the Bathgate community. The realisation of the dire prospects facing the town contributed to the support which the townspeople showed the Plessey workers. Donations came from all sources to the plant: from local shopkeepers, families, pensioners (in the form of finance and provisions), and from the few factories which still existed in the area, particularly from British Leyland. The workers were also supported by their local regional and district councils, and by their

MP, Tam Dalyell. The workers argued that the townspeople had realised the impact that the closure would have on the community, and on their children's prospects.

People could see the community going down and down. The British Leyland dispute was going on and everyone was worried there wasn't going to be any work left.

It let the workers know that the people outside did care about them, and were appreciating the fight the workers were putting up.

It may be the case that the domestic roles of many women workers, such as shopping, involvement in local schools, youth and community organisations, and also in informal neighbourhood groups and kin groups, provides the basis on which community support can be built, more so than is the case for male workers. Many women spend time and energy constituting these kinds of networks, and these may be of great significance in an industrial dispute, particularly where a dispute affects many members of the same community, as was the case at Bathgate.

It must be pointed out, however, that much of the solidarity which was built up during the dispute disappeared at the end. Many workers were extremely bitter about how the dispute ended, particularly those workers who had been made redundant. None the less, amongst those workers interviewed, even those who felt that the sit-in had ended badly, there was complete agreement that the sit-in had been a worthwhile experience, and most expressed satisfaction at having taken part:

When you consider how things were stacked against people, the occupation was remarkable, courageous and solidaristic.

The sit-in definitely brought people together. There was a great feeling of being together and of camaraderie during the fight.

The sit-in was a success as everybody pulled together – the majority took their turn at doing what needed to be done.

These workers argued that they would recommend the sit-in to other workers facing closure, where they felt that there was some possibility of either reversing the closure decision or attracting new capital. The general feeling was that the sit-in was an effective tactic against redundancy. In many ways, it was seen as the only action workers could take which had any hopes of success. They did point out, however, that workers who were considering occupying their factories should be fully aware of the difficulties involved in occupations, and should take into consideration the sacrifices of home life and social life which have to be made: 'Yes, I would recommend it to other workers, but everybody has to want to do it'. For the Plessey workers, the intangible benefits accruing from the direct action they took against Plessey were seen as crucial, and compensated in many ways for, what was for many, an unsatisfactory end to the dispute.

POSTSCRIPT TO THE OCCUPATION – ARCOTRONICS

The selection of the workforce for the Arcotronics plant was made by the Arcotronics management alone. It would appear that workers were selected on the basis of their ability to perform a number of tasks, as opposed to focusing on one particular aspect of production. There was no worker influence on employee-selection, save for the fact that the takeover agreement only permitted management to employ workers who had taken part in the sit-in. After the sit-in, there appeared to have been little change in the nature of employment at Arcotronics. Wages and conditions remained the same, although a wage-freeze was imposed for the first year of production.

Initially, the workforce was somewhat perturbed that the management of Arcotronics was to be carried out by the same management team as had operated at Plessey. In the first place, the workers had accused the Plessey management of inefficiency and incompetence. They had also argued that the size of the workforce did not warrant as many management personnel: 'Eight managers with high salaries for 53 shop floor girls? These salaries have got to be produced for, and it takes a hell of a lot of capacitors to produce that kind of money'.

From the beginning, the workforce at Arcotronics was convinced that the Arcotronics company would not succeed. Management kept workers well-informed of the difficulties in finding customers for their products. In the spring of 1985 the plant closed, with very little resistance from the workforce, despite shop stewards' encouragement of resistance. It can be argued that management's strategy of sharing their business problems with their workers had the effect of pre-empting any worker action against closure. This is not surprising, when one considers how important the workers' belief in the plant's profitability was in encouraging them to take the original action. What it does point out, however, is that management also learn lessons from industrial action, and will use this knowledge to attempt to prevent similar occurrences in the future.

CONCLUSION

This chapter has sought to assess the various strengths and weaknesses of the action taken by the Plessey workers, and to use the events of Bathgate to highlight a number of important issues. Conflict on a large scale was inevitable given the fundamental difference of rationality between the company and the workforce over the closure of the plant. On one side, the company's decisions were based on a notion of overall corporate profit position. On the other side, the workforce believed in the need to continue the production of a useful and profitable product, both for the sake of individual employees and the community as a whole. Essentially, the occupation represented a challenge to the logic of capitalist accumulation: a logic which fails to take into account the massive social costs of factory closure. Similarly, such action represents a challenge to the pluralist belief that collective bargaining alone can secure a fair resolution of conflict in industry. The basic contention of this chapter has been, therefore, that occupations have many strengths over conventional forms of action. However, these very strengths are likely to encourage significant retaliation by capital, which, as this case study shows, will use any means at its disposal to prevent or defeat such actions.

The Plessey case study also leads us to look behind the more tangible outcomes of industrial action, to see the real gains brought about through collective struggle in developing workers' organisational capacities and promoting labour solidarity. The dispute reveals the importance for the labour movement of utilising the capacities of women workers, and belies any notion of women's alleged passivity. Moreover, the Plessey dispute indicates that community support represents an important strength for the labour movement: a strength labour needs to develop in the difficult years ahead.

4 Closures: The Threat and the Future for Labour
Huw Beynon

In May 1981, the British TUC organised a People's March for Jobs. The march commenced in Liverpool on 1 May, and for the rest of that month unemployed men and women walked south to London. During that time, another 60 000 workers had joined the dole queue as a result of plant closures and the continuing massive run down of manufacturing production in Britain; a run down that continued through 1981 and saw British industry entering 1982 with its lowest output figure since 1967. In July of that year, 5.57 million people were employed in manufacturing, compared with 7.1 million four years earlier. It has been a collapse of dramatic proportions, and one which fitted into a general crisis that saw total unemployment in the countries of the OECD rise above 25 million.

Perhaps it was no coincidence that the 1981 march began in Liverpool. Merseyside has been particularly badly hit by the recession. In early 1981, sixteen per cent of the labour force of the area were unemployed, (twenty per cent in the city of Liverpool) and it had been reported that there were just forty nine jobs on offer for 13 505 youngsters registered unemployed (Lane, 1981). In 1964, Liverpool was hailed as the 'city of change and promise'. Its 'traditional industries', dependent upon the port, were being phased out and replaced by high growth, manufacturing plants from the vehicle and electrical engineering industries (Merseyside Socialist Research Group, 1980). A new city centre was built in celebration and optimism: cars and Beatles, music and motors – the Detroit of Europe. In 1981 it was a different story. The city was a graphic illustration of urban dereliction. Everywhere there were empty factories, boarded shop fronts and tracts of wilderness between mean streets. Everywhere people talked about the closure of this or that plant: British Leyland, Dunlop, BICC, Plessey, GEC, Lucas, Girling, Courtaulds, Unilever, Meccano, Tate and Lyle. The list was endless, because *every* industry had been hit. From the docks to flour milling and telephone equipment, from office equipment to animal foods, there had been closures. The story told on people's

faces; it was forever a topic of conversation in pubs and on pavements.
'Anything doing?' 'Working?'

In a pub off Colquett Street in 1980, an ex-British Leyland worker put
it like this:

> I don't know what's happening. It seems like there's just nothing
> doing for this town. I've got a mate, works as a tanker driver. Now
> there's no more secure job than that. Bleeding hell – an oil tanker
> driver! Well, he's been on short time and now he tells me they're
> making half the drivers redundant. If that's happening I don't know
> what chance there is for the other BL plant. It's hard to take in at
> times.

A week later, BL announced another cutback in the No. 1 BL plant (it
finally closed in 1982). In the same week, Burmah Oil announced the
closure of its refinery across the Mersey at Ellesmere Port. The *Financial
Times* (8 May 1981) expert was not surprised. In his view:

> there is little doubt that Merseyside . . . will have to come to grips with
> a small workforce. Compared with just under 600 000 in jobs now, it
> has been forecast that on the most favourable projections the area will
> be able to sustain only 575 000 jobs by 1986 and the figure could be as
> low as just under 500 000.

But in facing such a 'jobs crisis', Merseyside was not alone. Perhaps of
greater significance was the situation in the West Midlands. Here, in the
area around Birmingham, Coventry and Wolverhampton, metal
manufacture has its home in England. It is a region which gave England
the name, 'the workshop of the world'. Throughout the twentieth
century, its people have known prosperity, with its industries forming
the basis of a growing regional economy. Yet in 1981, John Warburton,
director of Birmingham's Chamber of Commerce described how
'people in the West Midlands are still shell-shocked by the events of the
past twelve months'. These 'events' were a series of plant closures which
had driven the unemployment rate up to fifteen per cent. Throughout
1980 and 1981, the region lost jobs at a rate of 1000 a week, and in 1983
the Thatcher Government was forced to create a minister with special
responsibility for the area.

Perhaps the city of Coventry provides the clearest example of the scale
of the changes affecting this region. In 1976, 186 000 people worked in
the city; in 1982 the figure had dropped to 150 000. The drop was
accompanied by a fundamental change in the structure of employment
in the city. In 1976 manufacturing industry provided 57.4 per cent of

jobs for the Coventry workforce, in 1982 just twenty nine per cent. In that area generally, workers and managers from the engineering industry have been made redundant. Many of them are unemployed and disillusioned. Two managers, Gerry Read and Robin Wilson, worked for W & T Avery which was taken over by GEC and then threatened with closure. They attempted to salvage the operation, taking it over themselves. But to no avail. Read put it like this: 'It broke my heart when we had to tell the lads that that was it. We'd put everything into that place, it was my whole life. But that was it. I've finished with engineering'. And Wilson: 'Engineering has lost the experience of people like ourselves and when things pick up they will be paying much more for their products'.

Throughout the region several companies have figured prominently in the collapse. Nationalised firms like British Leyland and the British Steel Corporation had major plants in the area and two of these companies respectively reduced their national payroll by forty per cent and fifty two per cent. In Coventry, Solihull and Longbridge, 40 000 car workers joined the dole queue. In Bilston, a steel town for 150 years, unemployment went past thirty per cent as the works closed and the plant was sold for scrap. In the private sector, GKN, the giant of the mechanical engineering industry, shed 18 000 jobs in 1980 alone, as component factories, screw factories, forges and foundries closed down. By the end of 1981, GKN's Heath Street site in Birmingham had seen its labour force cut from over 2000 to 965 – all in the space of eighteen months. At GKN Sankey, too, its major Telford plant shed a thousand workers in 1980, and another thousand in 1981. The Manager of Telford Development Corporation, shaken by an unemployment rate of eighteen per cent, commented: 'after last week's announcement by GKN we all lay awake and wondered what the hell to do next'.

The context of this man's insomnia was a world recession, whose impact upon the British economy had been particularly acute. The scale of the decline of employment in manufacturing industry has already been noted in chapter 1. This decline in employment has been long term in sectors of industry that were identified as the 'traditional smoke stack' base of the British economy. In 1945, for example, 750 000 workers were employed in the mining industry; this had dropped to 305 000 by 1983. In other industries the decline was just as dramatic: in shipbuilding (250 000 to 90 000), railways (500 000 to 180 000) and motor manufacturing (600 000 to 270 000). Against this background, the late seventies and eighties can be seen as an acceleration in the rate of plant closures, and an extension of it to those branches of industry – most notably to metal manufacturing, engineering and the automotive industry. Between 1978 and 1983, a quarter of a million jobs were lost in mechanical engineering and 110 000 in electrical engineering. By 1983, Spain had overtaken the UK as a producer of motor vehicles. British Leyland, which employed 239 000 workers in 1971, had reduced its labour force to 62 000 by the beginning of 1984. In 1984, it was the turn of the coal miners. Successful in 1981 in their attempt at halting closures, their year-long strike was preceded by announced cuts of four million tonnes in capacity. The strike was defeated and further cut-backs have been announced. In March 1983, 205 100 men were employed in coal mining; in the autumn of 1985 the figure had dropped below 150 000, as pit after pit closed down. It has been a transformation of quite dramatic proportions; and it is one which is more complicated than a mere 'run down', for it combines complex processes at the level of both economic organisation and subjective understandings.

To begin with, it is clear that while industries like the motor industry face decline in the UK, many of the companies involved in that sector, including some British firms, have expanded. For, as British Leyland proved its vulnerability in the face of the giant transnational car producers, so too did British component manufacturers re-order their operations on an international basis. As such, 'shake out' and 'run down' in the British Midlands was matched by grant-assisted development elsewhere. Commenting on this new 'flexibility' and 'competitiveness' of British firms, the *Sunday Times* remarked:

> It is something they have achieved by planning on an international base. As car production has migrated away from the UK, they have moved with it, taking the jobs with them. 'We've grown out of the West Midlands' says one executive, 'anyone tied to the fortunes of the local motor industry is now suffering too much'.

In Birmingham, the effects of changes like these can be seen in the changed operations of ten of its leading manufacturing employers. In 1978, those companies employed 686 694 throughout the world, with seventy five per cent of their total labour force in the UK. By 1982, this total labour force had fallen by twenty three per cent to 530 275: the UK component, however, had fallen by *sixty* per cent. Production overseas had increased by twelve per cent and the British output by just 1.7 per cent. What is true of Birmingham applies to the North East and the North West of England, and also applies nationally. British output of the country's top fifty manufacturing units *declined* by thirty six per cent between 1979 and 1983, while the output from their overall operation increased by forty four per cent.

What the figures point to is a process whereby manufacturing industry has become increasingly flexible and geographically mobile. While previous periods of industrial expansion (and recession) have been accompanied by the geographic stability of particular regions – as coal and steel communities, or auto-regions – the modern period is' predicated upon the near total dismantling of this link between localities and particular industries. This is even the case in the extractive industries like coal mining, where new coalfields are being developed both in the UK and abroad. In this process a number of things have become clear. To begin with, while comparisons are often made with the 1930s, aspects of the present recession are much more disturbing. This is made clear in this assessment of the coal and steel industry by a lodge official of the National Union of Mineworkers. 'In the thirties', he argued, 'there was hope. There were hundreds of pits still working two, three or four days a week. There were little steel works and fairly large ones dotted up and down the valleys. Now we are talking about the *total closure of industries in South Wales.*' (*Marxism Today*, 1980).

This view was echoed by another man, a life time employee of the Vickers Company on Tyneside. For a period of years, the shop stewards at the company's heavy engineering plants had documented the incremental shift in the company's investment profile. The combine shop stewards' newspaper carried articles which showed the way in which Vickers increasingly operated outside of Tyneside, outside of heavy engineering and outside of the UK. On the Tyne, one redundancy followed fast behind another and the closure of the Scotswood works in 1979 was, to many, the final straw. It was this which produced the following reflection from one of the plant's redundant workers:

> Well, let's face it; can *you* ever see the North East employing all these engineers again? I mean, these factories aren't getting redecorated. They've closed. Finished! I can't see engineering picking up . . . I think it's finished up here, in fact the way this Government's going it looks as though engineering's going to be finished in England! (Pyke, 1983).

The case of the steel industry is similar. In 1976, over 216 000 men were employed by the British Steel Corporation; today the figure is 80 000 and the prospect is for more major cuts in plants and manpower. In the late seventies, plants dotted throughout South Wales, the Midlands and the North (many, like Consett, old but profitable) were closed down in an attempt to concentrate production around five 'super-plants'. Yet in this ten year period of rationalisation, BSC's share of the UK market *has dropped by thirty seven per cent* to forty three per cent. In the face of steel imports from the Third World, 'rationalisation' has produced an increasing cycle of excess capacity, and the continuance of plant closure. This was made clear in July 1982 when BSC employed a firm of public opinion consultants to sample its work force, asking them if 'in their heart of hearts they thought BSC could survive without closing plants'. This question was followed by another which asked 'which plant?'. In October the corporation made it known that perhaps two of the super-plants were vulnerable to closure. This threat, and the conflict and competition *between* plants and groups of workers which it implied and, to some extent, orchestrated, was repeated regularly in the years that followed and was to have a crippling effect upon 'class solidarity' during the miners' dispute.

These events, taken together, are deeply disquieting – both for the future of British manufacturing, and for trade union organisation. They require sober reflection upon both the changing nature of industry, and the kinds of challenges posed to trade unions and other bodies which hope to fight closures and rebuild a manufacturing base to the British economy.

SIMILAR PROCESSES, DIFFERENT CONTEXTS: THE CASES OF COAL AND CARS

British industry was built around a domestic coal industry. Throughout the nineteenth century, this industry established itself as a leading producer, and the coalfields of the North East and South Wales became major coal exporters. The reconstruction of British industry after the Second World War was based upon coal mined in often appalling conditions by miners working for the National Coal Board. After 1957, with the influx of cheap oil and gas, the industry was rationalised. In the 1960s, production was increasingly re-organised around fewer collieries with mechanised systems of cutting and transporting coal. In one decade, over 300 000 men left the industry, while others were transferred from pit to pit – often between areas of the country. This period of restructuring, in which wages were also depressed, was achieved with little industrial unrest. In part, this was due to the *co-operation* of the trade unions, and this, in turn, was linked to the availability of alternative employment achieved through state direction of industry. In spite of this, however, unemployment rates in the coalfields increased.

In 1974, in the wake of the increase in the price of oil and the two successful national strikes, the NUM, along with the NCB, signed a new *Plan for Coal* with the incoming Labour Government. The aim of this Plan was to expand coal production through investment in existing pits and the development of new collieries in virgin areas. This was the clearest attempt at a Planning Agreement. Its ethos was expansionist and deeply optimistic about the future of coal as an energy source, and it provided a basis of high paid employment in the coalfield areas. Yet problems with the Plan were apparent almost as soon as it was signed. While the NCB and the Government pushed for greater output and productivity, the demand curve for energy, instead of continuing on its upward path, fell and flattened out. Coal stocks grew, and not only in the UK. Increasingly large amounts of steam and coking coal became available on the international market. In the UK itself, opencast production, dug by civil engineering firms on non-union or TGWU organised sites, rose in accordance with the Plan. As coal piles grew at the pit head, new imports supplied the steel plants at Llanwern, Redcar and Ravenscraig. So, too, did the open-cast operatives sell their output at a profit. There are two important pointers to the internal transformations that took place within the coal industry as the recession bit: demand dropped, but with it supply was re-allocated; and this involved a shift from NCB deep-mined coal to open-cast coal mined in the UK and around the world.

The EEC Commission in its 1981 statement on the coal industry, which has formed the background to all subsequent discussion in Brussels, made clear that, as the largest trading entity in the world, and the largest importer of coal, the Community has a vital interest in the promotion of free trade in that commodity. It was in line with this policy that the Commission (in a view supported by key sectors of the UK energy industry) argued for the closure of 'very unprofitable and uncompetitive' pits. Such pits produced 40 million tons of coal – fifteen per cent of EEC capacity. This capacity will be taken up by imports, mined and transported by transnational corporations. This fact has given rise to the fear of a world wide 'energy cartel' of private corporations. But the EEC has sought to defuse these fears by arguing that: 'this risk is limited by the natural forces of competition, the flexible and diversified structure of the world coal market, . . . and the existing anti-trust legislation in the main coal-exporting countries' (EC Comm, 82 Final, 1982, p. 28).

While the EEC considered how port facilities could be 'expanded and new ones contracted to cope with larger ships, to provide bigger coal storage areas, and to allow for an increasing number of coal preparation plants', many men in the British coalfields asked questions about the logic of this system. As one of them put it: 'we face massive closures in Durham – and the same in South Wales and Scotland – and it's not just jobs that will be lost: it will be the sterilisation of millions of tons of reserves. It's hard to get and we know that. But it's there. All they want us to do is to bury it'.

This view was informed by a sense of how trends in the international coal industry had reduced areas like Durham, Scotland and South Wales to the 'periphery' of European production. It was just such a realisation which helped keep the coal strike solid in these areas for so long. Even here, though – in the fulcrum of an emotional 'solidarity' – men at 'secure' pits like Bilston Glen, Ellington, Wearmouth and Cynheirdre sensed that their interests lay elsewhere. Here, too, in the most dramatic strike to have affected British industry since the war, the structure of the international energy markets came into play. In the 1960s, the availability of cheap oil was used to unpick the social network of production in the coalfields. In 1972 and 1974, the shortage of oil severely limited the options open to the CEGB and the Government in their handling of these coal disputes. In 1984, British miners faced a situation of abundant cheap oil and coal; supplied and delivered by agencies over which the Union had no control. Arthur Scargill's message: 'the cheapest deep mined coal in the world' was an important one. But like the Consett workers' message of a profitable steel plant, it missed the point. British coal was under attack not from German and deep mined production, but from world open-cast coal in near infinite supply.

If coal was associated with the first industrial revolution, vehicle manufacture was the base for the twentieth century development in mass production and what has become known as the 'Fordist' revolution. Yet the international crisis has also affected this industry, and perhaps in an even more dramatic way than coal mining. Here, too, the recession produced a major production crisis. Here, too, state plans for the industry were developed by the 1974 Labour Government – Ryder at BL and the much vaunted 'planning agreement' with Chrysler. Equally these plans proved to be woefully inadequate in the face of the kinds of structural changes that took place in the years that followed.

During the 1960s, the British vehicle market had been dominated by the British Motor Corporation whose forty per cent market share was seen as 'traditional' and, to many people, unchangeable. The company had a range of models with respected brand names tied in to a widespread dealership. Amalgamated with Leyland and Triumph, the company seemed strongly placed in an industry whose output increased steadily to 1.92 million vehicles in 1972. That was to be the high point, since that year the trend has been steadily downward. In 1980 only fifty per cent of those cars were assembled in British plants. Moreover, the industry's output dropped below a million for the first time since 1958. This collapse has been associated with a dramatic change in the level of competition in the British market. In an expanding market, *imported* cars took a bigger and bigger share throughout the 1970s, rising to nearly sixty per cent of all sales. Within this total, Ford had emerged as the market leader. In 1981, while BL's share of the market dipped still further to eighteen per cent, Ford's peaked to thirty one per cent. Yet in the 1970s, Ford's level of production in Britain *dropped*; a large proportion of its sales (about half in 1981 and *all* Capris and Granadas) being imported from its European plants. This fact alone points to the complexity of the issue involved. For while the question of imports may be the most visible indication of the way things are changing in the motor industry, they are only one part of the picture, and perhaps more of a symptom than a cause.

In the late 1960s, the locus of automobile production shifted. While investment had been directed away from established centres of production *within* states, perhaps the most significant change was the orchestration of investment *between* states. 'Ford Europe' symbolised this most clearly. If Ford's plant on the River Rouge (with its integrated production system from iron ore to the car on wheels) was the symbol of Fordism at its height, the modern system contrasts in the way industrial units are dispersed over a vast geographical expanse. Companies have always taken advantage of attractive locational sitings (the availability of grants, loans cheap labour etc.), but the new system, integrated as it is by detailed computer control of components and unit production, gives them an added flexibility. To begin with, it lessens their dependence upon *particular* groups of workers. Ford was beaten in 1941 because all his eggs were in the basket of the Rouge. This is no longer true. Today, Ford's main assembly plants all replicate each other, and production can be switched with some ease from one to the other. Furthermore, disaggregation – as the process of breaking up 'The Rouge' into smaller dispersed pieces has been called – allows the companies to take advantage of variations in labour markets across continents and around the world. Processes requiring skilled labour can more easily be separated from those needing large numbers of untrained workers. In these ways, the new system gives added powers to the companies in their dealings on the factory floor and in the market place (see Beynon, 1984). In Europe, Ford's British and German companies, while registered as individual and independent entities have, through Ford Europe, a degree of mutual co-operation described by the company chairman, Bob Lutz, as 'absolute'. Based upon the same models and plants, purchasing components through the umbrella company, the arrangement is one which allows them to 'have all the benefits of size without the drawbacks' (*Financial Times*, 7 July 1981). Furthermore the geographical spread allows Ford to operate in 'two domestic markets instead of one', thereby accelerating the advantage it has over companies like BL, Renault and VW whose European operations are so strongly based upon the 'domestic' market. In this way, Ford – and to a lesser extent GM – had by 1973 united marketing and production in a new form and to its advantage in Northern Europe. It was against this background that Lee A. Iacocca, when with Ford, had stressed the need to extend the relationship *beyond* the North:

> We are not Ford Europe. We are Ford of a half of Europe! And that is what we remain as long as we can't provide the cars that the other half wants. We can't go on forever importing foreign workers into Northern Europe. It's time to go and build our cars where the manpower already exists. Let's export the factories and stop importing the men. There is a common market; we should have a common company (Seidler, 1976, p. 41).

This was the argument which shifted Ford into the small car market and led to it establishing an assembly plant for the Fiesta in Spain. Iacocca (then President of the Company) had sent Dick Holmes (Ford's man in charge of new Business Opportunities, who was 'in Africa one day, in Asia the next and rarely in his office in London') to Spain:

> Listen, Dick, get down to Spain and forget everything else. We now have two top priorities. Brazil and Spain. Spain is your job. You must do everything possible to get Ford into Spain. It's vital. 'What will we make there?' I don't know, Taunus Escort, time will tell. The main thing is to get started. If you succeed, I'll promise you one thing Dick: we'll put our executive building next to the most beautiful beach on the Spanish Coast, we'll give you the best office on the top with a view of the sea, and we'll call it the Dick Holmes Building (Seidler, 1976, p. 43).

The move South became established around the Fiesta assembly plant at Valencia. It was the beginning of a pattern which, in a deepening crisis of over capacity, saw GM project and then establish an assembly plant in Spain. Ford's own strategy developed with its projected assembly plant in Portugal. In the American continent, this move South was mirrored first by the move out of Detroit into California and the 'Sunbelt States' of the South, and then outwards into Mexico (see Bluestone, Harrison and Barker, 1981). This change was accelerated by the oil crisis and the advent of 'the world car'.

As the 'small car' became established in the US market, so too did the possibility of one range of car selling throughout the world. This is the concept which Ford termed 'Project Erika' and which led up to the launch of the New Escort. GM had a similar project around their 'J car'; and VW produce and sell the Golf in Europe, the USA and Latin America. These cars are 'world cars' in the sense that they are both *produced and sold* globally. Hence, the Ford model that is assembled and rolled off the lines at Halewood, is the same as the one which is produced in Genk and Saarlouis in Germany. It is also produced at two plants in Michigan and by the Mazda Company (in which Ford has a twenty five per cent interest) in Japan. Commenting on the project, Philip Calwell, Ford chairman, argued that 'it is no exaggeration to say that Ford and the auto industry as a whole are currently engaged in the most massive and profound industrial revolution in peace-time history'. While the extent to which this departure represents a radical break with the past is debatable – Walter Hayes, Ford vice-president of public affairs, admitted that 'we invented the phrase "world car" . . . because we had to reinforce the faith of the US in the technical ability of our industry' (*Sunday Times*, 28 September 1980) – its publicity does serve as a pointer to the established trend within the motor industry. The Escort, with over a million produced a year, is built in plants around the world and also draws upon component suppliers on a global basis. The Escorts assembled at the Wayne Plant in Michigan will thus be made up of transaxles manufactured in Japan, shock absorber struts from Spain, reach brake assemblies from Brazil, British steering gears, Italian cylinder heads, hub and bearing clutch assemblies from France, door lift assemblies from Mexico, along with Taiwanese wiring and West German valve guide bushings. In this context, the observation of the industry correspondent of *The Times* (15 August 1980) was quietly understated:

Much of the discussion about the threat to the European car industry has centred on Japan . . . far less has been said about . . . the

American companies active in Europe – GM and Ford – yet they are much more firmly established than the Japanese and likely to become even stronger in the next decade. GM and Ford have both come to realise that national boundaries are irrelevant when rising costs demand the biggest economies of scale.

He went on to conclude that 'faced with Japanese efficiency on the one hand and the American world car on the other, BL, Fiat, Renault and the rest of the European manufacturers are in for a tough time. It is a situation that can lead only to more mergers, more government intervention, and, possibly, some casualties'.

THE FUTURE: A PROBLEM OF STRATEGY

In 1981, the *Financial Times* (21 January 1981) commented on the problems facing trade unions in the new industrial situation by citing the example of a shop steward who,

having spent his working life in a factory near London, protested recently that employers no longer play by the rules. He and his fellow workers had been told that if they tightened their belts and rolled up their sleeves, their factory would make a profit and continue to provide jobs and prosperity in its catchment area. They did and the profits duly materialised. But not long afterwards the company announced that the factory would close. It was explained that the plant was in the wrong place for the market it was trying to serve. The work would be moved to mainland Europe. Probably for the first time, it was brought home to workers what the investment strategy of a multinational corporation means, and how powerless his trade union is to oppose it.

This reality was rubbed home to workers time and again in the late 1970s and early 1980s. In 1979, for example, the Dunlop–Pirelli Company closed its tyre factory at Speke in Liverpool. The Company blamed cheap imports from Eastern Europe for causing a crisis in the tyre market. During the campaign to save the plant, research by the General and Municipal Union revealed that the importing company (National Tyre Suppliers) was a wholly owned subsidiary of Dunlop–Pirelli. While the Speke plant had been starved of capital over the whole of the post-war period, the company had been investing in a new plant in Eastern Europe. In order to facilitate such deals, Dunlop had in 1979 moved its headquarters to Geneva. The move there was described by Ken Gardener, the company's financial director, as a 'considerable coup'. Headquarters in Geneva free the company from the controls which the Bank of England exercises over international transactions and, to quote Gardener again, 'provides the company with considerable financial flexibility'. From Geneva, the company's holdings in the UK, the USA, South Africa, Nigeria, Yugoslavia, etc. are balanced, weighted, moved and controlled. A reality which, to quote one shop steward, 'the working man cannot really grasp. We just have no information about the kind of things that go on at that level'. As another shop steward put it:

> You are talking about a company that doesn't have a heart. It doesn't have any moral obligation to anybody it employs. It's run by accountants and professional hatchet men who manipulate and wheel and deal their products irrespective of the human cost involved. It's like playing a great game of Monopoly: 'Where shall we make tyres this week – give them a pound of rice there, this government owes us a favour'. I thought you couldn't find a worse company than Dunlop but when you talk to people in other multinational firms you see the same dirty trick all along the line. I think they must all go to the same college with Henry Kissinger or someone teaching him.

In 1981 Ron Todd, chief union negotiator at Ford UK, expressed the view that: 'we've got three million on the dole, and another 23 million scared to death'. His feelings, powerfully expressed, were that workers – in fear of their jobs and their livelihoods – were in no state of preparation for a major assault upon the employers or the government. A recession is a time for keeping your head down, not for heroics. Todd's view was supported by a union official in the Midlands: 'workers in the factories have had the stuffing knocked out of them. The union movement is in disarray, and workers are just anxious for a quiet life and to protect what jobs they have' (*Financial Times*, 27 April 1982).

Throughout the North of England, as the closure of factories, pits, shipyards and steel mills reached avalanche proportions, union representatives talked of representing 'a frightened workforce'. As one man put it: 'people are terrified; there's no other word for it. And the company is playing on this fear'. One factory convener describes how:

> One time, if I had a meeting with management, no-one in the factory could care less. You know the sort of thing; there would be union meetings, and regular negotiations with the company over one thing and another, and we more or less got on with it. Communicating with

the members through the Branch and the notice board. Not any more though. When we come out of that office now, I can see hundreds of pairs of eyes on me. Every time I'm called into the manager's office, the people I represent are afraid that they're going to close. And I feel that fear too.

This fear is not irrational. Too often, closures had hit 'out of the blue', as at the Plessey factory in Sunderland. In March 1977, the shop stewards were asked to attend a special evening meeting at the plant. As they arrived, security guards locked the doors behind them. No-one was allowed out. They had been brought together for sentencing – closure. One man hadn't been able to attend the meeting,

I'd arranged to meet the stewards in the workmen's club just around the corner after the meeting to find out what was going on. When I walked in I met one of the lads at the doorway and he just ran his hand across his throat. The stewards were all sat in the corner and their faces were all white. I realised then, without any words, I realised that it was closure (Austin and Beynon, 1980).

The key element in this new environment has been fear, and, in this, the experience of workers at BL has been of pivotal significance. In 1978, Michael Edwardes had been appointed as Chairman to the company. At the time, *The Economist* (14 January 1978) thought that he 'may have had the nod from Mr Callaghan to play it tough. The government is known to want a solution to the Leyland problem wrapped up by early spring'. And play it tough he did. In Liverpool, the dramatic closure of the Speke No. 2 plant was followed by an acceleration in redundancy and closures. As one union official put it: 'they've been given the green light now, if a nationalised concern under a Labour government can close its most modern plant in an area with high unemployment, anything goes' and within BL, Speke was the first of a long line of closures, and sackings. It was the beginning, too, of a strategy aimed at undermining trade union organisation. Management commentators write of the new 'macho style' (Purcell, 1982) of management in the plants that remain, workers talk of 'terror tactics'; and it has been clearly used as a model. Within the private sector, Massey Ferguson at Coventry was quoted as having taken 'a leaf out of Michael Edwardes' book', as the company bypassed the union and held a secret ballot on the future of the plant. BL, in the public sector, was compared in a similar way as it attempted to 'seek a Michael Edwardes style productivity deal when it met with the three trade unions' (*Sunday Times*, 12 July 1981).

So, too, at Ford. At Halewood, in a city with high unemployment, the workers have had it forced upon them time and time again that their jobs are vulnerable and their future depends upon their attitude. Since their major strike in 1978 (when the Callaghan government's five per cent norm was broken), there has been no national strike within the company. In 1980, a year of record profits for the company, the workers refused to strike, voting to accept the company's offer, in spite of the advice of their leaders to strike for more. In the wake of this decision, a group of workers and shop stewards at Halewood decided to develop a regular broadsheet called *Halewood Worker*. An earlier *Christmas Special* had proved a great success, and it continued in a witty, iconoclastic way to assist in the task of breaking down the isolation and 'lack of communication' between workers in the plants. In 1981 it asked the question 'the pay deal: why did we accept it?'.

On Thursday 5 February 1981 we felt the results of our decision to accept the wage and conditions agreement for 1981. The wage packet didn't actually bulge, in fact most people were absolutely shocked at the pathetic 'increase' in the rate. It is useless for individuals to claim 'I didn't vote for it' or 'I didn't attend the meeting'. The fact is, locally and nationally we did accept – why?

In trying to work out an answer they approached thirty six workers, each on separate sections. 'Why?' The answers were interesting. Aside from the occasional maverick response ('because we're a gang of bloody nutters') what emerges is the overwhelming reference to 'fear'. People talk of a 'sense of insecurity', of 'despair' and 'a lack of belief in our own strength', of 'stories about cutback', 'Maggie's policies', and arching over everything else, the 'fear of Ford pulling a Michael Edwardes' fascist trip on us'.

Fear works then; but in what ways? A senior shop steward in the plant saw it like this:

Industrial relations haven't improved as such, it's fear that has done it really. There's more sackings. Now they discipline people to the gate . . . It's not a new understanding or anything. It's just brute facts like unemployment and money. A lot of blokes have pulled their horns in a lot. When you know that Ford have got five thousand applications waiting for your job, it's a bit different isn't it?

But to those 'brute facts' Ford have added the pressure for more production. The plant, tooled up for the new Escort, was designed by Ford to produce in excess of a thousand cars a day; so, too, the twin plant in Saarlouis. In the months after its launch in September 1980, the workers were inundated with statistical comparisons of performance in each of the Escort plants. These comparisons had an impact. They helped to produce an increase in production at Halewood; and there is some evidence to indicate that, in the other plants, (especially in the USA) Halewood, as the least 'productive' was seen to be the legitimate candidate for closure, should a plant have to go.

But these processes do not work in one direction alone. While Ford increases pressure in plants by developing international comparisons, so, too, are their workers more *aware* of the form and scale of the Company's global operations. In the Far East, workers on strike in the Phillipines borrowed the 'Fraud' logo from the workers' combine committee in Britain. So, too, in Liverpool did one plant convener comment that his members saw: 'Ford making £386 million profit last year, but companies are leaving Merseyside and little is going into public services. The men feel they are being exploited' (*Financial Times*, 12 November 1980).

A similar feeling of 'exploitation' and injustice moved workers in the National Health Service to become involved in a protracted series of disputes throughout 1982. This strike (while disastrous on one level, revealing the phenomenal *weakness* of organised trade unionism in Britain) was important in the depth of feeling it revealed both within the health service and beyond. Talking of this, one miner in South Wales explained how:

> As I see it, it's a question of supporting our own kind. In an area like South Wales with the mining and steel industries we need a health service. It's our people who use the health service. It's not them; if the health service finishes they'll pay for their health. So I say we should be on the picket lines. Let the nurses do their job of looking after our kind in the hospitals, and let us do the job on the pickets.

In November, the Day of Action received support from every lodge in the South Wales coalfield, and to some extent it can be seen as a precursor to the major dispute that affected the coalfields in 1984 and 1985.

Unemployment has more than one meaning, and 'fear' is not an infallible guide to action. Certainly in the coal industry in 1984 many miners and their families recognised that, in a real sense, they had 'nothing left to lose'. While colliery closures had been achieved *without* compulsory redundancies (in transfers and a reasonably generous voluntary severance scheme tailored for vulnerable age groups), recruitment had virtually ended and with it the long-term future for many of the towns and villages based upon the pits. It was this sense of a threat far deeper than that faced in the 1930s which held people together through a year of deprivation and struggle. A sense of threat *and* a sense of hope. For what the coal strike managed to achieve (at its best) was a combination of the range of struggles which had preceded it. The solidarity of the strike was linked, through the community support groups, to a wider understanding of what is involved in 'jobs' and 'employment'. It gave some flesh to the rhetoric 'it's not your job to sell'. The experience of the strike – picketing open-cast sites; meeting supporters from other areas, industries and professions – served to broaden the social and political perspectives of many of the activists. In this respect, there is truth in the NUM President's claim that 'victory' can be seen to lie in the very – politicising – experience of the struggle itself. But if this also is not to turn to rhetoric, and the experience itself soured, there has to be some tangible sense of progress, of gain. In this respect, the struggles for jobs (in glorious defeat, and in the odd marginal gain) serve to raise the serious questions of long-term political strategy.

INDUSTRY AND POLITICS

When all these changes are taken together, they add support to the view that the framework of a new international division of labour is being laid out. In this changing situation it is not only trade union officials and shop stewards who have been slow to react; governments and Departments of State have also been inclined to understand economic policy (within and between states) through the established post-war framework. As such, in the wake of the defeat of the industrial action by the mineworkers, there has been much talk of a return to the 'political wing' of the labour movement, and of a solution being found under the umbrella of 'the next Labour government'. For its part, the Labour opposition encourages this view and within its leader's rhetoric there is a strong pull toward the policies of growth evoked in the 1960s and the style of Wilson as its most successful advocate. But times *have* changed. And the complex *industrial* transformations which have affected the British economy since that period make the prospect of reworking a 'modernising' strategy as a basis for full employment and socialist development questionable indeed.

In 1964, the Labour government, in one of its early and rare moments of idealism, set up the Ministry of Overseas Development with Barbara Castle as minister of cabinet rank. Since then the Ministry has changed its name and status many times, but in all this, as *The Times* pointed out, 'one fact has stood out: the movement has been downhill all the way'. Budgets have been cut, and so, too, has the nature of its aid. In 1977, under the 'Aid and Trade Provision', the aid was openly tied to the commercial interests of the companies. It was a policy justified by 'the aggressive use of aid funds by other donors to support their firms in winning business in developing countries' (see Elliott, 1982). There have been several consequences of this policy (for example, aid has increasingly been directed away from the poorest to the not so poor countries in the Third World) but what stands out is the way in which 'aid' has become a prop to an, often contradictory, restructuring of the world economy. In 1981, for example, the biggest grant in aid given by the UK Government went to help Davy Loewy obtain a contract to establish a steel mill in Mexico. As *The Times* (7 October 1982) pointed out: 'at present the government is both financing the steel industry and *subsidising* the export of steel mills'.

Equally as 'disaggregation' develops as a basis for location, so too does the extent to which sectors of particular national economies form but one part of an international chain of production. Malta's involvement in European vehicle manufacture, for example, is based upon the production of boot locks. In Ulster, the region's car industry produces carburettors and seat belts. Here the degree of autonomy available to regional and national planning is extremely limited. And this worsens the more regional (and national) economies develop around branch plants of giant corporations, performing just one stage in an internationally co-ordinated production process. The North East of England is a good example of this vulnerability. During the 1960s the 'traditional' sectors of this old industrial area were run down. Almost 100 pits were closed in Durham alone, as 50 000 men left the coal industry, encouraged by the prospect of employment in the new manufacturing sector developed in the area. With the incentive of state support, corporations in a range of industries (textiles and clothing, construction, vehicles, light and electrical engineering, food) moved into the area, joining the NCB and BSC as major employers of industrial workers. In the late seventies these plants closed. In the recession, it was the giant firms, and not the equally new 'small firm sector', which cut back hard, with devastating effects upon the region's economy. As one local study pointed out: 'what happens to manufacturing employment depends on the big firms. If you can't do something about them there's nothing you can do about job losses. The small end is quite trivial compared with what happens in giant enterprises' (*Sunday Times*, 3 October 1982; see Storey, 1982).

This is one part of the dilemma. The 'new system' also poses problems at another level. In Europe, in manufacturing industry generally, and in the acute and particular case of vehicle production, there is *over* capacity. Yet the major producers continue to establish new plants, designed and located in a way which will increase competitiveness and by implication and necessity close down other plants. Here the contrast between the technical sophistication – the machinery, the degree of planning and organisation on an international scale – of the *internal* operations of the major companies, and the chaos of the overall system is most glaring. The new international division of labour is riven with this contradiction, and it reveals itself *politically* in relations between particular regions and states, as their communities and governments compete with each other for private capital. Within the new production arrangements, regions like the North East of England and the North of Egypt have an equivalence as areas of labour supply allied with domestic capital and state support. In the words of the president of the Westinghouse corporation: 'The unschooled girls of Taiwan can do just as well at assembling complex TV components as the High School graduates of New Jersey. The untrained workers of Africa or Asian nations can be taught to produce complex products, ranging from tiny transistors to giant turbines as readily as the skilled workers of Philadelphia' (Barnet and Muller, 1974).

There is no denying this. Nor is there any case, morally or politically, for denying 'jobs' to the peoples of Africa, Asia and the Middle East. The danger though, and the reference to 'unschooled girls' is perhaps the giveaway, is that these new arrangements, orchestrated as they are by private capital, will service *its* interests principally. This is certainly the case in coal mining, where the switch towards imports is linked to the slave urban regimes of South Africa and Columbia as well as to the command economies of Eastern Europe.

In this way, the question of 'closures' in the UK directs itself irrevocably towards the question of international relationships between workers and the degree of independence allowed to particular states within the new international order. The political task for labour movements between now and the end of the century (and it *is* important to take such a timescale) is to attempt to resolve this dilemma. In this task, forms of organisation and understanding need to be encouraged which bridge the division between work and home; between workplaces and between countries. The kinds of developments which have accompanied struggle against closures could yet provide the basis for such organised forms.

5 Closing Down: Management Perspectives and Strategies
Cliff Lockyer and Lesley Baddon

INTRODUCTION

In this chapter we seek to identify and examine the nature of management policy and strategy relating to closure. Our concern is to illuminate two neglected areas in the literature on closure: first, the factors influencing the choice of establishment to be closed; and, second, the policies management adopt to minimise employee opposition to closure. We have chosen to examine management strategy within the context of a specific closure: that of the Linwood motor manufacturing complex in the West of Scotland. We recognise the potential dangers of seeking to erect general explanations and analyses based on the examination of the closure of one manufacturing plant. Nevertheless, our example does indicate serious weaknesses in much of the existing literature.

First, our case study supports the arguments of Massey and Meegan (1982) that the dominance of macro-analyses of closure and of the spatial redistribution of employment is based on essentially aggregate and determinist explanations of management decision-making. Such approaches ignore the logic of decision-making internal to an industrial organisation – a logic based on the unique circumstances of the enterprise and coloured by the internal political processes within management. We use our case study to illustrate the degree of choice open to management and the factors influencing that choice.

Secondly, whilst it is now commonplace to comment on the neglect of management and managerial work in the study of industrial relations (Purcell and Sissons, 1983) and to comment on its essentially prescriptive and didactic nature (Turner et al., 1977), few have drawn attention to the role of pluralist or 'official' analyses of redundancy in reinforcing and maintaining the legitimacy of closure and job loss, rather than being concerned with the needs of those losing employment.

Thus, a further aim of our analysis will be to develop the arguments of Hardy (1985) as to the management search for social legitimacy in the context of closure.

LINWOOD: EARLY HISTORY

We base our arguments on a study of the motor manufacturing complex at Linwood, Renfrewshire; a complex initially erected by the Ministry of Supply as part of the shadow war factory programme of the late 1930s to make special steels and forge gun barrels. The establishment of a substantial factory reflected more the interests of Beardmores, which held the agency agreement to manage the firm on behalf of the Ministry of Supply, rather than wartime needs. Beardmores' interest in the factory effectively ended in 1947 when the Board of Trade, under the Distribution of Industry Act, allocated use of part of the factory to Pressed Steel, then a major independent producer of car panels and bodies for the car industry.

The early history is significant to the management closure strategy of the factory in 1981. From the outset the factory was seen as marginal and vulnerable. The Pressed Steel board was divided as to the merits of establishing a manufacturing base at Linwood. Likewise, the community and relevant government departments recognised both the problems of encouraging large firms to move to the site and to be long-term major employers in the area. There are several references within the official minutes of the Board of Trade as to the likely difficulties in persuading firms to occupy the factory and thus to reduce the political problems of high levels of male unemployment. From the late 1940s onwards, there is evidence to suggest that the various firms occupying the complex played on the fears of vulnerability and unemployment to lever additional funds and support from the government. It was apparent in 1946–47 in the very generous terms offered to Pressed Steel to move part of its production to Linwood; in the reconstruction of Pressed Steel to meet the emerging boom in private car ownership during the 1950s; in the mid-1960s when the Rootes car assembly factory had been erected adjacent to the Pressed Steel complex; in the early 1970s; and in the financial support for Chrysler in 1975–76.

Governmental fears of vulnerability also enabled the successive firms occupying the site largely to ignore the government policies on which grants and subsidies were based. Thus Beardmores, managers of the plant during the war years, embarked on a programme of asset stripping. Pressed Steel who secured, in the 1940s, more than £1.5 million from government departments did not transfer any substantial part of its car body operation to Linwood – despite this being the rationale for such government financial support. As Sims and Wood (1984) note, there 'were no conditions attached to state investment concerning what type of production was located at regional plants'. Consequently, firms were free to locate peripheral functions. In essence, the history of Pressed Steel's occupation of the complex, apart from the production of railway rolling stock, was of the transfer to Linwood of a succession of marginal, small volume and peripheral activities.

The Pressed Steel company converted the Linwood complex to produce railway rolling stock, utilising the same methods as were used to produce all steel car bodies. The work force grew from 450 to over 2000. In addition, a toolroom and press shop were established. These grew in importance as the volume of railway rolling stock orders decreased. Increasingly the work of the Linwood factory shifted to the production of dies for a range of car manufacturing companies, stamping panels for a range of car bodies and for Ford and BMC lorry cabs. However, all the car production work was peripheral to the major developments of Pressed Steel at Cowley and Swindon.

By the 1960s, the Pressed Steel factory's production range included lorry cabs for Ford and BMC; car bodies for Volvo and Rover; lorry trailers and specialist rolling stock; as well as Imp car bodies for the newly established Rootes factory which had been erected across the road. In addition, the toolroom, die manufacture and tryout section was completing work for Vauxhall, Ford, Alfa Romeo and Rolls Royce amongst others. Meanwhile, the production of railway rolling stock, the mainstay of production in the 1950s, had declined to the production of small numbers of passenger coaches and specialist wagons.

ROOTES/CHRYSLER: LINWOOD'S VULNERABILITY

Rootes Motors had been persuaded to move to Linwood by the incentives offered by the regional policy of the then Conservative government. Between 1960 and 1962, the company erected assembly, machining and diecasting facilities at Linwood. But Rootes was wracked by continual financial difficulties in this period, and only an injection of capital by the Chrysler Corporation in 1964, and its eventual purchase of the Rootes Company in 1967, ensured the survival of Rootes. The logic behind this purchase was not solely to enable Chrysler to follow the pattern of Ford and General Motors – to become a multinational – but rather to use Rootes as a springboard into Europe when Britain eventually entered the EEC. This strategy became evident in the restructuring of the company in the 1970s and in the eventual sale of Chrysler Europe to Peugeot–Citroen.

Rootes/Chrysler purchased the Pressed Steel factory in 1967, following the acquisition of Pressed Steel by BMC, and merged the managements of the two companies in the following year. By the time of the merger, it was clear that Pressed Steel did not value its Linwood operation: the Linwood complex was of marginal importance as far as vehicle production was concerned, and of minor interest to corporate staffs. Yet for Rootes/Chrysler, the Pressed Steel plant was of vital importance; for BMC's acquisition of Pressed Steel had left the Rootes motor company without a major car body supplier. Traditionally Rootes had only produced approximately ten per cent of its stamping needs. British Light Steel Pressings, Rootes' stamping facility, was outdated and incapable of expansion. Moreover, Rootes had never had an effective die manufacturing capacity.

Hence, the Pressed Steel factory at Linwood offered the company the ability to produce virtually all its car body panels and to produce a range of sets of dies for new models. It was essential, if the company did not want to be dependent upon a larger competitor for its car bodies. Chrysler, the new owners, saw the facilities at Linwood as the means to facilitate expansion of its European operations. Paradoxically, this policy heightened the sense of vulnerability amongst the labour force, since it was achieved at the expense of terminating all other existing contracts. Thus the production of the Volvo and Rover car bodies, BMC and Ford lorry cabs, a range of specialist railway wagons, extensive refrigerated trailer production, minor fabrication work and extensive die manufacturing work were all stopped.

But, once Chrysler had introduced a new European model range, the Linwood die shop was less essential. Consequently, as Chrysler's finances worsened, the die shop was the first to be run down. By the mid-1970s Linwood was incapable of providing dies for minor model changes within Chrysler UK; for example, dies for the 50 series Dodge truck came from the United States. Likewise, the assembly line at Linwood became less essential once the reconstruction of Chrysler's other UK assembly plant, at Ryton, had been completed. Linwood was relegated to producing ageing models (with the exception of the Sunbeam) and low volume derivatives. All new models, apart from the Sunbeam, were produced initially at Ryton.

In the public statements of the company in the early 1970s, Linwood was an integral part of Chrysler UK and Chrysler Europe. It was to be integrated into these operations through a policy of rationalisation and modernisation. To this end, Chrysler UK's management re-allocated functions between plants. Yet, the operational policy of the company was fundamentally different. The expansion at Linwood was cosmetic, involving largely the transfer of old equipment from other locations into the plant. The policy was one of maximising output at the expense of forward planning, replacement of equipment and even basic maintenance. Models were introduced with inadequate planning and engineering design. Moreover, the policy of short term gain was accompanied by transferring dies, machine tools and machines abroad and by a policy of transfer pricing.

Thus, whilst an automated door assembly line had been installed in 1969, much of the expansion of the Press Shop had been by equipment from British Light Steel Pressings. By 1976 only two per cent of the major presses were less than eight years old; forty eight per cent were between thirteen and twenty two years old and nearly twenty nine per cent were more than twenty two years old. The picture was more depressing in the minor presses and decoil areas, where respectively fifty per cent and thirty nine per cent of the equipment was more than twenty two years old. Between 1972 and 1975 the management of the machine block at Linwood requested £1.5 million in investment and replacement, £500 000 was approved but only £385 000 spent – less than the costs of machine breakdown for one year alone. In 1975, for example, machine breakdown in the machine block alone accounted for thirty eight per cent of all lost hours and twenty five per cent of the overbudget. Such figures do not include the costs of rejected parts or reworking.

The introduction of Avenger production from Ryton was planned to be completed within six weeks. The production of both the Avenger and Sunbeam was undertaken by an inadequately trained labour force. Senior production management expressed concern at the implications of such production decisions on both the volume and quality of output. It was widely believed amongst Linwood management that after 1976 there was a squandering of the financial support from the government and overproduction for reasons that were not associated with securing the future of Linwood.

The Talbot Action Group (1981) highlighted both the extent to which design work and die manufacture was not credited to Chrysler UK, and the method of costing which credited Linwood with a 'notional manufacturing price' rather than the price to dealers. *Labour Research* questioned whether the poor profitability of the company was due to the low price per vehicle exported. Almost all exports from the UK went via Chrysler International SA, a subsidiary registered in Switzerland (or its British owned subsidiary – Chrysler Overseas Trading Company), which handled the marketing of UK products in 140 countries. *Labour Research* suggested that if Chrysler exports had been sold at eighty per cent of the average figure for BL exports rather than the actual figure, it would have made Chrysler UK £31 million per year better off for the period between 1972 and 1975. The Chrysler Overseas Capital Corporation, a finance raising agency for Chrysler activities outside the USA, possibly acted as a further avenue for transfer pricing. Like the other agencies, it regularly operated at a 'loss' in currency conversion, indicating either 'a sophisticated form of transfer costing or exceptionally poor judgement' (Joint Trade Union Research Group, 1978).

CHRYSLER UK: 'RESCUE' AND SELL-OUT

The oil crisis of the early 1970s created severe problems for Chrysler both in the United States and in Britain and prompted a re-assessment of its UK operations. Ostensibly the Chrysler Corporation proposed closing down the United Kingdom operations because of the intolerable drag on company profitability imposed by these operations. Riccardo, the chairman of the Chrysler Corporation, commenced a series of discussions with the Labour government after 1974 in which he stated that it was impossible to continue to finance the UK operations. The Chrysler Corporation suggested the government either nationalise Chrysler UK or take a majority holding. The government, for a combination of political, electoral and balance of trade reasons, offered four alternatives, three of which envisaged an enhanced role for Linwood at the expense of Ryton and the commercial facility at Dunstable. Both the cabinet and the chairman of Chrysler UK agreed that the priority was to keep Linwood open. Eventually a plan was agreed which involved the government accepting liability for £162.5 million, including loan capital of £55 million for investment in new models and equipment, and a reduced role for Ryton – the most vulnerable plant in all the proposals. Nevertheless, Ryton was reorganised to assemble Alpines from French kits at a rate of 40 000 per annum. In addition, the agreement between the Chrysler Corporation and the government called for full integration of Chrysler UK with the European operations. The importance of Ryton to the production and successful launch of the Alpine meant that Chrysler was loath to agree to any new proposal involving the closure of Ryton, yet it publicly played this down.

There is much to suggest that Chrysler's espoused policy was not its operational one; that the degree of vulnerability of the UK operations was not as great as the directors publicly implied. The inadequate assembly capacity at Poissy for the production of the Alpine necessitated a shift of some production to Ryton (Wilks, 1984, p. 141; Chrysler Corporation, 1975, p. 5). First, Chrysler recognised the vulnerability of the Labour government to the growth of the Scottish National Party. Politically, Linwood had to be kept open, as long as the costs were not too excessive. Secondly, there was a degree of opportunism in Chrysler's strategy; it noted the degree of support given to British Leyland and sought to link its UK operations to the general rebuilding of the British car industry. At least it would get a cheap new model range from government assistance! Thirdly, as Hood and Young (1982, p. 69) note, the agreement between Chrysler and the government may be seen as a cynical attempt to improve the saleability of the UK operations. Fourthly, and more importantly, was the Iranian CKD contract. This entailed the supply of Hunter car parts, including engines to Iran for local assembly. The terms and scale of the contract, some 160 000 car kits in 1975, rising to 250 000 kits by 1980 (see Wilks, 1984, p. 119) are significant, for the timing of contract matched that of the rescue plan, and for later developments including the changing ownership, volume and nature of production of Chrysler UK.

The first stage of the Iranian contract involved supplying virtually complete car kits, with only minimum local content. The second stage, scheduled to commence in 1978–79 involved a more substantial local content. The third stage envisaged the substitution of a Simca made engine. Moreover, the kits were supplied directly to Iran but went via a series of export companies (see above p. 121). There is much to suggest that this was an elaborate transfer pricing mechanism for shifting profit abroad and generating artificially high losses in the United Kingdom. Equally, it can be seen that once a French engine had replaced the UK version, and the degree of local components was increased, there was less need, or value to Chrysler, in retaining its UK operations. Evidence for this was noted by the Expenditure Committee (HC 596, 1976) which was not optimistic as to Chrysler UK's ability to generate sufficient profits after 1979 to maintain a model programme and to repay the loans. The Committee also noted that Chrysler's agreement with the Labour government did not include any guarantees that there would be integration with Chrysler Europe. Nevertheless, the government was concerned to ensure that the UK operations did not become marginal to the larger French operations. Hence, its pressure for integration and the requirement that certain components for Chrysler's European models be produced in the UK (Dunnett, 1980, p. 163). This requirement was later modified in an effort to ensure that cars assembled in the United Kingdom had a certain percentage of UK made parts (this was subsequently bypassed by Talbot).

As far as integration was concerned, it was strangely skewed. It was the integration of a market rather than of a rational production policy involving Chrysler Europe facilities. A comparison of the Peugeot–Citroen–Chrysler car model range by 1977 illustrated the degree of model duplication and the need to rationalise components (there were some fourteen basic engine types as compared to Ford's four). Moves towards integration were confined essentially to defining and sourcing markets. Hence the transfer of production from France to Ryton could be seen as the first step in opening Chrysler UK's 590 dealers to UK labelled, but foreign made, cars. This development was to attain even greater significance after the transfer of ownership to Peugeot and the abandonment of the Talbot marque.

By 1978, rumours as to the future of the Linwood plant were again rife. This speculation culminated in the announcement of the sale of Chrysler Europe (Talbot) to Peugeot–Citroen (PSA). PSA took control of Chrysler Europe in 1979 and appointed new managing and personnel directors. The French company was primarily interested in the share of the market held by Chrysler and the associated dealership network of some 3000 outlets in Europe. On the manufacturing side, PSA embarked upon a policy of contraction and closure in Britain. At first it was unclear as to which facilities to close. Within the company, Ryton was initially thought to be most vulnerable, given a combination of available facilities, its history of labour relations and political pressure.

Yet, within a very short period a decision was reached to close Linwood. Linwood's position had been undermined by the policy of restricting the sales of the Scottish produced Sunbeam so as not to affect sales of the comparable, French-built, Horizon. And despite government offers of financial help, PSA notified the British government, in February 1981, of the decision to close Linwood in May 1981. By 18 March, opposition to the closure had ended. Despite weeks of campaigning, and offers of support from many other groups, the employees at Linwood voted by a majority of two to one against fighting the management's decision.

ANALYSIS OF MANAGEMENT'S CLOSURE STRATEGY

Within six weeks of the announcement of closure, management had successfully weakened and subsequently destroyed what was popularly regarded as a well-organised, militant workforce and trade union opposition. From an analysis of management's actions it is possible to identify and define first, the nature of the strategy; second, the factors influencing management and workforce; third, the components of management's strategy; and, finally, the centrality of industrial relations issues in the process.

Purcell (1983) notes the importance of labour and product markets, planning and technological factors on corporate industrial relations. Thurley and Wood (1983), in stressing similar considerations, question whether industrial relations strategies relating to corporate strategy should be seen as relatively autonomous, as a function of a professional self conscious approach to labour problems, or should be seen as essentially informal, spontaneous and opportunistic. However, our analysis suggests first, the need to consider conditioning factors, that is aspects of work and industrial relations which reduce employee opposition to closure but which were not explicitly introduced to bring about closure; and secondly, operational closure policy. In many respects conditioning factors determine the contours of the closure policy.

a) Conditioning factors

The widespread belief in the vulnerability of the Linwood complex was undoubtedly a major factor affecting the workforce. The complex had been threatened with closure in the 1940s, in the 1960s, and again in 1976 and in 1978. Thus, announcement of closure was met with resignation, as illustrated by the following comments by employees:

> It was never meant to work. They were forced up here by the Government. If they wanted the money they were forced up here . . . I thought it would close sooner. It was tipped every year as soon as the Yanks were the owners.

> No [the closure] wasnae a shock, it kept changing hands so often. I knew it was going downhill because everything pointed to closure. We could see no way over it. It was just getting worse and worse and worse. If you took over a business you'd go in and see everything.

Nobody did. They say they sent a delegation in . . . I never saw a Frenchman in there since they took over.

Many recognised that PSA was primarily interested in the dealership and market shares; the lack of interest in Linwood was seen as a clear indication of closure. To some of the shop stewards, the announcement of the closure was 'a relief' and a recognition that given the years of rundown and the scale of previous redundancies the complex could not survive in strict financial terms. Hence the campaign against closure was essentially based on securing a rescue rather than seeking a further refunding of PSA.

Amongst Linwood management there was an acceptance of what was seen as inevitable: 'It was presented in such a fashion that there was no recourse other than acceptance. But then we were told that it was all important to get an orderly closure in order to ensure that the people would get their redundancy money'. The fortunes of Linwood had always been associated with the fortunes of Scotland, the complex demonstrated the successes and failures of attempts to rebuild the Scottish economy. Linwood suffered from a surfeit of media attention. Ultimately the announcement of closure appeared to support the prophecies of the media and their apportionment of blame to the workforce, to its strike-proneness and its poor quality work.

The history of the Linwood complex, with its frequent threats of closure, was invoked by PSA corporate management to weaken potential opposition. The past performance of Linwood enabled corporate management to present its actions as commonsense – as rational and legitimate decision-making. Indeed, as noted above, the economic rationality of closure served to undermine the possibility of opposition on the part of local management at Linwood. Moreover, this possibility was further reduced by the internal divisions within local management: some were offered other appointments in the company; those near retirement age were offered enhanced redundancy terms; whilst the remainder looked outwards to employment elsewhere.

Similarly, corporate management sought to portray any trade union opposition to closure as being not only futile but potentially damaging to the size of the workforce's redundancy payments. Indeed, both arguments were voiced by management in a series of letters sent to employees at Linwood between February and March 1981. However, trade union opposition had already been fundamentally weakened by the development of company-wide bargaining which had arisen from the spate of participation proposals which in turn were a feature of the

1976 'rescue' of the company. The development of company-wide bargaining served to weaken the links between senior stewards and the rank and file, it bureaucratised the steward hierarchy and incorporated it into an agenda of issues generated by management. Stewards argued that the last offensive strikes took place in 1972–73, thereafter they believed that the initiative shifted to management. The extensive committee structure, established in 1976 as part of the participation proposals, firmly placed the declining economic fortunes of the company at the centre of the 'information' agenda. Productivity, duality, costs and losses became the language of discussions between management and trade unions and the criteria to assess any proposals or wage claims.

In this respect, the vulnerability of Linwood became a core issue. Divisions emerged within the shop steward organisation, as the senior stewards and conveners were increasingly regarded by other stewards as primarily the purveyors of company information rather than representatives of the workforce. The conveners and senior stewards felt trapped in this situation, yet could not abstain from it. National trade union officials were also ensnared by the same logic. Talbot was seen as a lost issue in the deepening recession. By 1980, for example, the TASS national officer for cars had spoken of the 'awesome' problems at Talbot.

The moves towards company-wide bargaining were but one feature of a general centralisation of industrial relations and other management functions. Importantly, for instance, sales and any other outside activity, such as purchasing or tendering for die work for the toolshop, were centrally controlled. Linwood had become by the late 1970s the classic branch factory, incapable of altering the terms of its existence.

b) Operational closure policy

The operational closure policy at the corporate level most probably started in 1978. The results of Chrysler's attempts to create a European car division, along the lines of Ford and General Motors, had been to create a Europe based corporate centre. This relied on Simca rather than Chrysler UK. Thus, by the time of the sale to PSA, the locus of power at the corporate level was outside of the UK. Additionally, the then relative success of Simca implied that rationalisation in the form of cuts in production capacity would initially affect the UK rather than France. There is much to suggest that Chrysler overproduced in the period 1976–78, the period of government support, and was prepared to cut production at Linwood in 1978. Thus, in January 1979, target production levels were cut from 2880 to 2564, with further cuts in May and October 1979. In 1980, production levels were progressively cut in January, August, September and October. These cuts were accompanied by redundancies and short time working. Moreover, weekly production records note an increasing proportion of production losses arising from a combination of shortages of parts and machine breakdowns.

The first element of the operational policy was thus to reinforce the traditional fears of vulnerability. This was heightened by the motivational scheme which stressed the poor quality of production. Frequently the rate of first time 'buy-offs' (cars coming off the production line and meeting the quality standards) was often below fifty per cent of production (see Table 5.1). The impression created was that the complex was nearing closure, management would therefore have to take some action to stem the 'obvious losses', and the only possible action by management would be to cease production.

The second element of the corporate strategy was to maintain orderly production during the restructuring and closure. Thus, until the announcement of the closure of the complex, the official statements of the managing director were optimistic about the future for the company. Indeed, in the final quarterly briefing for all management, supervisors and stewards conducted by the managing director in late 1980 there was no suggestion of closure. 1981 was presented as a year in which the fortunes of Talbot would improve, although there were a few uncertainties. A senior manager noted that whilst this optimistic view was being presented, Linwood's personnel managers were being notified to attend meetings with central staffs to be briefed as to the procedures for closing the factory.

Whilst the espoused policy was not to mention closure until early 1981, almost the last possible date to meet the notifications of redundancy requirements, the operational policy was to finalise arrangements for closing the complex. The uneconomic, and hence vulnerable, state of the complex was further extended by the refusal of the central staff to tender for additional work for Linwood. It has been suggested, for example, that British Leyland approached Talbot to ask if the die shop at Linwood could undertake die work associated with the production of the Maestro. Yet, Talbot central staffs indicated that Linwood was not interested in the work and should not be approached by British Leyland. Clearly, the operational policy was directed at closing rather than saving the Linwood complex.

Table 5.1   Average weekly production figures 1978–1981

Month	Target production level	Actual production	Man assigned level	First time buy-off
1978				
March–April	2880	2674	3232	1543
April–May	2723	2299	3049	1410
May–June	2865	2369	3216	1385
Aug.–Sept.	2880	2516	3232	711
Sept.–Oct.	2647	2222	2972	1159
Oct.–Nov.	2880	2173	3232	1129
Nov.–Dec.	2880	2415	3232	1591
1979				
Jan.–Feb.	2564	2129	2849	966
Feb.–March	2564	2048	2849	1105
March–April	2564	1757	2849	983
April–May	2174	1892	2398	1059
May–June	2304	2121	2541	670
June–July	2304	1928	2541	889
August	2304	1815	2541	981
Oct.–Nov.	2223	1876	2461	1122
Nov.–Dec.	2141	1984	2381	718
1980				
Jan.–Feb.	1756	1577	n.a	850
Feb.–March	1760	1615	n.a.	937
March–April	1760	1624	n.a.	741
April–May	1777	1280	n.a.	683
May–June	1840	1509	n.a.	735
June–July	1456	1132	n.a.	524
Aug.–Sept.	997	743	n.a.	366
Sept.–Oct.	871	771	n.a. ~	480
Oct.–Nov.	795	733	n.a.	436
Nov.–Dec.	582	545	n.a.	269
1981				
Jan.–Feb.	872	803	n.a.	470
Feb.–March	1310	1179	n.a	568
March–April	1456	1292	n.a.	697
April–May	1309	1104	n.a.	392

Source: Management Production Figures, Talbot Scotland Limited, Linwood.

Notes

i)   These figures are derived by combining weekly statistics into four and five week periods and expressing the figures as a weekly average.

ii)   Minor fluctuations in target and man assigned production levels reflect the impact of holidays on production levels.

iii)   Figures under first time buy-offs indicate neither the severity of faults in cars, nor the reasons for low production. Thus a significant percentage of failures to meet standards reflect minor shortages of components. In addition, industrial action, by reducing the volume of cars produced affects first time buy-off rate. Nevertheless, the impact of this is more clearly shown in the difference between target and actual production. Machine breakdowns would be included in these figures.

iv)   Production figures achieved can include production generated in overtime and on short time.

Orderly production was further engendered by the bonus scheme. On the announcement of closure, production was increased and full-time working restored. The bonus scheme, which had been introduced at the end of the 1970s, began to yield more attractive bonuses. All the letters to employees between the announcement of closure and its acceptance by the workforce stressed the impact of bonus scheme payments in increasing redundancy payments. As a letter of 24 February 1981 made clear (see Figure 5.1), orderly and efficient production with maximum co-operation from all employees was linked to the bonus scheme. In turn, bonus payments were stated to have a potentially significant effect on the redundancy package.

The third element of the strategy was to divide the workforce. The letters to employees offered a number the possibility of being given work after the closure – dependent upon management choice. More specifically, redundancy terms were set to be attractive to those nearing retirement and to those with limited service. Not surprisingly, these groups opposed attempts to resist closure as they perceived resistance as a threat to their redundancy terms.

The fourth element was to ensure that those managing the closure were also to be declared redundant – a number of senior managers moved, leaving behind those with long service or who were locals. The argument was that employees would see the inevitability of closure more clearly and work more efficiently if they saw the managers as being in the same position as themselves.

Fifthly, corporate management was prepared to increase the terms to 'buy' acceptance of the closure, but was still uncertain as to the degree of resistance. Thus, as soon as production ceased, facilities in the car assembly building were either removed, disconnected or broken to prevent any occupation of the building. Very few records were made available to Scottish archives; most of the material was transported to corporate headquarters. Finally, Talbot changed its name to Talbot Peugeot and, more recently, has introduced models solely under the Peugeot marque.

The indications are that the above operational strategy arose from a corporate plan to rationalise production and cut capacity. The policy stressed the need to keep only limited production facilities in the UK; to close rather than find alternative products. There was to be no attempt to preserve any part of Linwood, in either the short or medium term. Thus the industrial relations strategy can be seen as a response to the corporate policy, and subordinate to it. Dating the commencement of the closure strategy as late 1978 would suggest the existence of a

Dear Employee,

Although I am aware that your trade union representatives are continuing to campaign for the decision to close Linwood to be reversed or, at least, delayed, it is necessary, for my part, to proceed with the task of ending all major manufacturing operations by May 22. I trust you will understand, therefore, that I must draw your attention to the requirement to achieve the run-out production programme of 1380 units per week as efficiently as possible.

Given the sad but inevitable fact of closure, I believe it is now in the interest of everyone to implement the decision in a continuing orderly manner. This is important, not least of all, because, with the plant entering the closure phase on a full-time working basis, maximum co-operation leading to the efficient achievement of the weekly programme will optimise Incentive bonus payments, and, in turn, protect and improve the level of redundancy compensation. I do not apologise for mentioning this aspect of the matter because, without doubt, it will be of importance to every employee in three months time.

What contribution, then, can employees make to this objective? There is no new formula.

- Continuity of output must be maintained by avoiding disputes and meetings in production time

- Quality standards must be met first time to avoid re-work

- Lateness and absenteeism must be kept to minimum levels every day to avoid slow start-up, excessive labour transfers and mass relief all of which affect both output and quality

- Supervisors, service and administration staffs must give maximum support to this effort.

Consistent attention to these matters will be very important between now and closure when the Company is required, by law, to calculate the average weekly wage earned by each employee during this period as a basis for redundancy payments.

The accumulative effect of this average earnings figure (which includes bonus) on the various elements of the redundancy package can be significant. I trust, therefore, that the request for co-operation on which the Company has conditionally based its offer will be given by each employee in the interests of all.

Yours sincerely,

Figure 5.1   Extract of a letter from the managing director of Talbot Scotland Ltd (S.C.B. Deason) to the Linwood employees

24 February 1981

coherent policy with little recourse to opportunism. Nevertheless, the details of the strategy were clearly related to the experience and history of the Linwood complex. However, there is little to suggest that this moulding of policy was conducted at the factory level. Of importance in operational policy were the interests of management. Teulings (1985, p. 408) suggests that a consequence of the specialisation of management has been a reduction in the powers of the individual manager. Moreover, implicit in his argument is the belief that rivalries and struggles between management (the politicisation of management) partially replace the operation of the market. In our case study, it can be seen that rather than market forces dictating the survival of Linwood or the other components of Talbot, rivalries between management are a significant factor. Management is far more than a neutral factor responding either efficiently or inefficiently to market pressures; it reflects the vested interest of managers struggling to survive and progress. PSA's policy required Talbot UK to cut models, reduce capacity and retain essentially an assembly facility for the production of French sourced cars. Facilities relating to the Iranian contract had a value so long as the Iranian contract lasted. Thereafter defence of market share became the key element in the strategy. PSA's definition of markets and production policy undoubtedly favoured the survival of the Ryton assembly plant at the expense of Linwood, as the former was more modern and had been assembling French made cars since 1976. However, the larger the scale of the UK operation the more Linwood could have emerged as the logical facility to preserve. If PSA envisaged UK sourcing of pressings, model development and the machining/ assembly of power train components, then Linwood could, as an integrated complex and with greater government support, have become the more obvious choice to maintain. Even though this latter option was only a remote possibility, none the less it attracted opposition from the central staffs at Talbot. UK central staffs management saw their prime need to preserve as much of the Midlands based operations as possible. They were aware of the vulnerability of the design and styling centre and of the Stoke engine plant. They feared that PSA might, if losses were not contained, further radically reduce the scale of the UK operations. Paradoxically, management was supported by a number of trade unions which drew attention to the company's breach of the agreement that more than fifty per cent of the value of the car would be generated in the UK. This breach of agreement with the government raised fears of protectionist policies.

At a personal level there were other interests. The managing director,

George Turnbull, had recently returned from the Far East where he had been vice-president of the Hyundai Motor Company of South Korea. Amongst Linwood management it was suggested that his move to Talbot was part of a longer term strategy to seek to return to British Leyland as a possible successor to Michael Edwardes. As such, his strategy was possibly coloured by personal interest as well as implementing corporate strategy. There are, for example, clear differences between his espoused attitudes towards the personnel function at Talbot, outlined in *Personnel Management* (1982), and the operational policy of the company. Success appeared to be defined in meeting established and defined corporate objectives, rather than acting in an independent manner.

THE CONTEXT OF MANAGEMENT STRATEGY

Our focus on conditioning and operational policy, whilst illuminating the interplay between closure strategies and factory cultures and, additionally, the significance of the interests of individual directors and managers, has paid insufficient attention to the factors highlighted by Purcell (1983) and Thurley and Wood (1983). It is possible to subdivide conditioning factors into two categories. First, into general contextual influences: reflecting broad changes at the level of national economic activity; political influences; and the employment and industrial relations framework. Secondly, industry-wide factors: changing technology and its impact on optimum size and distribution of production; the operation of and differentiation within the market; patterns of management control; changes to the pattern of the integration of production; and the peripheralisation of individual production units.

a)   General contextual factors

A consistent finding in surveys of workplace industrial relations over the past twenty five years has been the growing importance attached by management to the personnel function and the move towards single employer bargaining (Brown, 1983). Batstone (1984) indicates that government legislative changes in the 1970s and 1980s underlay much of this reform and increased its importance. Other legislative changes in respect of the introduction of redundancy payments, reductions in trade union immunities, restrictions on lawful picketing and, more recently, pre-strike ballot requirements have all combined to restrict opposition to closures. The deepening recession and growing unemployment, together with a growth in part-time employment, sub contracting, and the ending of union-only contracts, have all combined further to weaken trade union opposition to closures, to 'rob employees of an important structural source of power' (Hardy, 1985; Bright, 1983). Moreover, the commitment to a version of neo-liberal principles by the Conservative government since 1979 has fundamentally weakened the political influence of the trade union movement and its ability to mobilise government support against closures.

Yet it would be wrong to see the contextual factors which facilitate closure simply in terms of a changed legislative and political environment. The rise in unemployment has been associated with a diminution in the 'subjective commitment to resistance' (Hardy, 1985). Of equal importance is the extensive legitimacy accorded to management actions over redundancies. Closure is deemed a 'legitimate act'. The dominant paradigm of pluralism reinforces this legitimacy through presenting management behaviour as a rational response to market conditions. Thus redundancy is seen as a rational action of last resort by management in order to preserve the employment of remaining employees. The criteria for determining the legitimacy of redundancy becomes not the redundancy itself but the way in which it is managed. The provision of counselling, opportunities for retraining, and a well developed social conscience on the part of management are presented as indicators of good and acceptable redundancy practice. Fryer (1973) notes that public policy defines redundancy in management terms: 'how best to facilitate managerial decision-making and encourage workers to accept the inevitability, indeed the desirability of redundancy'. Surveys of redundancy schemes (Incomes Data Services Studies, 1978, 1981, 1982, 1984 and 1985) indicate the extent to which 'the interests of the business' have replaced agreed and traditional criteria for the selection of those to be made redundant. Jackson (1983) and Tyson (1985) stress the value of redundancy as an aid in introducing more intensive forms of production and control. The emergence of the 'business manager' approach to the personnel function indicates a growing awareness of the strategic functions. The social responsibility aspects are more clearly separated from the inculcation amongst employees of the achievement of business objectives (Hunt, 1984; Tyson, 1985).

Yet Hardy's (1985) assertion that management defines the legitimacy of closure to other groups is possibly incorrect. The works of Morley

(1976) and Hartmann (1975), for example, indicate the significance of a 'dominant ideology', a one sided commonsense interpretation of economic events. Such an interpretation identified trade unions and employees as largely causing their own job losses; managements, on the other hand, merely respond rationally to market forces (which may or may not be within their control). The impression of self-induced redundancy was particularly noticeable in the press coverage of the closure of the Linwood complex. One national Scottish newspaper filed all stories of Linwood under strikes; every story of Linwood, including the closure, was presented, and could only be logically interpreted, in terms of strikes and the failings of the labour force. The history of marginality and vulnerability of the complex clearly meshed into the wider perspective of the media, each reinforcing and legitimising the other.

b)   Industry-wide factors

A number of industry-wide trends are apparent in influencing closure strategy. From the 1960s onwards, all British car manufacturers sought to reduce the influence of the shop steward organisation. The development of multi-plant bargaining and the increased bureaucratisation of stewards (whereby senior stewards were linked to bargaining structures which reduced their powers and distanced them from their members) was a feature of both Chrysler and British Leyland's personnel policies. Within Ford, which already possessed company-wide bargaining, similar attempts were made to weaken shop steward organisation. Industrial relations policy in the British car industry now fits a sophisticated version of Kinnie's (1983) 'integrated model'. Such a move has not been without problems (Gill, 1974; Willman, 1984). Nevertheless, the result has been a strong shift towards centralisation with controlled and limited plant variation. Chrysler and British Leyland, who suffered the most from decentralised and autonomous bargaining structures, followed remarkably similar strategies to centralise bargaining. Both adopted participation schemes as a means to centralise bargaining and to air proposed changes. Participation acted to 'augment the legitimacy of the need for change' (Willman and Winch, 1985). Both adopted incentive schemes to bolster performance under measured daywork systems of payment. As a result, by the 1980s, both companies had re-asserted management control over the shop floor and had reduced shop steward influence on pay and workplace issues. Both used participation as a method of restructuring industrial relations and company organisation (Lockyer et al., 1984; Whipp and Smith, 1984).

The more recent basic labour challenges facing car manufacturers have arisen from the near saturation of markets, increased international competition, costs of technical change and overcapacity. These have generated the need to: reduce labour input; re-adjust traditional work organisations to new technological and economic circumstances; strengthen the commitment of workers to efficient and high quality work; and to re-assert managements' rights to manage (Marsden et al., 1985; Streek and Hoff, 1984). Hence threats of directing investment abroad, using fears of redundancy, the adoption of Japanese working practices and the adoption of harder personnel management policies have become more common features of the car industry.

The impact of technical change was increasingly felt in the 1970s. The low investment strategy of some car manufacturers became less tenable. Some firms, especially Chrysler, were less able to substitute labour for technology to maintain comparable and competitive levels of efficiency (in terms of quality and quantity of output) with those firms which pursued medium or high technological investment strategies. On this point, Linwood was increasingly vulnerable as the company used less technologically advanced methods of car body construction, downgraded production specifications in the pursuit of quantity production and reduced the manning levels of quality control. Together these measures made decline inevitable. Some indication of the consequences of such a strategy can be seen from Table 5.1 in terms of the discrepancy between target production levels and first time buy-offs.

Technological factors are complex, the car industry comprises a number of distinct stages: stamping, body build, paint and trim, parts assembly and final assembly. The degree and type of automation varies considerably both between and within each stage. Traditionally, automation and technological advances have been concentrated at the early stages of production – stamping and body build – but now is progressively spreading into the later stages of trim and final assembly. Cumulatively current technological developments will reduce manning by a further twenty five per cent by 1990, with reduction of forty per cent in stamping and up to thirty per cent in final assembly. The ability to reduce manpower, either by automation and changed work practices or by reducing off-standard work, is largely generated in the design and development phases. Recognition of this led firms to centralise design and development work, thus reducing most plants to 'branch' status.

More recently all such work in the UK, apart from British Leyland, has been centralised in Europe, making all multi-national owned establishments in the UK essentially 'branch' factories, incapable of determining their futures.

Initially the focus in design was to engineer for ease in efficient and quality production. More recently, it has meant the development of new production concepts and layout methods to enable robot production, for example, the assembly concept of the open roof as a precondition for automated seat assembly (Jurgens et al., 1984). Chrysler faced problems arising from designs that were hard to engineer, cars that were slow and complicated to build. The Imp, Avenger and Sunbeam were all harder to build than comparable rivals. Such deficiencies in engineering for production, coupled with low levels of maintenance expenditure and investment in new equipment, made Chrysler unable to maintain high levels of process yield. High levels of machine down-time, material losses and defects in production rendered Chrysler less competitive than other UK and European manufacturers, who, for similar reasons, were less competitive than Japanese competitors. Again, Table 5.1 illustrates the consistent inability of Chrysler to achieve planned levels of production and to maximise process yield.

There is a further dimension to production efficiency relating to the availability of components. Until 1969, Linwood production suffered from an inability to secure continuous supplies of components and, subsequently, from the costs arising from the need to maintain buffer stocks. It had been unable to develop parts movements to the sophistication of the 'just in time' Japanese model. Moreover, Chrysler, in common with British Leyland, suffered from the costs of excessive parts movement – a consequence of non-rationalised production.

Rationalisation of production processes and models combined to complete the peripheralisation of car manufacturing within the United Kingdom. All the four major car manufacturers have restructured production towards integrated production at geographically distant factories. None has adopted the Japanese 'car city' model in the United Kingdom. For British Leyland this has meant operating within the confines of the United Kingdom, apart from collaborative ventures with Honda. For the other three manufacturers it has led to rationalisation and integration of production on a European basis. This has enabled the relocation of investment and considerable product switching. Table 5.2 illustrates the degree of rationalisation in terms of in-company sourced components. Table 5.3 illustrates the extent to which the integration of production has meant in-company importing of completed cars. Thus

Table 5.2 Components of UK-built cars

Model	Total (a) UK sales	Percentage imported	UK content of (b) British-built units (%)	Components of UK-built (c) cars by country of origin
FORD ESCORT	125 571	41.96	85	UK: 1.3, 1.6 all diesel engines; manual gearboxes, bodies, interiors. Other: 1.1 engines (Spain); automatic gearboxes (France) fuel injection (W. Germany).
VAUXHALL CAVALIER	110 621	35.88	47.5	UK: glass, wheels, tyres, paint, steering wheels, soft trim, minor engine parts (eg filters), steel for bodies. Other: 1.6, 1.8 engines, estate car panels (Australia); 1.3 engine (W. Germany); manual gearboxes (Japan), automatics (France)
FORD FIESTA	103 874	38.35	62.1	UK: 1.3, 1.6 engines; bodies and interiors. Other: 1.1. engines (Spain), all transmissions (France)
AUSTIN/MG METRO	100 143	Nil	97	UK: all except glass (Belgium), oil coolers (US), and alternators (France)
FORD SIERRA	83 807	32.43	74.47	UK: bodies, most engines, gearboxes, interiors, rear axles. Other: 2.8V6 engines, gearboxes (W. Germany), 2.3 diesels (France)
AUSTIN/MG MONTEGO	61 463	Nil	95	UK: all except gearboxes – 1.3, 1.6 from VW (W. Germany), 2 litre Honda (Japan), sunroof mechanism (W. Germany)
VAUXHALL ASTRA	60 656	38	52.5	Same as Cavalier, except bodies pressed in U.K.
FORD ORION	53 761	63.58	83.2	As Escort, but Spanish-built 1.1 engine omitted from range.
VAUXHALL NOVA	52 924	100	N/A	N/A
AUSTIN/MG MAESTRO	47 947	Nil	95	As Montego, except glass sourced from Belgium

Source: Financial Times, 26 October 1985.

Notes

(a) First nine months 1985.

(b) Measured by ex-factory gate prices including overheads.

(c) There are some UK parts on imported vehicles, e.g. Ford UK is the sole source of supply for all Escort diesel engines.

Table 5.3   Registration of new cars in UK and exports 1981–83 by make

	1981	1982	1983
BRITISH LEYLAND			
New cars registered in UK	285 071	277 260	332 725
FORD			
Produced and registered in UK	256 074	244 140	278 306
Imported into UK	203 291	230 052	239 742
Produced in UK and exported	82 354	60 937	31 717
GENERAL MOTORS			
Produced and registered in UK	68 265	102 573	123 114
Imported into UK	58 876	79 164	139 027
Produced in UK and exported	5 536	300	320
TALBOT			
Produced and registered in UK	47 942	31 607	35 953
Imported into UK	37 911	44 176	43 512
Produced in UK and exported	85 296	27 216	80 799

Source: Society of Motor Manufacturers, 1984.

Notes

i)   This table is derived from two sources. The UK and imported cars are taken from the registration of new cars statistics; exports from the UK are derived from manufacturers' allocations for exports. Figures are thus broadly rather than directly comparable.

ii)   Figures do not identify proportions of foreign components in UK produced cars, see Table 5.2 for an indication of this. Talbot UK produced cars are essentially French sourced kits.

iii)   Talbot exports are virtually all car kits to Iran.

Table 5.4   Pattern of car imports and exports in 1983

	UK Exports No. of cars	UK Imports No. of cars
Belgium and Luxembourg	21 955	39 894
Denmark	574	49
France	37 703	127 791
Germany	7 329	471 335
Greece	287	7
Irish Republic	9 675	22 162
Italy	17 405	59 862
Netherlands	2 018	40 782
Spain	2 729	58 296

Source: Society of Motor Manufacturers, 1984.

General Motors imports more cars than it produces in Britain. Talbot, excluding the Iranian contract, similarly imports more cars, and almost all those produced in the United Kingdom are French sourced kits. Table 5.4 illustrates the extent to which the United Kingdom has declined towards the status of a car assembler, serving the UK rather than other markets.

A consequence of rationalisation has therefore been the ability to switch production and to relocate investment and management functions in Europe. Thus Chrysler moved management functions and investment to France (Kujawa, 1980). Such a structure enables easier transfer pricing (Wilks, 1984) and so reduces tax liabilities and tariffs. Rationalisation, coupled with over capacity, rendered Linwood a disposable plant: a branch factory administratively easy to cut. Its closure inevitably meant the retention of Ryton, hence the motivation within Talbot UK management to facilitate the closure of Linwood rather than seek its preservation.

Dunning (1985) highlights the ability of multi-nationals to determine what is produced where, and to engineer a new international division of labour. Marsden (1985) illustrates the restrictions of minimum efficient scales of operation on choice of location (these range for example from between 200 000 to 300 000 for final assembly, although it is likely that these figures are decreasing as a result of new production methods). However, such estimates would suggest that there is considerable assembly below minimum efficient levels.

This apparent discrepancy indicates the peculiar nature of the market. The market operates via oligopolistic hierarchies competing both within and between one another. Increasing collaborative measures reduce competition to agreed levels and with political and economic factors (for example, transfer pricing) combining to keep the existing manufacturers in the market (Altshuler, 1984). Maintaining market penetration is aided by satellite assembly units which give firms a national identity and hence favourable treatment by national governments (Ridgers, 1979). Table 5.3 illustrates this clearly, as it demonstrates that the majority of imports of cars are via manufacturers that 'produce' in the United Kingdom. The effect is to preserve an artificial and inefficient market. Manufacturers patrol their shares of the market and the high market price of United Kingdom cars encourages firms to collaborate to protect the market against the imports from non-European firms, even though they are major importers themselves. By this view, the decline of firms is explained in terms of factors largely internal to the company rather than the actions of multi-national firms. Linwood 'failed' because of the militancy of its employees and their inability to produce efficiently. Some criticism is attached to the model policy and the location. However, the subjective rationalism of multi-nationals, the substitution of the market by the internal dissensions and rivalry between subsidiary companies and executives within multi-national enterprises is ignored (Wilks, 1984; Teulings, 1985).

CONCLUSION

Linwood closed because of the long term failure of Rootes and Chrysler UK to move with developments in the industry. Industrial relations issues and quality of work were consequences of this failure rather than the causes of closure. Our analysis stresses that management failures reinforced and augmented the sense of vulnerability which dominated factory life. This was the key to the successful closure strategy. Moreover, this image of vulnerability was deliberately heightened by management. The legitimising of closure is, therefore, a key factor in any examination of management strategy. The centralisation of control, development and rationalisation inevitably meant that there would be a contraction in the size of Talbot UK. Yet, the decision to close Linwood rather than Ryton was essentially a decision made by Talbot UK management within a corporate policy that favoured Ryton. It would have made little difference to that corporate policy if Linwood had been chosen to be retained. The personal interests of senior management at the Talbot UK level and rivalry between management at Linwood and Ryton played a significant role in the decision to close Linwood. Personal factors therefore need to be considered alongside more general contextual influences and industry-wide factors in any assessment of the pattern of industrial closure.

6 Labour and Management Strategies in the World Market: The Plot Thickens

Nigel Haworth and Harvie Ramsay

INTRODUCTION

The speed of change in the nature and distribution of international production has given rise to a number of analytical problems: in practice, are broad trends identifiable? Can we speak of broadly-defined managerial strategies within such trends? Do managers themselves have clearly analysed strategies predicated upon the imperatives of the international market? If they do, how are they produced, and what are their effects? International capital restructuring has been the order of the day throughout the current recession. The relocation of production within a global framework, linked to technological transformation, has been a particular hallmark of management strategy since internationalisation of production became an imperative after 1945. Such has been the urgency of these developments that research and analysis has found it difficult to understand either the broad trends or the nuances of the process. It has been equally complex for management itself. Internationalisation has required managements to appraise constantly the complete range of international production and distribution options available. No sooner have one broad trend and associated characteristics been identified than alternatives have appeared to confuse the observer.

A better understanding of these issues has a far wider importance than simply offering an insight into international managerial practice since the last war. They define the context in which both national and international labour organisations and their constituent memberships have confronted the post-war explosion of transnational production. Labour's understanding of the needs imposed upon the global workforce has lagged behind the reality of relocation and restructuring.

Labour has 'tail-ended' managerial strategy, in the process often responding not to the contemporary impositions of capital, but to the imperatives of previous phases of investment. Consequently, unions have been confronted with *fait accompli* after *fait accompli*, and as often as not have resorted to accusations of foul before succumbing to the blandishments of redundancy pay-offs. Recession has in the case of many unions resulted in ineffective and tokenistic threats of action if plants are closed and jobs lost, and the outcome has been almost universally in line with management demands.

Some would argue that this bleak scenario reflects nothing more than the reality of capital's power during recession. Economistic bargaining traditions lose their effect, and the one-sided nature of the employment contract is re-asserted arbitrarily by management. Such a view might go further, and suggest that the options available to international production are such that the one-sidedness is exaggerated by capital's ability to choose between different locations, technologies, products and, crucially, workforces. Yet this sombre view cedes all initiative to international capital and its national allies. It presumes the impenetrability of international capital's carapace, and offers a grimly deterministic understanding of the logic of capital's international strategies. If, however, the reality of management strategy fails to conform to this logic, do alternative labour strategies exist which can capitalise upon the contradictions between broad trends in accumulation and the specific forms of managerial practice within the international economy? In somewhat problematic terms, would these contradictions, if shown to exist, create 'space' in which national and international labour organisation could seize the initiative and overturn the power of international capital? Is management decision-making sufficiently heterogeneous a process as to open up the possibility of worker-inspired usurpation of strategic prerogatives, even across international boundaries and in a period of global recession? We address this chapter to these questions in the light of our previous contributions to the debate about labour's international strategy (see Baldry et al., 1983, 1984; Haworth and Ramsay 1984, 1986; Haworth, 1984). Perhaps two points should be made at this early stage. First, some aspects of the following discussion draw heavily on our previous publications and we refer the reader to these for further detailed clarification of our broad analytical stand on labour-capital relations in MNCs. Secondly, our argument in this chapter is essentially abstract, with only passing reference to case studies either of our own or of others.

SURVEYING THE MODELS

A comparison of orthodox and radical approaches to the MNC provides a framework in which to put these questions. In particular, the somewhat arbitrary comparison of Dunning (1981) and Frobel et al. (1980) highlights inadequacies in both traditions when considering managerial strategies within the MNC. Broadly, the nuances of management decision-making within MNCs are either ignored, given little significance or presented as simple functions of the managerial division of labour. Generally, this is a consequence of an intellectual division of labour in which radical political economy tends to see management actions as undifferentiated effects of capital accumulation, and orthodox managerialist analysis found in the world's business schools focuses exclusively on the productivity and profitability effects of decision-making. In both traditions, the actions of labour are understudied and underestimated, except as secondary effects of management strategy. More importantly, these intellectual traditions have also been important in the formation of labour's own view of their links with the MNC. Unions have accepted intellectual understandings of international production which *a priori* assume that workers respond to, rather than initiate, action. This reinforces the practical sense in which unions find their circumstances apparently predetermined by MNC decision-making. Essentially this is another context in which labour finds itself tail-ending managerial practice, though in this case within the ideological framework imposed by contemporary intellectual paradigms.

FROBEL ET AL.: A RADICAL MODEL

The work undertaken by Frobel et al. (1980) on the 'new international division of labour' has become a touchstone of the contemporary radical debate about the internationalisation of capital. It builds empirically on the wealth of radical interpretations of internationalisation which emerged in the 1960s and 1970s; this in turn was impelled by perhaps three contributions – Baran and Sweezy's (1968) controversial analysis of monopoly capital, the radical tradition inspired by the later Hymer (1975) work, and the 'dependency' analysis (see Cardoso and Faletto, 1979). All are concerned with the international expansion of capitalist production and the particular vehicle bearing it across the globe – the MNC. All offer important insights. All suffer from one fundamental weakness – the failure to provide a textured, nuanced understanding of decision-making within the MNC. At the risk of over-generalisation, they are not particularly concerned with the internal mechanisms which lead to MNC location and production strategies. These are broadly ignored as internal functions of 'capital' or 'capitals', interesting in their consequences, but not their technical qualities.

The Frobel et al. approach illustrates this weakness well. Their starting point is the post-war transformation in international accumulation, which induced a relocation of investment from 'centre' to 'periphery', stagnating or declining investment rates accompanied by rising structural unemployment in the 'centre', and the growth of export-orientated manufacturing in the 'periphery'. Underpinning this transformation is the worldwide reservoir of labour power concentrated in the Third World as a result of structural economic changes in those economies. This international reserve army of labour can be mobilised because technological development permits the technical decomposition of production processes and their re-location into areas where cheap labour can operate within appropriate systems of work organisation. Technological change also permits the geographical dispersion of related products and enterprises and the replacement of skilled, high-cost labour with cheap, often female semi- and un-skilled workers.

New production areas consequently manifest suitably uniform basic characteristics. The labour force tends to be female, between sixteen and twenty five years old, production-orientated and semi- or un-skilled. Wages are low, job security is limited, working conditions are poor, and state protection via industrial relations legislation limited or non-existent. These conditions are enforced by the supply elasticity of the labour market, limited worker organisation and naked repression where necessary.

Empirically, much that Frobel et al. describe is correct. One major trend in international production has involved substantial re-location of production to various Third World economies, using a mixture of direct ownership, sub-contracting and other organisational methods. Their analysis has been a great motivator of important investigation of global production and it strengthens our belief that any understanding of the context in which labour acts must be based upon the study of capitalist accumulation in all its guises. However, important criticisms have been made of the model, focusing particularly on the issue of its universality. It has been pointed out that the 'new international division of labour' is only one aspect of internationalist capitalist restructuring in the current crisis. Trends contrary to those identified by Frobel et al. can be seen in certain sectors – electronics, for example – where re-location has occurred in the developed capitalist economies impelled by a complex of factors including R & D provision, marketing requirements, skilled labour supply, state aid, productivity levels and technological advances.

Two particular examples of alternative radical analysis of the international division of labour may be found in the work of Elson (1986) and of Jenkins (1984). The former has produced a far more textured understanding of global production rooted especially in the textile sector. It shows the range of production possibilities open to textile employers, and also the location of options available to them. Jenkins focuses on the over-generalisations which may be traced on what he considers to be the 'one-dimensional' Frobel et al. approach. We stress these contributions in order to establish that the search for a 'multi-dimensional' understanding of global accumulation is afoot. The debate between the Frobel et al. tradition and its critical offspring offers the most sophisticated way forward for the analysis of international accumulation, and simultaneously provides substantial collateral for our own arguments.

Criticisms of the Frobel et al. model implicitly highlight two unfortunate tendencies within radical approaches to international production. The first is the focus on 'capital' or 'capitals' as abstract agents of capitalist accumulation. As discussed briefly above, the real-world internal processes governing capitalist decision-making are essentially undiscussed. 'Capital' acts, and that is deemed sufficient information upon which to base an understanding of international accumulation. Despite the structuralist discourse which brought our attention to the factional aspects of capitalist practice, radical thought has, with one exception, passed over the empirical dimension of contradictions within the beast. The exception has been the Labour Process debate, which in its later manifestations confronted the real-world production relations governing manager and worker.

The second tendency is a specific aspect of the first. Radical analysis has failed to confront the MNC as a site of contradictory decision-making within capitalist accumulation. There are two dimensions of this failing. First, at the level of popular rhetoric the MNC is usually presented as the paramount expression of capitalist power, and therefore the primary target of radical economic reform. The equation is simplistic; MNCs are the highest form of capitalist organisation; they are consequently all uniformly powerful, and uniformly to be attacked.

Attached to this view is an equally simplistic understanding of the practice of cartels in which MNCs are thought to 'arrange' the division of the world economy. This popular view has its political uses as it allows the generation of clear anti-MNC slogans, and, in tandem, anti-United States attitudes.

Secondly, at a more analytical level a similar failing is common. In a way which parallels much analysis of the capitalist state, internal decision-making within MNCs is seen as a struggle internal to capital, a confrontation between different capitalist strategies any of which will be disadvantageous to labour. It often appears as if two separate universes exist in the real world. On the one hand, the world of capital, from the internal decision-making of which emerges a strategy. On the other, the universe of labour awaits the presentation of the capitalist strategy, retreats into its own internal strategic conclave, and emerges onto the battlefield to counterpose its strategy to that of capital. This is more than a strategic 'tail-ending'. It is a misunderstanding of the relationships between labour and capital in the strategic ordering of capitalist production. To invoke a relic of earlier debates, these relationships exist not in a dual and exclusive structure but in a 'unity of contradiction' based upon the collective prerequisites of capitalist production. The manner in which these contradictions are resolved has been at the core of the 'job-redesign' debate, which has focused its attention on the potential for non-zero-sum outcomes of labour-management negotiation around work organisation (see Knights et al., 1985). Although there is little agreement in this debate about the possibility of non-zero-sum consequences, it has opened up for debate two things: the range of managerial strategies open to capital at any stage, and the immediacy of labour inputs to the potential implementation of any of these strategies. Perhaps the term 'dialectical conditioning' sums up the complex inter-relationships between labour and capital in the process of defining work organisation. Extending the argument beyond the immediate context of production, that conditioning effect operates to a greater or lesser degree on all management decision-making, and therefore constitutes a major analytical and empirical qualification of the 'two universe' tradition of MNC analysis.

However, this point can be taken further. We have argued elsewhere (1984, 1986) that relationships between labour and capital in the MNC are based on the existence of two conflicting political economies: that of labour and that of capital. Furthermore, we argued in relation to this duality that within the MNC the political economy of capital –

particularly in relation to its financial decision-making criteria – may occur at a level so distanced from the realities of worker involvement in production that worker organisation against, say, company financial decisions is likely to be ineffective, or even on qualitatively different levels within the production process as a whole. This argument may be qualified in its absolutist implications by reference to the previous argument relating to the conditioning effects of the 'unity in contradiction'. The qualification is in part necessary to remove 'dual universe' overtones in our original argument. However, it also serves to reveal the contexts in which labour organisation may hope to use its power to qualify, even transform, management decision-making in the MNC.

Schematically, the argument may be presented in terms of a traditional radical understanding of any future transformation of capitalism. Let us assume three things: that the complete transformation of capitalism into an alternative system is not imminent; that the labour movement's strategic thinking has to encompass both long-term and short-term realities; that substantial sections of the international labour movement are – in the short term at least – wedded to accommodative economistic practices. Clearly, if these assumptions hold, then the focus of labour movement activity will be on the relatively short-run movements in the 'frontier of control' between labour and capital. Equally, the debates in national and international labour movement organisations will look to the different effects of dialectical conditioning on managerial practice when defining strategy. This argument holds for both zero-sum and non-zero-sum analyses of labour–capital relationships in production. In the former, strategic thinking will be orientated towards the enhancement of labour's power at the expense of capital's, a search for a shift in the balance of power within production wherever such a shift may be achieved. Non-zero-sum theorists will accept this thinking, but complement it with a view stressing the potential of restructured labour–capital relations which satisfy quite diverse requirements on the part of labour and capital.

A NEO-CLASSICAL VIEW

We now turn to the work of Dunning (1981), a major neo-classical interpretation of MNC activity. Our use of Dunning's work in no way supersedes our commitment to the radical tradition discussed above. We reject the intellectual approach adopted by neo-classical economics, and similarly have little sympathy with its political counterpart. However, such a rejection should not blind the observer to a recognition that the insights into MNC behaviour offered by Dunning may inform radical analyses of the MNC. In a sense, we are attempting to give greater analytical insight to the radical tradition by poaching selectively certain interpretive concepts developed by Dunning. We suspect that he may not regard this as the highest praise yet to be given to his work, but if the World Bank can appropriate the cooperative as a development strategy, the labour movement can reciprocate by turning neo-classical insight against the MNC.

Dunning's work has been particularly influential in the establishment of an orthodox neo-classical understanding of MNC activity. His analysis highlights a number of broad strands of thinking which underpin his own interpretation of MNC behaviour. They arise from the long-standing debates about the nature of international trade and capital movements within the world economy, many of which do not have the particular case of the MNC in their sights. In recent years, he believes that two approaches have come to dominate the broad debate about trade and capital movements. On the one hand, neofactor, neotechnology and scale economy models illustrate attempts to define location-specific and enterprise-specific attributes which influence international economic behaviour. On the other, analysis of the contexts in which direct foreign investment take place took off after Hymer's classic doctoral work. These various approaches tended to overlap in their foci, and led to a specific concentration of interpretive effort on the role of the MNC as an economic agent.

MNCs, in Dunning's view, make their decisions on the basis of potential comparative advantages to be gained by international production, the calculation depending upon, first, the performance of host-country firms, and, secondly, the balance of location factors present in domestic and foreign countries. This approach therefore defines two sets of factors which will be considered in any MNC production strategy. Location-specific factors are those which are peculiar to any particular economy, region or product, and which consequently exist external to the enterprise. Such factors might be minerals and raw materials, labour supplies, industrial relations and work organisation traditions, specific market features, trade access points, state policies, infrastructural provision, education facilities and the like. Ownership-specific factors, internal to the enterprise, consist of the various functions and ideologies within the firm which contribute to efficiency and the decision-making process. In this case, such factors might include capital, investment decision-making, patent control, management skills, control over new technology, research and development factors and the like. The argument notes that for a variety of reasons – in particular market imperfections and public intervention – firms have found it advantageous to internalise many functions in order to maximise returns to investment. If monopolistic and oligopolistic practices have ensued from this internalisation process, these are essentially the consequences of rational managerial practice in an imperfect market. The logic of this argument provides a basis for the explanation of international production by a firm. Returns to investment may be maximised by the internalisation of production across national boundaries through the agency of international affiliates and subsidiaries.

Dunning develops his eclectic model of MNC behaviour as a result of his explanation of the relationship between location-specific (external) and ownership-specific (internal) factors. Linking approaches based on technological superiority and the consequences of imperfect competition, it aspires to a systematic understanding of ownership advantages in relation to international trade and production. To quote Dunning (1981, p. 33):

> The theory suggests that, given the distribution of location-specific endowments, enterprises which have the greatest opportunities for and derive the most from, internalising activities will be the most competitive in foreign markets.

We are not concerned here either with the elaborations of Dunning's approach, or with the various alternative and critical neo-classical approaches which have arisen to support or qualify this specific view (see Hood and Young, 1979). It is the insight into managerial practice provided by the eclectic approach which attracts our interest. Dunning provides a theorised insight into the real world context in which managerial decisions are made within MNCs. If there are two broad categories of decision to be made – appropriate to location and ownership – each brings with it a range of different decision-making criteria for the different management functions responsible for policy. It is clear that these different sets of criteria may in certain cases be complementary – for example, in a situation where a firm's location-specific and ownership-specific requirements broadly coincide over, for example, appropriate technology investment. Equally, the two sets of criteria many contradict each other – for example, location-specific factors may point to a particular configuration of ownership-specific policies, which, however, contradict the requirements of particular managerial functions within the enterprise or, perhaps, the interests of other affiliates of the firm. However, the texture of the problem for MNC management is substantially more complex than this simple image. The eclectic approach suggests that a three-dimensional matrix defines the space in which MNC management must operate. The essential dimensions are:

i) the requirements – complementary or otherwise – of location-specific and ownership-specific maximisation
ii) the requirements of the different managerial functions within the firm – investment, R & D, production management, human resource, finance and so on – which may or may not coincide individually or collectively with the location – ownership-specific requirements
iii) the divisional requirements (if such a structure exists), or the requirements of the different constituent elements in the firm.

Of course, it could be argued that the number of distinct dimensions in the model should increase to take account of other contexts which impinge on managerial policy, but the simple three-dimensional model suffices for the purposes of this argument.

The matrix model highlights the complexity of the decision-making process in which MNC management works. First, it undermines simplistic views of dictatorial management practices in MNCs, which suggest managers ride roughshod and unimpeded over all levels of opposition. Simply, it can encompass circumstances in which MNC decision-making finds itself compromised by conflicting pressures which perhaps may considerably constrain management's freedom of action. Secondly, it suggests that power bases within an MNC may vary over time in their ability to impose their solution to a problem. Different conjunctures will produce different criteria for assessing possible solutions, different practical responses and different political alliances within managements. Thirdly, and, perhaps, most importantly, it illustrates the scale of the problem which confronts management when it comes to make and implement a decision. What often appears in the media and some academic treatments as a simple, rational response to a set of problems disguises a complex assessment of the available options within the defining matrix. It is not simply that managements may make decisions which are wrong. More importantly, the matrix effect highlights the extent to which MNC decision-making, albeit often in an oligopolistic or monopolistic context, may reflect compromise imposed by the contradictions within the matrix. Second-best decisions may be the normalcy within MNCs rather than first-choice policies produced by a simple unitary practice. Of course, second-best choices may be as repellant to workers as first choices, and, arguably, may have worse consequences in the long run if a strictly neo-classical view of the economy is taken. However, this does not detract from the analytical insight into MNC management decision-making offered by Dunning's eclectic approach.

THE ARGUMENT SO FAR

It is useful to bring together the threads of the argument before looking at the possible components of labour strategy in detail. So far we have argued that for all its faults, the Dunning eclectic approach provides a useful way of beginning to think about the complex factors and contexts which define managerial decision-making within MNCs. There is no reason to take on the baggage of neo-classical analysis in order to make use of aspects of the model. To use elements of the eclectic approach is merely to recognise the usefulness of its empirical orientation. Paradoxically, though radical analyses provide an impressive theoretical insight into international capitalist accumulation, they tend not to look at the internal decision-making processes in the enterprise. This is unfortunate, because short-term – that is, non-revolutionary – prospects require a careful strategic understanding by labour of the nuances of capitalist decision-making, a case made with force in the 'job redesign' debate. This omission is particularly noticeable when we look at labour responses to MNCs. Arguably, labour strategy in MNCs must seek to consolidate labour potency within a framework of dialectical conditioning, whilst not losing sight of the continuing degrees of coherence and power which MNCs display in their actions.

CONSTRUCTING A MATRIX

One useful way of conceptualising the targets at which labour strategy may direct its actions is to lay out a radicalised version of the Dunning-inspired matrix outlined above. The three aspects of this matrix – location and ownership-specific factors; the requirements of the different management functions; the structural–spatial aspects of MNC decision-making – provide a three-dimensional framework which broadly highlights the potential for contradictions within MNC decision-making and stress a further point of some importance. Labour's strategic use of a matrix-based approach will be empirical, and consequently will produce widely-differing responses from different groups of workers in different locations.

Taking the first aspect – location and ownership-specific aspects – it is clear that each has different implications for labour strategy. Location-specific factors are more amenable to the intervention of workers' organisations than ownership-specific factors. They are relatively immobile, spatially-specific and, often, culturally-defined. They are also regionally and/or nationally-specific, which raises the issue of state action around the question of MNC investment. At one extreme – the case of important mineral deposits, for example – location-specific factors may be paramount in the decisions made by state, labour and capital when extraction is considered. At the other extreme – the case of labour skill-profiles, for example – it may be that a number of locations offer broadly-similar advantages, thus reducing the location-specific aspects of MNC decision-making to marginal importance. There may also be contradictory location-specific factors which further complicate the MNC decision.

On the other hand, ownership-specific factors based upon the degree to which internalisation of functions is necessary or possible may be remote from the workers' point of contact with the international firm. Decisions may be taken which are not encompassable by union action, or at such a senior level within the union hierarchy that union pressure has no effect. Such decisions within a MNC may be categorised as management-specific as opposed to others in which unions and workers might gain purchase over management deliberations. Of course, there are potential circumstances in which management-specific decisions may find themselves challenged by labour; for example, where the organisational structure of the MNC permits devolved decision-making at, say, divisional level, in which case the powers accruing to labour as a consequence of location-specific factors may be brought to bear.

Cutting across location and ownership-specific factors are the requirements of different management functions within the MNC. Many of these functions contain both management-specific and contestable aspects, and the task for labour is to make strategic decisions about which functions may be challenged with the greatest likelihood of success. On the one hand, work organisation functions – job design, bargaining procedures, payment structures and so on – within MNC management are open to challenge on a variety of different bases and historically have provided one of the major foci of union action in MNCs. On the other hand, investment and finance functions may again be spatially-remote from the circumstances in which workers' organisation can achieve purchase over management decision-making, and may therefore be contexts not immediately conducive to labour action. As a rule of thumb, the nearer to the point of production the management function, the greater the potential for worker intervention to gain leverage over management prerogatives. This suggests that the national context will have particular importance as it is also more likely to reflect spatially-specific cultural and state definitions which may reinforce the potential for effective worker challenge. In this context, the definition of issues will take on a great importance. Unions will attempt to widen the range and scope of issues which may be contested; management will attempt to minimise the issues open to question by workers, particularly using formal definitions of management functions as a means of delimiting legitimate worker concern. The policy adopted by the MNC defining its own particular solution of the devolved decision-making versus centralised control models of management control will be a major factor in the setting of the issues agenda and will vary between different MNCs.

The issue of devolution of power within the MNC leads to the third element of the matrix – the structure of the MNC as a potential basis for contradiction in decision-making. The adoption of divisional or equivalent structures as a means of rationalising decision-making within diversified MNC operations provides the basis for potential clashes in both regional/spatial and management-function terms. Divisional structures provide yet another potential focus of management strategy formation, potentially different in its expectations from either plant or aggregate corporate level. Of course, this level is the most variable in its impact as it will effect the matrix only to the degree in which divisional structures have been adopted, or allowed independence in planning and action. The potential for contradictions to appear within the macro-organisational structure of the MNC may be exacerbated by differences in management function responses. This contradition may be further developed by, for example, state requirements placed on MNC subsidiaries which promote cleavages between centralised MNC policy and the divisional response. Similarly, product development, market power, R & D, investment and technological change could also be alternative foci of tension between core and periphery within MNCs.

At this point, it is necessary to draw back from the matrix and reiterate the corollary of fragmented decision-making – the continuing power of the MNC. Fragmentation goes hand in hand with decision-making and implementation on a day-to-day basis. To recognise potential divisions is also to recognise a continuing potential for agreement and coherence in decision-making. Perhaps the latter case is the more normal; the task of labour is to turn the normal into the abnormal by the application of appropriate strategies.

Before offering an assessment of different labour strategies designed to capitalise on the contradictions outlined above, two general conditioning factors which define the context in which the matrix operates require passing comment. First, the cyclical nature of the international economy will act to condition all management decisions, but international boom and slump tends to have a differential effect across global production. Hence, MNC managerial decision-making will take on board these differential effects, seeking to maximise returns by relating the matrix components to the contemporary dynamic governing international economic performance. Secondly, state power and its associated policies are a constant in the calculations made by international capital. Although empirically differentiating between the actions of individual states, MNCs will aver that their conditions of existence require a constant recognition of the formal issue of national sovereignty to which – in principle at least – MNCs are subordinate. If cyclical economic processes are a defining factor in MNC policy-making, it is more questionable whether national states do have the priority which the principle of sovereignty suggests in relation to MNC activity. We have outlined our analysis of these issues at greater length elsewhere.

WHITHER LABOUR?

Labour faces the complexity of MNC management strategy with its own phalanx of possible responses. If labour is to understand and take advantage of the contradictions in management strategy traced above, its responses must necessarily be tempered in terms of the optimisation of organised effort against the most susceptible targets. Effective union organisation will be based on a *mélange* of spatial, institutional, strategic and resource factors which hopes to pre-empt, or at least countervail, the intentions of management decision-making. An understanding of the management decision-making matrix will advance union action in two ways: first, it will provide the basis of an effective intelligence system which, when properly resourced, will plot the progress of MNC activity in its various spatial and policy dimensions; secondly, it will inform the strategic choices made by unions as they calculate the form, location and intensity of union action. This approach implies that the labour movement must systematise and heavily resource its anti-MNC activities in a number of ways which are perhaps best understood by tracing the four central components of worker strategy – the spatial context, the institutional framework, the strategic choice, and the provision of larger, and perhaps different, resources.

THE SPATIAL CONTEXT

It is relatively easy to reel off the spatial levels at which workers' organisations can operate – local plant level, regional, national, supra-national (as in the case, for example, of the EEC) and globally. It is equally easy to recognise that the wider the spatial context in which workers organise, the greater the potential dilution of solidaristic coherence. To quote a previous statement of this problem:

workers create cooperative supportive relationships between themselves for a variety of reasons. Probably the most important is the sense of identity, shared experience, common interests and proximity which the workplace offers. This level of response is perhaps elementary, but it is dissipated the further away from the workplace we move (Haworth and Ramsay, 1984, p. 71).

In Thompsonian terms, it is real-world experience which gives form and life to effective organisation. Self-evidently, this experience is richest and most durable when immediate. It can exist across great distances – the cases of international worker solidarity around Chile and Vietnam are but two important examples – but the resource implications and the efforts needed to maintain actions of this type are perhaps exponentially greater than for organising solidarity actions within, for example, the British coal industry. Arguably, although some institutions and some strategies will span the range of spatial levels noted above, others will be level-specific, reflecting the particular exigencies of their spatial context. Similarly, the resource implications will vary between levels in terms of type and intensity of resource application, a point to be taken further below. However, the matter of consciousness will not be resolved by institutional and resource strategies. In relation to this, two questions must be addressed. First, can simple trade union and worker action, often located within a specifically economistic tradition, hope to transcend the distance difficulty? Is the alternative to this basis of action a more overtly political strategy, drawing on class unity as a way forward to internationalism? In practice – and dispensing with the catch-all that all actions are political, even economistic ones – most commentators recognise that moving beyond the immediacy of the plant is inherently a political step, in terms of the institutional linkages such a step implies and the content of issues discussed on a wider basis. Arguably, more effective international linkages will constitute the basis for an upsurge in internationalist interest, though it must also be recognised that such a development will also engender a variety of critical responses from existing vested interests within union and party circles. It may also be argued that a political worker response of this type is more likely to be established within a national framework, wherein class-based political action may aspire to state power, or, at a less dramatic level, hope to confront the existing national state.

THE INSTITUTIONAL FRAMEWORK

If the spatial aspects of worker action raise a number of difficult issues, many of which are yet to come to the fore, the institutional and organisational context is already the focus of both effort and controversy. We can structure this context in two broad strands – the formal and the informal. Formal organisational activity parallels in part the dimensions which define the spatial framework. Thus plant-level official worker representation may be aggregated to national union level, perhaps through regional levels of representation. National union bodies similar to the British TUC lead into supra-national formal union bodies such as the ETUC, whilst superimposed at a global level are the ICFTU-type institutions. Another strand of formal organisation emerges from the national union level of activity. This is the sector-based formal response which has taken the form of MNC-based bodies – the World Councils – and the international sectoral bodies – the ITSs. It is to the ITSs that many people look for the most effective sectoral response within the labour movement.

The informal institutional responses emerge out of plant-level rank-and-file action, pass through (usually) unofficial combine structures which in turn may internationalise their activities into international combines. Another informal way forward, though often with either explicit or implicit support from some formal institutions, is the international consultation, such as the events held for General Motors (1986) and Ford (1985) workers in Liverpool. In these events, rank-and-file representatives from all the plants in a MNC come together to study company strategy and look for means to improve international information flows, contacts and solidarity action.

In a sense, both formal and informal aspects were inevitably going to arise in response to MNC power, and in ideal circumstances they should not find themselves in conflict. However, if we look at the tensions internal to both, and also between the two, the picture to emerge is fraught with difficulties. Within the formal context, for example, tensions may exist between each of the elements in the chain of organisations. Perhaps the key issues giving rise to conflict are sovereignty, representativity, relevance and political affiliation. Local unions find themselves in disagreement with their national bodies in MNC-related issues as elsewhere, and the right to determine strategy is hard fought. At the international level, few national union confederations are prepared to submit to the will of other national bodies or the will of supra-national agencies. As one moves from the local union branch through the ever more remote echelons of leadership, questions arise as to how representative the larger formal bodies are of their constituent membership. This raises other questions about the relevance of the larger bodies to either the rank-and-file at plant level or to the strategic debate about anti-MNC action. To this fear may be added a far broader concern about the range of issues which the formal bodies consider important and worthy of action. For example, much attention has been focused on the sexual division of labour utilised by international capital, with particular emphasis being placed on Free Trade Zones and similar developments in various parts of the Third World. Many would argue that a traditional protectionist response to the effects of these new types of international production is either inappropriate or wrong, and that formal union bodies, steeped as they are in a now-aged view of anti-MNC action, cannot take on board new styles of action needed to confront these new conditions. Cutting through this is the thorny issue of political affiliation, which split the WFTU in 1949 and continues to this day to be the origin of a host of cleavages within the international union structure.

All four of these problems affect informal organisations too, though perhaps to a different degree. However, for informal types of action it is the clash with the formal institutions which raises the most difficult questions. Formal levels of organisation are at best ambivalent about informal contacts and the agencies outside the labour movement active in their generation. There are many cases where a degree of cooperation has been offered, but the general fear still exists that informal contacts cut across the rights and responsibilities of the formal bodies. Other problems faced by informal organisations relate to their longevity. Although many such links are by their nature short-lived (consultations, for example), most require extended periods of operation in order to bear fruit, and the resource implications thus implied are not easily met. It is remarkable how resilient are many of the informal contacts in the face of such constraints, and the inputs of agencies outside the labour movement proper have been important in this respect.

Given this resilience on the part of the informal sector, and given the resource strength of the formal level, it is possible to envisage forms of cooperation and action between the two sectors and their constituent parts which, if not overcoming all the difficulties in their entirety, would create a more structured and effective base for anti-MNC activity. However, the choice of appropriate strategies thus takes centre stage.

THE STRATEGIC CHOICES

Effective unity will be based in the final analysis on the correct choice of strategies for worker action. Contemporary thinking about strategy tends to focus on five types of action: collective bargaining in its various guises; statutory participation systems; direct action by workers; political attack on the MNC; and alternatives to MNC-defined production. Each is a curate's egg offering both advantages and disadvantages; none can be said to have been applied effectively, for reasons which often have much to do with problems at the institutional level. We have given our views of the various versions of the collective bargaining strategy at great length elsewhere, particularly taking to task the seminal Levinson (1972) position in line with Olle and Schoeller's critique (1977). Suffice it to say that neither theoretically nor empirically does the collective bargaining strategy lend itself to overcoming the problems of 'tail-ending'. Of course, this is not to reject outright collective bargaining strategy, but to expose its weaknesses if proposed as the *sole* union strategy for coping with MNC power. This is more than adequately borne out by the experience of closure during the 1970s and 1980s.

A second strategic strand has been the Vredeling-type extension of European participatory intervention into management functions (see Horn 1981; Blanpain, 1983; Rojot, 1985). Voluntary codes of conduct might be seen as forerunners of aspects of the Vredeling proposals, whilst the British planning agreement initiative of the 1970s is another progenitor of interventionist strategy. A number of points relate to these initiatives. First, they have been stillborn (Vredeling) or rapidly rejected (planning agreements) or ineffective (voluntary codes of conduct). This does not, of course, mean that future attempts in this mode will face the same fate, but it does point to the constraints which tend to undermine them. Secondly, their capacity to cause a truly international company to change course is open to challenge. Making Chrysler stick to the provisions of the planning agreement with unions and government struck in the late 1970s proved to be impossible, and voluntary codes of conduct appear to suffer from the same inefficacy. Thirdly, particularly in relation to Vredeling-style proposals, the provision of information about the MNC becomes an end in itself, rather than a necessary function of strategy formation. An aspect of this is the view held by some that information equals power. Others have argued that the equation is not so obvious; indeed, it has been suggested that the provision of information in certain contexts may act to misdirect or undermine worker action (see Gold et al., 1979; Gospel and Willman, 1983). All such proposals also face the likelihood of concerted MNC attack through propaganda and sanctions. Finally, all such proposals require state commitment to their application, a response not always immediately forthcoming – the Thatcher government's feelings about Vredeling have been less than warm, for example.

The question of the state raises the broad issue of overtly political responses to the MNC. Again a distinction might be made between the formal and informal aspects of anti-MNC political practice. Formally, established political channels may be mobilised around a number of strategies and institutions at a number of levels. Thus state policy might be to support local and national union bodies in their demands against MNCs, and perhaps to extend such support into international agencies such as the EEC. This has certainly been the case in a number of countries in the past, but it suffers from perhaps two flaws. First, party control of the state may well change, such that unions cannot rely on consistent state support for their demands. In this case, state support will be contingent upon the predilections of parties-in-power. Secondly, state willingness to support workers' demands may well be qualified by wider questions. For example, supporting one group of workers might threaten MNC investment within the economy, and therefore threaten other jobs. Governments will fear sanctions from large MNCs, particularly where things like R & D and new technology are concerned.

Such responses might be forced on Third World economies in particular by the exigencies of development plans. Even in the developed world, many strategies proposed by governments derive from an import control/protectionist tradition which, arguably, may not necessarily offer the best support to workers confronting an MNC. In the final event, MNCs may be willing to forgo access to particular markets in the short term in order to discipline recalcitrant governments. Finally, the problems arising in the organisation and application of control policies over MNCs has been pointed to as a material constraint on state action.

Informal organisation in support of worker claims against an MNC is an underdeveloped alternative/complement to formal political intervention. Local political mobilisation at community and regional level is a well-established approach to building campaigns, but the possibility of extending these beyond the immediate issue and the local region has yet to be explored. Sustained campaigns have been waged against Coca-Cola (Guatemala), Brooke Bond in Sri Lanka, Wilson–Rowntree in South Africa and many other individual MNCs, often with a degree of success over time. Cases such as these point to the amount of effort and time needed to create pressure on an MNC. They also suggest that the more extreme behaviour of the MNC, the greater the potential of a wide political alliance against its actions. Hence, a 'reasonable' MNC, such as Ford, may not attract the commitment that the grosser companies generate. Informal political organisation allows the adoption of a variety of novel tactics – the boycott, the picket, the share purchase and the like – which have been shown to have a substantial propaganda potential. However, such strategies may not attract the praise of the labour movement institutions to which the solidarity action is directed. Many European labour movement bodies display an innate conservatism when confronted by novel ideas emerging from outside the labour movement's own confines. Thus informal political options need to be developed further if they are to be both effective and accepted.

Finally, we mention in passing the alternative product/cooperative strategy for coping with MNCs. More often than not arising in the face of MNC closure threats, this approach seeks to transform the MNC subsidiary into an alternative enterprise, either in a similar capitalist mode, or as some form of alternative style of enterprise. Following the Lucas Plan tradition, it has been argued that such approaches could be turned into offensive weapons for the labour movement, rather than continuing simply as crisis responses (see Wainwright and Elliot, 1982). Again, this strand requires more development before it is generally accepted.

This sober assessment of labour strategy highlights the scale of the task which has to be confronted if effective anti-MNC policies are to emerge. To this should be added the overriding contextual factor – the phase of the international production cycle in which action is planned. Melding elements of the above strands, and simultaneously taking them forward in new ways, will be substantially dependent on the cycle. Simply, most – perhaps all – labour strategies will succeed more readily when the power of labour is benefiting from the upswing; equally, they will be less effective in a downswing (or period of massive technological innovation) when the power of capitalist decision-making may be enhanced.

However, the elements of labour strategy have to be brought together in new ways if the contradictions in MNC decision-making discussed in the first part of this chapter are to be exacerbated in the interests of labour. How this is to be done cannot be laid down in terms of a programme or blueprint. The imponderables are too great, and alternative melds of action will be defined empirically when appropriate circumstances arise. However, we can go beyond simple exhortation of workers to capitalise upon the range of strategic options available. First, we can suggest that certain correlations of labour strategy with contradictions in management decision-making may be more likely than others. Secondly, we can outline the resource and planning implications raised by a more effective labour strategy.

The process of laying out *a priori* potential correlations which may emerge brings the discussion back to the management decision-making matrix. Let us assume a decision made by an MNC management based initially on location- and ownership-specific factors. Clearly, using the criterion of immediacy, it will generally be the case that the more location-specific a decision, the greater the potential for labour to intervene using traditional established tactics. Thus collective bargaining strategies may be an appropriate starting point, in line with much contemporary practice. Where ownership factors play a proportionally larger role, the appropriateness and efficacy of traditional collective bargaining will tend to be reduced. Practically, for example, work organisation decisions, even if they are imported from distant parts of the MNC, will have to be negotiated and sanctioned by the workforce to some extent, a process which gives a role to collective bargaining strategies. However, a financial decision made at MNC headquarters may be less amenable to such pressure (though, of course, not necessarily without some opportunity for the collective bargaining approach to be used). The case of the financial decision also raises the other potential contradictions emerging from an analysis of the matrix –

it could encompass a functional contradiction (finance versus, say, marketing functions) or an organisational problem (headquarters versus the sub-division expected to implement the financial decision). We must stress that such contradictions are not inevitable; possibly only a small proportion of such decisions create contradictions and, importantly, become sufficiently difficult to attract labour movement attention and action. However, again assuming that this is just such a decision, a number of things must happen if labour is to capitalise on events.

First, planning and resource work – detailed below – must target the decision before it becomes a *fait accompli*. Essentially the labour movement must be able to parallel the debate about decisions taking place within the MNC as far as possible. Secondly, appropriate tactics need to be set in motion. The need is for a new melding of different tactics designed to confront the management decision. Instead of the usual (and important) trinity – collective bargaining at a local level, appeals to the national state, and some information exchange and limited international joint action – ownership-specific decisions require the last option to be as developed and structured as the first from the inception of strategic thinking. Instead of a decision being confronted by a steadily widening but usually simultaneously weakening response, it must be thrown off balance by internationally-coordinated action which does two things. It immediately brings home to management that what they see as a particularly-directed decision has far wider consequences which have to be considered before it is implemented. Perhaps, more important, it threatens to cause internal dissension in management in different regions and functions, as one decision is seen to carry with it unforeseen consequences for other managerial functions and locations.

This hypothetical case captures the essence of the strategy we believe is necessary if labour is to confront the MNC with a hope of success. Workers have to wage a concerted guerrilla attack across the MNC showing that actions bring unexpected consequences which in some cases will be more costly than the implementation of the decision. In this strategy, most, if not all, of the tactical components outlined above will play a part – the art will be in choosing the combination of tactics which most wrong-foots management. It should be said that this is not a pipe dream. Mobilisation around appalling work conditions in MNC subsidiaries in South Africa adopted relatively low key and unstructured actions around the world and forced MNCs to reconsider their local employee policies. A massive increase in the quantity and quality of this type of action offers the way forward on the basis of labour initiatives, rather than a terrain laid down by capital. In a non-revolutionary context, it is perhaps the most subversive attack on capitalist power available, providing national, international and supra-union options for political and economic action. In passing, it may also provide a way of linking Third World action with that undertaken in the developed world. We are aware of the difficulties which confront this strategy – varying from the innate conservatism of many existing institutions to the divisive consequences of cash-nexus based and nationalist/sectional traditions – and we have laid out their possible consequences in earlier work. However, these difficulties must be prevented from standing in the way of moves to develop a new effective response to MNC power.

Two practical steps have to be made if the basis for this strategy is to be laid. Neither can be outlined in detail, but it is clear that planning and resource work will be needed on an unprecedented scale. The planning aspect will emerge at its most effective when a unity of purpose binds the existing institutions of the labour movement into an effective international practice, but initial steps towards structured, integrated action can be set in train before such unity is achieved. We leave this aspect to one side for now, as it requires more sophisticated analysis than the limits of this chapter allow. Resource work has priority over all tasks to be undertaken. The intelligence network needed to back up the wrong-footing strategy must parallel the resource base on which MNCs operate. Management strategy must be predicted with a reasonable degree of accuracy if tactical success is to be gained. This means an international structure of information gathering, processing and dissemination, which itself acts to unsettle MNC management and which is immediately accessible in language, data-handling and political terms to all who challenge the power of international capital. This requirement means that, apart from the obvious logistical questions of money and language, information gathering and dissemination will depend on new technology-based networks which provide data for a sophisticated research effort similar to that which the MNCs maintain. Work goes ahead already around this requirement, pointing to the existing moves in the direction we trace above (see Waterman, 1984).

CONCLUSION

We have perhaps been over-ambitious in this chapter, given space constraints. However, the argument may be reduced to a very basic level. Orthodox management analysis can help the labour movement move from a traditional tail-ending strategy if applied in a radical action framework. It suggests that alternatives to existing labour strategies do exist, which may increase the efficacy of labour action against MNCs. Many problems face attempts to move towards these alternatives, and changes must be thought of in terms of a long term strategy. Perhaps some of the obstacles may be insuperable – commentators might point to nationalist and political commitments as potentially immutable difficulties – but moves are already afoot in the directions we lay out indicating that others have recognised that it is the real alternative to existing labour strategy. Above all, it is a positive response to the problems created by the actions of international capital. It seizes the initiative from capital and may therefore subvert its imperative. It is a positive political response to the negative economism which dogs much of the comtemporary debate about union responses to MNCs. In the final analysis, it moves labour's thinking about strategy away from the parochialism which currently forms the basis of international action.

7 The Politics of Closure
David Judge and Tony Dickson

Closure of manufacturing plants in Britain and the general decline of manufacturing capacity is not part of an ineluctable process: this has been a recurring theme of the chapters in this volume. There is no single, universal and inescapable economic law of downturn and closure. Whilst companies and governments may seek to legitimise their actions by invoking immutable laws of economics, recourse to such legitimating devices is itself a political act. In these instances, impersonal economic rationality is called upon to obscure the discretionary choices made by firms and governments. In a simple and definitive statement of economics – that there is no alternative – the intricacies of political and social considerations can be dispensed with. What the preceding chapters have pointed to is that there invariably are alternatives – but that alternative strategies to closure are complex and contain contradictory elements.

In this concluding chapter, we seek to pull together the discrete threads of analysis developed in each of the separate chapters within this book. In so doing, not only do we wish to provide a comprehensive analysis of the complexities of the closure issue, but also to unravel these strands of analysis from the corset of economic rationality and determinism. The danger with this approach is that what we might be left with is a handful of disparate analytical threads with no overall perspective on closure, and hence no comprehensive or simple solutions. But this should not deter us, for recognition of the complexity of the problem confronting us is itself a precondition for devising an effective conceptual framework within which alternatives to closure can be formulated. So our intention is not to offer short-term 'solutions'; we seek instead to identify the crucial variables and the contradictions which need to be resolved in the construction of alternative strategies, as well as to indicate some of the possible implications of these strategies.

IS MANUFACTURING DECLINE AND CLOSURE A PROBLEM?

This question needs to be addressed at the outset, for, if manufacturing decline is not a problem, then the discussion of alternative strategies to combat closure is either futile or positively harmful to the rejuvenation of the economy and employment prospects. One answer is that as the capitalist economy is founded upon the accumulation of capital and production for profit then the 'imperatives' of this system will lead to constant restructuring and reordering of the production process in accordance with market forces and competition. Given this dynamic, closure of old industrial plant and the generation of new industries based on new technologies, investment patterns and the exploitation of new sectoral markets has been a recurrent feature of capitalist economies. Therefore, to frustrate these forces of competition and to prevent capital seeking out new arenas for profitable accumulation would be self-defeating. By this argument, defence of manufacturing in the abstract, defence of existing production processes in general would be detrimental to the revitalisation of the British national economy. It is capital in the abstract, and the capitalist process in general, that is the focus of attention. Within this process the relative strength, importance and performance of one economic sector *vis-à-vis* others is determined by competitive forces. Capital merely requires a framework within which such competition can take place – and looks to the state to provide these conditions. Manufacturing is accorded no special priority in this model, and constitutes but one fraction alongside finance and commercial capital in the accumulation process and in the state system itself. Indeed, this is the model subscribed to by the Thatcher government in its avowed intention to 'increase the competitiveness and adaptability of the whole economy, not just one particular sector' (Cmnd 9697, 1985, p. 4). The corollary of this approach is that state policies should not discriminate in favour of manufacturing, particularly as the connection between overall economic performance and that of manufacturing is limited – with manufacturing accounting for just under one-quarter of GDP. As long as the service and financial sectors are buoyant and combine with oil revenues to offset the deficit in trade on manufactures, then the government sees its role as pursuing macro-economic policies which will sustain the performance of these sectors – if needs be, to the detriment of manufacturing.

But this answer by the government (more accurately by the Treasury) has elicited alternative responses from the major representative organisations of both sides of industry and from parliamentarians of all parties. The Association of British Chambers of Commerce, which claims to be the largest non-sectoral representative body for service industry, does 'not accept the proposition . . . that Britain should concentrate on developing its service sector and allow much of manufacturing to die' (ABCC, 1985, p. 3). Instead, the ABCC points to the impossibility of filling the short-fall in the non-oil balance of payments account through relying on service industry. First, because the 'majority of service industry is essentially local in its content and application and is non-exportable'. Secondly, a three per cent increase in service exports is required to off-set a one per cent fall in manufacturing exports. Thirdly, because the prosperity of service industry is directly linked to the prosperity of manufacturing – with manufacturing industry absorbing twenty per cent of the outputs of service industries. And, finally, there is 'almost certainly a correlation between the existence of manufacture exports and the growth of service exports' (HL 238ii, 1985, pp. 615–6). Similarly, the CBI has cautioned against too much reliance on the growth in services and argued that it would be 'unlikely that our service industries will be able fully to bridge a gap in our balance of payments arising from reduced oil exports' (HL 238ii, 1985, p. 48). In the CBI's view, Britain's economic problems can only be resolved by seeking the maximum contribution from both the manufacturing and service sectors.

Parliamentarians in each of the major parties share the same sentiments. Senior members of the Conservative party, for example, have emphasised the need for a dynamic and innovative manufacturing sector alongside a competitive service sector. In Peter Walker's words: 'The only sane solution is that we must do well in both' (*Guardian*, 19 February 1986, see also Heseltine, *Guardian*, 21 February 1986). Recent speeches by Neil Kinnock and his industry spokesmen have emphasised that concentration on service industries 'does nothing to prevent the growth of imports, which Labour [believes] threatens the balance of payments' (*Times*, 4 January 1986). In a campaign entitled 'Party of Production' Labour identified the reversal of Britain's manufacturing fortunes as its central economic objective. Not to be outdone, Dr. David Owen also places the regeneration of Britain's industrial base at the head of the political agenda in the run-up to the next election (*Observer*, 5 January 1986). But the most explicit and broadest party-based criticism of the Conservative government's answer came in the Report of the House of Lords Select Committee on Overseas Trade:

> The Committee believe that manufacturing is vital to the prosperity of the country and that services important as they are, are no substitute for manufacturing because they are too heavily dependent upon it and only 20 per cent are tradeable overseas. . . . The Committee believe

that expansion of the manufacturing base is the principal means of achieving growth. (HL 238i, 1985, p. 43)

Given that manufacturing still represents over one-fifth of economic activity in the UK, around one-quarter of employment and over forty per cent of overseas earnings, it still constitutes a significant part of the British economy. Yet the size of the manufacturing base is itself now perceived to be a problem. There has been a dramatic fall in production since 1979, as shown in chapter 1; and by February 1986 manufacturing production was still 6.6 per cent below the figure for the second quarter of 1979, and still four per cent below the level of output in the first quarter of 1974 (i.e. the time of the three-day week under the Heath government!). Thus, although certainly 'leaner' than in 1979, British manufacturing is hardly significantly 'fitter' despite the cold splash of competition which, in the rhetoric of the Conservative government, should have tautened its productive muscles. Pessimism as to whether manufacturing production can now be significantly increased is widespread (see HL 238, 1985).

One simple reason for such pessimism is that many manufacturing industries have ceased operations. The long-term adverse effect of this demise is that 'once a country, or company, has opted out of a particular industry it is virtually impossible ever to re-enter because of the substantial costs involved in capital re-equipment, re-establishing access to markets, and catching up with changes in technology' (HL 238iii, 1985, p. 427). The basic problem for Britain's industrial future is, in the words of the chairman of ICI, that 'some whole areas of industry seem to . . . have virtually gone from the United Kingdom' (HL 238ii, 1985, p. 465). Many small, domestically-oriented firms have collapsed, and British MNCs have relocated significant manufacturing capacity overseas. Even in those industries which still remain, should they seek to expand their manufacturing capability, investment in new plant, technology and production processes reaps results only in the long term. Manufacturing decline and plant closure appear to be with us for the foreseeable future. Moreover, as the Overseas Trade Select Committee concluded: 'there is . . . no reason to suppose that events will change their course by way of an automatic recovery' (HL 238i, 1985, p. 46).

LEVELS OF ANALYSIS: KNOWING THE PROBLEM

We have stipulated both that manufacturing is important, that its decline is likely to continue in the short-term and that remedial action is urgently required. Yet before remedial action can be taken, it is important to specify the problem accurately. Part of the problem is itself the diversity of factors contributing to industrial decline generally and industrial closure specifically. Only through locating the specific within the context of the general can a full understanding of the phenomenon of industrial closure be gained.

i) Britain and the international economy

a) Finance capital

We outlined in chapter 1 the special position of finance capital within the accumulation process and the British state. In the chapter, it was argued that the basic parameters of economic policy had been set, since the late 19th century, by the international orientation of finance capital. Very simply: the state has internalised the 'universal' interests of the City in its economic policies. In so doing, the state has accepted the demands of the City to be unfettered and to let the play of market forces determine exchange and interest rates (or more accurately the City has sought freedom from government control but licence for City institutions to regulate stabilisation policy). The characteristic of financial markets is that they are extremely fluid, universal and international. As such they do not reflect simply *British* finance interests but the transactions of money and credit dealers throughout the capitalist world. The City is truly international, therefore, both in the scope of its markets and, increasingly important, through the operations of foreign banks and finance houses in London.

The very internationalism of the City with its multitude of diverse institutions, dealers and brokers – indeed, the very fragmentation of the financial system itself – leads to a common desire within the finance sector to develop simple indicators to help structure decision-making in the international market. The accuracy of these indicators is 'relatively unimportant compared to the question of whether financiers agree on their acceptability' (Fine and Harris, 1985, p. 77). Out of the fragmentation of the system arises the need for a unity in establishing criteria for judgement: criteria, which in practice, are subject to rapid changes and fashions. But the important feature of these fluctuations is that 'by buying and selling financial assets in accordance with such indicators the dealers determine movements in interest rates and exchange rates which shape and constrain state policies toward the economy as a whole' (Fine and Harris, 1985, p. 77). State economic policies thus constitute reactions to market forces which the government has been unable to control, and for significant periods has not sought to control. In the absence of control, the needs of the domestic economy, and especially domestic industry, have tended to be subordinated to the maintenance of the City as the nodal point of international financial networks.

In addition, industrial development in Britain has been influenced by the separation of industrial and finance capital. British industry has been far more dependent than its major competitors on self-financing and correspondingly has been less interconnected with financial institutions. Traditionally, as we noted in chapter 1, investment by banks and financial institutions in British industry has been short-term, flexible and largely devoid of operational involvement in industry. At this micro-level, the fragmentation between industry and finance capital has stunted industrial investment, but equally at a broader level the predisposition of finance capital in favour of free markets and limited state intervention has itself contributed to the blocking of coherent policies by the state towards the restructuring of industrial capital.

The international orientation of finance capital in Britain is clearly the first factor to be addressed in an analysis of the present (and past) difficulties of British manufacturing industry. But, as we made clear in the introduction to this chapter, it is not our intention to offer simplistic solutions to this malaise. Indeed, were such obvious panaceas readily available, they would undoubtedly have been tried and the problems which lie at the heart of the discussions in this volume might seem less formidable. Our intention here is to outline the main alternative strategies which have been advanced in response to this international orientation of the economy and the state. Only by highlighting the weaknesses inherent in these strategies can we move on to pointing the way toward what seems to us to be a more productive line of development.

The Thatcherite strategy has been to applaud the internationalism, the fluidity and the *laissez-faire* orientation of finance capital. International competition, so productive for financial interests, was to be the preferred medium through which British industry could be regenerated. The national economy was to be more firmly coupled to the international economy, with free trade and free markets bolstering the internationally competitive sectors of the economy. The reverse of this, of course, was that those sectors which were uncompetitive on the world market would suffer a necessary and *inevitable* contraction. This logic merely underlined the subordinate position of manufacturing, both in terms of output/employment and impact on state policies. In this position, the various voices of industry, even when articulated in a single low groan by the CBI, sounded like the merest whisper against the chatter and clamour of the finance sector.

The danger of this strategy is plain to see. Thatcherite commitment to international competition rests upon the assumption that free trade is the dynamic of the international system. In practice this assumption does not hold. As witnesses from major manufacturing companies repeatedly informed the House of Lords Select Committee on Overseas Trade: 'Free trade . . . was a dead duck and it seemed as though only the United Kingdom had failed to recognise the fact' (HL 238i, 1985, p. 77). But the British government could not acknowledge this fact, given the hegemony of finance capital and its interest in securing the freedom of the money and exchange markets. Even in these terms, however, the strategy of the Thatcher government is flawed, as the operations of the financial markets have no conception of a 'national economic interest' with which to work. The interests of finance are simultaneously more restricted (in terms of profit maximisation by individual institutions and dealers) and more diffuse (in terms of an internationally recognised and changing definition of national economic performance – which places little emphasis on the actual performance of the productive sector of the economy). These interests are becoming increasingly volatile in the 1980s as exchange rates come to be determined 'more on the buyer's expectations of the [currency's] resale value, than on underlying economic developments' (*Guardian*, 15 January, 1986). Indeed, one estimate of the consequence of free trade in the foreign exchange markets is that 'at least 90 per cent of deals done . . . are not to facilitate import or export trade, but for speculation' (*Observer*, 12 January 1986). As Keynes observed some years ago: 'The position is serious when enterprise becomes the bubble on a whirlpool of speculation'.

To counterpose the Thatcherite strategy an alternative strategy – literally the Alternative Economic Strategy – has been formulated by the left grouped around the Labour party. An essential ingredient of this strategy has been exchange controls as part of a programme to regain and extend control of international capital movements. Initially, exchange controls would be used to prevent speculative dealings against the pound, but would be extended to prevent investment abroad at the expense of the domestic economy. It is clearly envisaged that sterling would no longer be freely convertible and so cease to be an international currency. Foreign holdings of sterling would be frozen. The exchange rate would no longer be determined through the exchange markets, but in accordance with British trade and industrial policy. This decoupling of Britain from world financial markets would be accompanied by the safeguarding of domestic industry through regulated trading agreements, or in cruder versions of the AES 'import controls'. Clearly, the British national economy is to be insulated from the anarchy of world markets.

Although bold in outline, the AES is weak on the precise details of how these policies would be implemented. This is particularly important given the sheer volume and scope of financial transactions passing through (but not of) the City of London, and given the massive outflow of British capital overseas since 1979. The financial world has moved on since the drafting of the AES in the early 1970s – it has moved further away from national state direction and control!

b) *Multinational corporations*
Much of this volume has been directly or indirectly focused upon the activities of MNCs, primarily because the major closures in Britain in the 1980s have resulted from the policies of MNCs. Nearly one-third of all jobs lost in manufacturing in the decade 1972–83 stemmed from the decisions of 58 leading British MNCs alone (see *Financial Times*, 5 December 1985). That Britain is not the sole, nor even the primary, focus of the activities of these companies is revealed in the fact that whilst jobs in Britain were reduced by more than 600 000 in this period, British MNCs created 200 000 jobs overseas. The international orientation of British MNCs and the secondary status of the domestic market was well illustrated by Mr. Harvey-Jones (chairman of ICI) in his evidence to the House of Lords' Select Committee. There he recorded that ICI had reduced its UK manpower by 30 800 between 1979 and 1984 and that 'a number of plants have been closed to reduce over-capacity' (HL 238ii, 1985, p. 452). At the same time, Harvey-Jones outlined ICI's strategy and performance:

> expansion abroad has been essential in order to maintain and improve ICI's position as the free world's fifth largest chemical company. Not only does the United Kingdom market represent less than 5 per cent of total chemical sales, but it is growing at a slower rate than elsewhere. . . . The health of the United Kingdom chemical industry and its ability to generate a positive trade balance is closely related to the fortunes of manufacturing industry as a whole . . . between 1978 and 1981 . . . a substantial part of the manufacturing base was lost and manufacturing production has remained weak since then. In ICI's case, we estimate that we lost about 20 per cent of our customer base

in our petrochemicals and general chemicals businesses. As a result of this . . . ICI moved out of the production in the United Kingdom of several commodity products (HL 238ii, 1985, pp. 451–2).

The trend of ICI's development is not unique; most other British MNCs have extended their international operations under the Thatcher government. This has led some commentators to argue that MNCs are becoming 'denationalised' (Smith 1981, p. 173) and that their international orientation leads their economic interests to diverge from those of their country of origin . A seemingly logical extension of this argument is to conceive of an integrated system of global production – of 'one world capital'. But this is to overstretch the meaning of the international orientation of British MNCs and, by extension, to overemphasise the homogeneity of MNCs *en genus*. Only by caricaturing the intent and organisation of MNCs in *global* terms can the 'denationalisation' argument be sustained. Thus as Coakley and Harris (1983, pp. 177–9) argue, the international integration of capital is constrained by the nationally based dimensions of MNCs: MNCs are predominantly owned and controlled by national capitals; profits are recorded in national currency units (giving MNCs a vital interest in national exchange rates); and strategic decision-making is concentrated on the domestic headquarters. MNCs may subsequently pursue apparently contradictory strategies, depending upon the relative emphasis placed upon national or international considerations at any particular time.

If the strategic vision of MNCs appears to be blurred on occasion, so too can the locus of decision-making within their internal organisation appear ambiguous. In theory, the formal structure of decision-making may be hierarchical and unproblematic, but the sheer number and spread of decision-points in any MNC makes the process of decision-making conditional and ambiguous. MNCs are not, therefore, monolithic organisations in practice; nor can a single and uniform MNC interest in 'global capital' be adduced.

These discontinuities of interest and in decision-making are of some importance in the discussion of closure, because they point to a potentiality to expose and widen the divergence of interests within and between MNCs, to enable the expression and articulation of alternatives (both strategic and operational) over general investment patterns and specific closure plans. Chapters 5 and 6 have revealed the disjointed practice of MNC decision-making. Moreover, as the process of disinvestment in particular plants is invariably a gradual, and in some cases – such as Linwood – a protracted procedure, there exist a number of potential arenas within which specific decisions can potentially be contested. At different times, at different levels and in different locations, changing alliances of labour, national and local governments and management can be used to formulate alternatives to specific closures. The outward appearance of MNC monolithic power needs to be challenged by penetrating and widening the organisational disjunctions that exist within MNCs. The exact nature of this challenge will vary from one decision to the next and be contingent upon the contextual factors of the decision-process – but the important point is to recognise that the potentiality to contest MNC decisions does exist. MNC decision-making is not as 'rational' as MNC managements would have their workforces believe.

ii) National level: the state, government and parties

Manufacturing industry's position within the wider economy has been structured and defined by the intermediation by the state of class forces in Britain. Without repeating the arguments of chapter 1, the absence of a coherent industrial 'strategy' on the part of the British state has been a characteristic feature of industrial development. The distancing of the state from industry has been described by Wilks (1986, p. 35) as a 'Pontius Pilate posture' and has differentiated Britain from most of its major industrial rivals. More than most, the Conservative government since 1979 has sought to keep its hands clean of intensive involvement in industry. Whilst in practice its hands have been rather more soiled than Thatcherite rhetoric prescribed, none the less, industrial policy has been minimalist, with the major emphasis being upon the creation of a general 'climate' for enterprise through macro-economic policy. The British state's persistent abdication of planning and intervention has found its logical culmination in Thatcherite policies. The state's 'arm's-length' approach to industry has its logical justification in the market-oriented individualism of Thatcherism. 19th century liberal emphases are invoked by Mrs. Thatcher in the 1980s in an effort to engender the industrial conditions that gave rise to the first industrial revolution.

The consequence of Thatcherism's liberal 'experiment' has been the decimation of manufacturing industry in Britain. Thatcherism cannot be wished away and neither can its results: the demise of whole sectors of industry; massive unemployment; occupational restructuring of the working class; privatisation; and the closer incorporation of the national economy into the interstices of the international economy. This is the starting point of any post-Thatcher alternative.

Consistently, throughout Mrs. Thatcher's period in office, alternative policies have been articulated within the Conservative Party itself, but the disparate origins of, and support for, these alternatives have never constituted a single and coherent strategy with which to counterpose the hectoring free market rhetoric of Mrs. Thatcher and her acolytes. Pronouncements by Mrs. Thatcher that 'there is no alternative' have drawn forth the simple exclamation from within the 'damper' sections of her party that 'there has to be an alternative'. But only towards the beginning of 1986 did something resembling an orchestrated, though still remarkably untuneful, response find expression against the 'de-manufacturing of Britain' (P. Price MP, *Guardian*, 5 February 1986). Conducting one movement within the Conservative ranks was Edward Heath and his calls for the 'abandonment of dogma' and a return to the 'British tradition of empiricism' (for empiricism read Keynesianism). In a wide-ranging speech to the Employment Institute in Birmingham in March 1986, he argued that:

> The key element of Britain's industrial policy over the next seven years, before oil revenue begins to decline sharply, should be a deliberate and purposeful strategy to recreate modern British industry. . . . (Part of which would be to) educate the financial markets to accept the need for more capital investment in the infrastructure (*Guardian*, 5 March 1986).

Echoing through this speech was the corporatist modernisation strategy favoured by Mr. Heath in his later years as Prime Minister. Similar resonances could also be detected in Mr. Heseltine's public pronouncements after his resignation from the Thatcher cabinet. Thus in his evidence to the Select Committee on Trade and Industry (HC 193, 1986), he pointed to the devastating effects that the Treasury ethos and its belief in unfettered market forces had had upon British industry. This ethos was out of synchronisation with the political 'sophistication' that was evident in most other capitalist countries. Heseltine's belief in the pervasive and pernicious impact of Treasury and City policies was repeated in an 'Agenda' article in the *Guardian* (21 February 1986). There he called for 'national strategic judgement' to offset Treasury influence. The reorganisation of the DTI as a 'strategic department' would go a considerable way to providing this judgement:

> Its Secretary of State should be one of the most senior members of the government and should chair a cabinet committee charged with the responsibility for the health of British industrial and commercial

activities ... we have a financial strategy. There is an economic strategy. We need now an industrial strategy.

Quite how this strategy, devoid of central state planning, would fare in an era of continuing privatisation, increased MNC activity and internationalisation of the economy, has yet to be articulated by Mr. Heseltine. None the less there are signs that some factions within the Conservative Party are beginning to retrace their steps back to the Keynesian consensus of the 1960s and early 1970s. Yet it was precisely the industrial policies of that time which were condemned by Thatcherites and 'leftists' alike and precipitated the polarised alternatives of the late 1970s and 1980s. Out of this reaction on the left came the AES.

Without dredging through the details of the AES, the essence of the strategy can be simply stated. At its centre was the state. The state was to be involved directly in industry and in maintaining the conditions for growth and investment in that sector. The industrial strategy subsequently revolved around: obligatory planning agreements; public ownership in key firms in each sector of manufacturing industry; co-ordination of planning through some form of National Planning Commission; and control of financial and investment decisions (see Labour's Programme, 1976). Doubts as to the efficacy of the AES were raised at the time of its inception, and these doubts have deepened with the passage of time. The economic and industrial world has changed since the mid-1970s; in particular, the state and the labour movement are now far more constrained than was conceivable a decade ago. In which case, as Aaronovitch (1986, p. 21) argues: 'though the need for radical changes are objectively greater than they ever were, the Left's economic strategy must come to terms with where we are now and cannot have the "grandeur" and ambition of the AES'. Undoubtedly, Aaronovitch is correct to note the changed circumstances of the 1980s, but we would argue that what weakened the AES in the first instance was a *lack* of ambition and a limitation of its analysis of the problems confronting the British state and the national economy.

In all of its dimensions – political, economic and industrial – the perspective of the AES is restricted. At the political level, significant sections of the Labour party and organised labour have never reconciled themselves to the logic of the AES and have constantly sought to disentangle preferred parts of the strategy from the overall package (see Aaronovitch and Grahl, 1985, p. 30). The AES's roots within the British

Labour movement have taken on a stunted appearance. But, even if these roots had tapped deep into the friable soil of Labour's ideology, the fundamental issue would still remain of whether the state can be used as a mere 'instrument' to implement such a strategy. The very class forces structuring Britain's industrial decline are the same ones that condition the range of options open to the state to redirect industrial and economic policies. This is not to argue that the mode of production determines directly and inexorably the form of the state – only to recognise that the respective strengths of the various fractions of capital, and labour, serve to constrain state policies. In this conjunction of forces, the pre-eminence of finance and multinational industrial capitals – with their international orientation – has attuned state policies to meeting the requirements of international markets and competition. It is illusory, therefore, to argue that internationalisation can be reversed, that the British national economy can effectively 'opt out' of the world economy behind protectionist barriers, and that national economic sovereignty can accompany the reassertion of national political sovereignty outside the EEC and other international political associations.

The nature of capitalist development in Britain is such that the most important sectors of the economy are no longer nationally delimited. In industry, the only group of large enterprises that are unambiguously 'national' are those in the public sector (Radice, 1984, p. 127) – and this is a rapidly diminishing sector under the Thatcher administration. The growing internationalisation of the economy has led one percipient commentator to conclude that in 'the *dynamic* sense . . . the British industrial economy no longer exists as an economic unit' (Radice, 1984, p. 135). As a consequence, there are few significant capitalist interests with an exclusive interest in the regeneration of the British national economy. Just as state policies, as epitomised by the Treasury, have long accepted this fact, so too must any 'alternative' strategy.

So, effectively the British national economy has 'disintegrated' under the centrifugal forces exerted by the international operations of the most important fractions of British capital. This disintegration has been twofold: first, in the sense that Britain as the locus of production and investment is merely a part, and often not the most important part, of international industrial operations; and secondly, in the literal sense of the demise of significant sectors of manufacturing industry. Any successor to the Thatcher government will be confronted by this reality. In particular, any radical socialist government will have to launch its transformative programme from this point. Yet only belatedly have significant sections of the 'left' in Britain come to recognise this and to countenance a socialist *international* strategy to offset the chauvanist suspicions of the initial formulations of the AES (see Holland, 1982; 1984; Coates, 1986). At the heart of a new international strategy would be the acknowledgement of:

> the need for involvement in the EEC and to work with all the forces available to change its policies with regard to co-ordinated economic expansion, industrial collaboration, assistance to the developing countries, relations with the socialist world, co-ordinated approach to the control of multinationals and the supervision of the banking and financial systems (Aaronovitch, 1986, p. 26).

Within this enlarged frame, co-ordinated policies for the regulation of the transnational activities of MNCs and the reduction of their capacity to 'play-off' one national government against another are feasible; as indeed is the regulation of trade patterns and capital flows.

Clearly, the logical extension of this argument is for 'socialists in any particular locality . . . to work . . . for the emergence of socialist options at a global level' (Spence, 1985, p. 135). In practice, and for the forseeable future, the EEC, with its putative supra-national political institutions and trans-national party groupings, provides the initial focus for attempts to generate what, by any stretch of the imagination, would prove to be a difficult process of co-operation amongst labour movements and national governments. Fortunately, here we can short circuit the detailed discussion of the forms of organisation and agitation required to promote such co-operation, as our remit is restricted to formulating an agenda for future analysis and discussion of the options available to reverse industrial decline and manufacturing closures.

One item on this agenda therefore is the need to utilise the international orientation of the state's policies, to work within the logic of state apparatuses and to invert this logic in favour of labour. Obviously there are contradictions inherent within this strategy, not the least of which is that, in seeking to control capital at a European level, Britain's manufacturing industry may well be further weakened in the short run. For unless all member governments can be persuaded to adopt uniform supra-national perspectives and policies, then competition within the EEC would only be heightened. Under these conditions, British industry would be most severely affected as its major competitors – most particularly Germany, but also France – have retained national industrial cores that are less dependent upon the international economy. Thus, although all leading capitalist economies are inextricably linked to international networks, the British economy is far more enmeshed than most and correspondingly least secured upon an independent manufacturing base. One danger, therefore, is that any strategy designed to fit the logic and determinants of the British state may fit uneasily with existing reality in the EEC and other domestic socialist strategies within EEC states. (Though there is evidence of developing commonalities of strategy and a convergence of planning-by-agreement approaches among leading European socialist parties [see CSE, 1980; Holland, 1984; Harris and Corbett, 1986]). Whilst it is easy to invoke the concept of international socialist co-operation, practical steps towards this goal are far harder to secure!

iii) Local state: community action and enterprise

Just as the AES has been criticised for its preoccupation with the national economy rather than the international economy, so it has attracted criticism for its 'top-down' centralist and bureaucratic perspective on economic planning. A recurring theme of the debate surrounding the AES, therefore, has revolved around the need to offset centralisation by the extension of workers' democracy, local enterprise initiatives and local/regional planning mechanisms. Attention has come to be focused on the 'local state' and the desirability of constructing locally based cross-class alliances. Thus Rustin (1985, p. 111) argues that 'one object of [local and] regional government should be to achieve class coalitions in which capital's local interests oblige it to co-operate in socialist economic programmes'. Similarly, in the CSE's version of the AES, a major advantage of local/regional planning mechanisms is that 'struggles against closure and for new job creation tend to be conducted best via an alliance of forces in which local authorities and local/regional trade union organisations are allowed to play a progressive role' (CSE, 1980, p. 84). Optimism in the efficacy of local action is widely shared on the 'left' (see Boddy and Fudge, 1984; Gamble 1985; Aaronovitch, 1986, p. 22). As Des McNulty made clear in chapter 2, several Labour local authorities have adopted a positive (pro-active), rather than a reactive role in the process of industrial restructuring. The creation of enterprise boards by the GLC and the West Midlands County Council, and the Employment Department in Sheffield, has provided a blueprint for local industrial planning: in McNulty's words, 'each successful economic initiative is . . . a demonstration that local and regional economies can be revived through the actions of public sector bodies'. Indeed, the national Labour party has learned from this experience and acknowledged the importance of local action. Hence, its *Programme* (1982, p. 51) pledged to 'build on the existing work of local co-operative development agencies and the initiatives of Labour-controlled authorities such as Greater London, Sheffield and the West Midlands'. Yet the importance of community as an organising focus of solidarity should not be overestimated. Only within the wider context of national and international relationships can the scope and possibilities of community action be properly understood. The community might prove to be an initial source of popular mobilisation, but too often in the past working class mobilisation at this level has been reactive, defensive and conservative, operating in relative isolation from wider labour, social and political movements. Community based action has demonstrated not only a potentiality to unite but also to fragment working class solidarity (see below p. 182).

None of the above means that 'local socialism' is inappropriate for fighting closures and managing structural economic change, but simply that local initiatives *by themselves* are incapable of reversing the decline in manufacturing production and employment. Local initiatives, either serially or cumulatively, have not thus far constrained the central state – as the experience of the Thatcher government has demonstrated. None the less, these initiatives, in articulating alternative approaches and in creating local administrative agencies to challenge the central state bureaucracy on its own terms, are pointers for the future. But these approaches can only effectively develop within a wider and concerted challenge to capitalist hegemony at all levels – local, regional, national and international. Thus far, the 'left' has tended to compartmentalise its analysis into discrete spatial levels of analysis. What is needed, however, is a systematic and inclusive analysis to reveal the forces leading to closure and the possibilities, and the difficulties, in combating these forces.

THE LABOUR MOVEMENT AND CLOSURE: TOWARDS AN ALTERNATIVE POLITICAL ECONOMY

The focus of labour's attention is far more closely delimited than either that of the state or of the most important fractions of industrial and finance capital. As we have seen, British capital has at its heart a universal and international dimension, whereas the interest of labour is essentially introverted and framed within the specific work community. Collective organisation amongst workers, given labour's restricted horizons, is most easily and successfully established at plant and workplace level. As Baldry et al. (1983, p. 160) note: 'labour relies. . . . on identity, consciousness, solidarity and determination. . . . generated essentially in the work community'. Generally, therefore, the workplace has been identified as the logical focus for defensive action against closure.

The significance of community based collective action has been displayed in several of the preceding chapters. Patricia Findlay's chapter particularly highlighted the contribution of women in developing local solidarity and community support. Women's shared life and work experiences may provide a dynamic for an enhanced consciousness capable of transcending particular struggles to form the basis of a strategy of wider resistance and co-operation. Yet contradictory pressures are also at work – for, if women's political consciousness is generated out of a particular struggle, past experience suggests that collective action seldom survives that struggle. The potentiality and the contradictions of women's heightened consciousness was clearly revealed in the 1984–85 miners' strike. One year after the end of that strike, one assessment of the political legacy of the Women Against Pit Closures movement concluded: 'It hurts to say it, but it must be said: the miners' wives have gone back to the kitchen, in their thousands' (Lewycka, 1986, p. 17). None the less, a residue of committed women, whose lives had been transformed, remains (see *Guardian*, 1 April 1986). A further contradiction is that whilst women have demonstrated ferocious resistance to closure in several *causes célèbres*, more employment opportunities (admittedly part-time and low paid) are often available for women than male manual workers confronted by closure. Female resistance to closure may be undermined by the existence of these alternative prospects.

If contradictions are apparent in the development of solidarity amongst women faced by closure, so too are they apparent in the experience of wider trade union solidarity. In theory, trade union resistance to closure is most likely to develop out of the organic cohesiveness of labour at plant level. But local solidarity in itself is insufficient to address the problem of closure – a wider and more universal solidarity is required. Yet the requirements for both specific and universal solidarity invariably conflict. Frequently there are divergences of interest between workers in different plants within the same company, let alone between workers in different companies and different countries. Calls for forms of organisation and understanding that interconnect workplaces at home and abroad are undoubtedly correct (see chapter 4). But the practical problem remains of how to translate community solidarity into a wider *class* solidarity and how to develop a consciousness which, whilst rooted and located in the locality, none the less transcends inter-plant and international divisions. Assuming, along with Haworth and Ramsay, that there is no automatic tendency for labour to develop international solidarity (or for that matter national solidarity – as the 1984–85 miners' strike demonstrated) then a strategy has to be devised to counterpose the internationalisation of capital with wider labour co-operation and solidarity. The problem is that the inward-looking, community orientation of labour is in contradistinction to the expansive and increasingly international orientation of capital.

This disjunction has led generally to doubts as to whether labour and capital are fighting on the same territory, and specifically to fears that capital defines the very terrain upon which labour has to do battle. In this latter and specific sense, labour has to contest closure on the grounds stipulated by capital, i.e. its response is essentially reactive and defensive. The case studies in this volume have illustrated the extent to which labour 'tail-ends', to use Haworth and Ramsay's phrase, the decisions made by capital. One consequence of this is that resistance to closure invariably constitutes a specific and *post-facto* response on the part of labour. 'Fighting closure' essentially means entering the ring after the bell has gone – after management has already decided upon closure. In these circumstances, the assessment of management's case, the drafting of alternative plans and trade-union campaigns – whilst commendable – are often tokens of resistance. This problem cannot be overcome simply by calling for more formal restraints on capital through agreements on planning, participation and the disclosure of information. The paradox of such formal procedures, as noted in chapters 5 and 6, is that labour is led to confront capital on capital's own terms. Formal agreements upon participation and the disclosure of information therefore tend to operate within the parameters of the economic rationality of capital.

If *post hoc*, locally based responses to closure are often inappropriate to counter decisions made within the frame of 'universal' capital requirements, then a precondition of a successful counter-strategy (i.e. one that sets closure within a wider social and political frame and does not simply react to predetermined economic rationality) is for labour to develop an operational perspective with which to contest the expansive logic of capital. Such a perspective would have to encompass local, state and international strategies. Yet vague and theoretically ungrounded calls for greater contacts and communications between workers at inter-plant and international levels do little to advance the understanding or operationalisation of co-ordinated action. It requires fundamental changes in the attitudes and practices of British trade unions and the labour movement more generally. For example, as Haworth and Ramsay argued in chapter 6, the potentialities of new technology (particularly information technology) must be firmly embraced so that a co-operative network of information is instantly available to all sections of labour across the boundaries of different companies, trade unions, and states. This not only implies an international perspective largely alien to British trade unions, but also a massive effort aimed at the education and co-operation of their members. Only by the aggressive utilisation of such 'information power' does labour have a chance of avoiding 'tail-ending' management strategy and instead creating the capacity to mobilise at plant, community, national, and international level to pre-empt the possibility of closure.

Similarly, there is a need to look beyond the bounds of workplace and community and to understand the significance of the state in an international perspective. The external implications of this have already been referred to above, in terms of the need to work within supra-national entities such as the EEC. But there are also important dimensions within national boundaries. We talked earlier of the requirement to invert the logic of the state in favour of labour. Nowhere is this more apparent than in relation to the legislative role of the state. The extent to which the law has been crucial in disputes over closure has been a theme running through most of the preceding chapters. Patricia Findlay, in chapter 3, showed how, in a rare instance of the labour movement using the law to its advantage to prevent the eviction of workers occupying a factory, the state moved rapidly to close the loop-hole. The effects of post-1979 legislation (particularly on pre-strike ballots, secondary picketing, and the sequestration of union funds) in weakening trade union resistance to closure has been referred to at various times. The use of such laws in the miners' strike of 1984–85, together with the court's interpretation of existing legislation to destroy effective picketing, are further examples. Finally, the cynical manipulation of these laws and the company acts by Robert Maxwell and Rupert Murdoch in 1986, is yet another illustration. In these latter cases, the newspaper proprietors resorted to a combination of injunctions against picketing and industrial action, and the formation of new companies to which control of their newspapers could be transferred, as formidable weapons in their attempt to enforce large-scale redundancies and restructuring on their labour forces. All of these examples provide testimony to the need for a broader, reformulated strategy which takes the debate beyond the sphere of particular trade unions and localities, even if these provide the bedrock upon which it is launched. By compartmentalising its organisational forms, and hence its areas of debate, the labour movement has fragmented its case.

To overcome the disjunctions of labour structures an alternative 'political economy of labour' - one that can 'universalise' labour's position and situate local struggles within this universal perspective - is required. The basis of an alternative 'political economy of labour' is an understanding that the 'economy is people, that its basic relationships are social relationships' (Bowles et al., 1984, p. 9). In this alternative, the needs of people are placed before those of impersonal market criteria in the ordering of the production process. People, not money, would be the organising principle of economic relationships. The advancement of this principle requires political action within workplace, community, national and international organisations.

It can be argued, however, that the more ambitious strategy that we are advocating is both altruistic and long term. In some senses it has to be conceded that it is. At the same time we would argue that there are crucial grounds for its adoption. First, the alternatives are so barren. They amount to either abandoning the manufacturing base of the British economy and accepting a continuing pattern of closures and industrial decline, or to holding on to a crumbling façade by our collective fingertips in the hope that a major change in international trade will lead to a convenient ladder being placed beneath our feet to assist us in clambering on to some new structure whose nature is not as yet guessed. Neither of these prospects, for reasons we have outlined above, seem especially attractive. Secondly, and on a more positive note, elements of this alternative political economy already exist and have been identified in the case studies within this volume. The clearest demonstration of the articulation of this alternative, and of the current barriers to its development, came in the miners' strike of 1984–85.

A detailed examination of the intricacies of the 1984–85 dispute is clearly beyond the limits of the present discussion, but one of the issues raised by the strike - that of 'uneconomic' closure - is central to our discussion. For at one level, the NUM's campaign sought to 'universalise' the nature of the miners' struggle:

Alongside workers in all of Britain's once proud basic and manufacturing industries, we will fight – not just for ourselves and our families, but for the entire nation – and the future (Scargill, *Sunday Times*, 11 March 1984).

An essential part of this fight was the articulation of social criteria for assessing the viability of coal production and of closure. In these terms, the NUM could portray its strike as 'the contest in which economics is assembled on one side, humanity and compassion on the other' (Samuel, 1985, p. 367). Crucial to the dispute, therefore, was the issue of the legitimacy of closure. By claiming that jobs in the mining industry were the property of those working in it, the NUM directly challenged the right of the NCB (management), of the government (and, by implication, of capital in general) unilaterally to decide to close plants. By drawing on the strength of social relationships in mining areas, and public perceptions of the importance of such community solidarity, the NUM in its struggle touched a basic chord which resonated with the wider significance of work for social life. The tragedy of the 1984–85 strike is that this simple but immensely powerful appeal was lost in the violence of the dispute, the government's counter-propaganda and the distortions of the media. Moreover, the NUM's own strategy was equivocal on the issue of 'social costs'. On the one side, documents were produced to show the devastating impact of closure on mining communities. Plus, even on strictly 'economic' criteria a case was made that the closure of loss-making pits would not have benefited the wider public purse. On the other side, however, the NUM was drawn into contesting closure within the parameters of the economic debate set by the NCB. Yet the presentation of the NUM's economic counter-arguments became clouded in the old-style and simplistic class rhetoric of the NUM leadership. In this rhetoric, the strength of the social audit case, upon which wider, cross-class support could have been developed, was dissipated.

Yet the confusion over whether to counter the claims of the NCB on 'economic' or 'social' grounds was exacerbated by the indecision within the political wing of the labour movement. Alienated by the rhetoric of the NUM leadership, significant sections of the PLP gave only ambiguous support to the strike and largely failed to utilise the available data to challenge the NCB's case of closure on 'uneconomic' grounds. The unwillingness, or inability, of Labour politicians to 'universalise' the fundamental issue of the social costs of closure left a political vacuum within which the economic rationality of the NCB and the Conservative government prevailed.

Whilst demonstrating the weaknesses and discontinuities of the labour movement, the miners' strike also provided the potentiality to generalise and 'socialise' the issue of closure. The counterposing of economic rationality with the needs of people; the appeal both to community and beyond; and the politicisation of the issues of closure were basic, if not always fully, developed, ingredients of the 1984–85 strike. These ingredients need to be reconstituted in future campaigns against closure. Why they need to be is evident from the analyses of the chapters in this book. Whether and how they can be depends, in our view, on the possibility of constructing a broad and dynamic strategy based upon an alternative political economy.

References

AARONOVITCH, S. (1981) 'The Relative Decline of the UK', in S. Aaronovitch and R. Smith, *The Political Economy of British Capitalism* (Maidenhead: McGraw-Hill).

AARONOVITCH, S. (1986) 'The Alternative Economic Strategy: Goodbye to All That?', *Marxism Today*, February, pp. 20–6.

AARONOVITCH, S. and GRAHL, J. (1985) 'An Alternative to the Alternative – Labour's New Economic Strategy: Interview with Roy Hattersley', *Marxism Today*, October, pp. 25–31.

ALT, J. (1978) *The Politics of Economic Decline* (Cambridge: CUP).

ALTSHULER, A.; ANDERSON, M.; JONES, D.; ROOS, D. and WOMACK, J. (1984) *The Future of the Automobile* (London: Allen & Unwin).

ANDERSON, P. (1964) 'Origins of the Present Crisis', *New Left Review*, 23, pp. 26–53.

ASSOCIATION OF BRITISH CHAMBERS OF COMMERCE (1985) *British Manufacturing Decline 1975–84* (London: ABCC).

AUSTIN, T. and BEYNON, H. (1980) *Global Outpost: The Working Class Experience of Big Business in the North East of England* (Durham: Mimeo).

BACON, R. and ELTIS, W. (1978) *Britain's Economic Problems: Too Few Producers* 2nd edn (London: Macmillan).

BALDRY, S; HENDERSON, S; HAWORTH, N. and RAMSAY, H. (1983) 'Fighting Multinational Power: the Massey Ferguson Closure and its Implications for the AES', *Capital and Class*, 20, pp. 157–66.

BALDRY, S.; HENDERSON, S.; HAWORTH, N and RAMSAY, H. (1984) 'Multinational Closure and the Boundaries of Resistance: Implications of the Case of Massey-Ferguson, Kilmarnock', *Industrial Relations Journal*, 15, pp. 17–27.

BARAN, P. and SWEEZY, P. (1968) *Monopoly Capital* (Harmondsworth: Penguin).

BARNET, R.J. and MULLER, R.S. (1974) *Global Research* (New York: Simon and Schuster).

BATSTONE, E. (1984) *Working Order* (Oxford: Blackwell).

BENN, T. (1980) *Arguments for Socialism* (Harmondsworth: Penguin).

BEYNON, H. (1984) *Working for Ford*, 2nd edn (Harmondsworth: Penguin).

BEYNON, H. (ed.) (1985) *Digging Deeper* (London: Verso).

BLANPAIN, R. (1983) *The Vredeling Proposal* (Deventer: Kluwer).

BLUESTONE, B.; HARRISON, B. and BARKER, L. (1981) *Corporate Flight: The Causes and Consequences of Economic Dislocation* (New York: Progressive Alliance).

BODDY, M. and FUDGE, C. (1984) *Local Socialism?* (London: Macmillan).

BOWERS, J.; DEATON, D. and TURK, J. (1982) *Labour Hoarding in British Industry* (Oxford: Blackwell).

BOWLES, S.; GORDON, D.M. and WEISSKOPF, T.E. (1984) *Beyond the Wasteland: A Democratic Alternative to Economic Decline* (London: Verso).

BRIGHT, D. (1983) 'The Industrial Relations of Recession', *Industrial Relations Journal*, 14, pp. 24–33.

BROWN, W. (1983) 'Industrial Relations in the Next Decade', *Industrial Relations Journal*, 14, pp. 9–21.

CAIRNCROSS, A. (1985) *Years of Recovery: British Economic Policy 1945–51* (London: Methuen).

CALVOCORESSI, P. (1979) *The British Experience 1945–75* (Harmondsworth: Pelican).

CARDOSO, F. and FALETTO, E. (1979) *Dependency and Development in Latin America* (California: University of California Press).

CATALANO, A. (1984) *A Review of UK Enterprise Zones* (London: CES Paper 17).

CBI (1985) *Fabric of the Nation II* (London: CBI Publications).

CHAMPION, A. and GREEN, A. (1985) *The Booming Towns of Britain* (Newcastle: Centre for Urban and Regional Development Studies, University of Newcastle, Discussion Paper 72).

CHANDLER, G. (1984) 'The Political Process and the Decline of Industry', *The Three Banks Review*, 141, pp. 3–17.

CHRYSLER CORPORATION (1975) *Annual Report of the Chrysler Corporation* (Detroit: Chrysler).

CITY OF SHEFFIELD EMPLOYMENT DEPARTMENT (1982) *An Initial Outline* (Sheffield: City Council).

CLARKE, T. (1977) 'The Raison D'Etre of Trade Unionism' in T. Clarke and L. Clements (eds) *Trade Unions under Capitalism* (Glasgow: Fontana).

CLARKE, T. (1979) 'Redundancy, Worker Resistance and the Community', in C. Craig, M. Mayo and N. Sharman (eds), *Jobs and Community Action* (London: Routledge and Kegan Paul).

CMND 6527 (1944) *Employment Policy* (London: HMSO).

CMND 9697 (1985) *Balance of Trade in Manufactures. The Government's Reply to the Report of the House of Lords Select Committee on Overseas Trade. Session 1984/5* (London: HMSO).

COAKLEY, J. and HARRIS, L. (1983) *The City of Capital* (Oxford: Blackwell).

COATES, D. (1980) *Labour in Power?* (London: Longman).

COATES, D. (1985) 'The Character and Origin of Britain's Economic Decline' in D. Coates and G. Johnston (eds), *Socialist Strategies* (Oxford: Martin Robertson).

COATES, K. (1981) *Work-ins, Sit-ins and Industrial Democracy* (Nottingham: Spokesman).

COATES, K. (ed.) (1986) *Joint Action for Jobs: A New Internationalism* (Nottingham: New Socialist/Spokesman).

COCHRANE, A. (1983) 'Local Economic Policies: Trying to Drain the Ocean with a Teaspoon', in Anderson, J.; Duncan, S. and Hudson, R. (eds.) *Redundant Spaces in Cities and Regions: Studies in Industrial Decline and Social Change* (London: Academic Press).

CREWE, I. and SARLVIK, B. (1983) *Decade of Dealignment* (Cambridge: CUP).

CROUCH, C. (1977) *Class Conflict and the Industrial Relations Crisis* (London: Heinemann Educational Books).

CROUCH, C. (1979) *The Politics of Industrial Relations* (Glasgow: Fontana).

CROUZET, F. (1982) *The Victorian Economy* (London: Methuen).

CSE (1980) *The Alternative Economic Strategy: A Response by the Labour Movement to the Economic Crisis* (London: CSE London Working Group).

DUNNETT, P. (1980) *The Decline of the British Motor Industry* (London: Croom Helm).

DUNNING, J. (1981) *International Production and the Multinational Enterprise* (London: Allen & Unwin).

DUNNING, J.H. (1985) ' Multinational Enterprises and Industrial Restructuring in the UK', *Lloyds Bank Review*, 158, pp. 1–19.

EATWELL, J. (1982) *Whatever Happened to Britain?* (London: Duckworth).

EC COM. 82 FINAL (1982) *The Role for Coal in Community Energy Strategy* (Luxembourg: Office for Official Publications of the EC).

ELDER, A. (1982) *Plessey: A Multinational in the 1980s* (Edinburgh: Unpublished Honours Dissertation, University of Edinburgh).

ELDRIDGE, J.E.T. (1968) *Industrial Disputes: Essays in the Sociology of Industrial Relations* (London: Routledge and Kegan Paul).

ELLIOTT, C. (1982) *Real Aid: A Strategy for Britain* (London: Christian Aid).

ELSON, D. (1986) *Women's Employment and MNCs in the EEC: Textiles and Clothing Industry* (Manchester: Conference Paper, Conference on Organisation and Control of the Labour Process, UMIST).

ELSON, D. and PEARSON, R. (1981) 'The Subordination of Women and the Internationalism of Factory Production', in K. Young, C. Walkowitz and R. McCullagh (eds), *Of Marriage and the Market* (London: CSE Books).

FEVRE, R. (1983) *Employment and Unemployment in Port Talbot – a Reference Paper* (Swansea: University College, Swansea Working Paper).

FINDLAY, P. (1984) *Worker Reaction to Closure: A Case Study of the Occupation of Plessey, Bathgate* (Glasgow: Unpublished Honours Dissertation, University of Strathclyde).

FINE, B. and HARRIS, L. (1985) *The Peculiarities of the British Economy* (London: Lawrence and Wishart).

FOTHERGILL, S. and VINCENT, J. (1985) *The State of the Nation* (London: Pluto).

FROBEL, F.; HEINRICHS, J.; and KREYE, O. (1980) *The New International Division of Labour* (Cambridge: Cambridge University Press).

FRYER, R.H. (1973) 'Redundancy Values and Public Policy', *Industrial Relations Journal*, 4, pp. 2–19.

GAMBLE, A. (1985) *Britain in Decline*, 2nd edn (London: Macmillan).

GAMBLE, A.M. and WALKLAND, S.A. (1984) *The British Party System and Economic Policy 1945–83* (Oxford: Clarendon Press).

GILL, C. (1974) 'Industrial Relations in a Multi-Plant Organisation', *Industrial Relations Journal*, 5, pp. 22–35.

GOLD, M.; LEVIE, H. and MOORE, R. (1979) *Shop Stewards' Guide to the Use of Company Information* (Nottingham: Spokesman).

GOSPEL, H. and WILLMAN, P. (1983) 'The Role of Codes in Labour Relations: The Case of Disclosure', *Industrial Relations Journal*, 14, pp. 76–82.

GRANT, W. (1982) *The Political Economy of Industrial Policy* (London: Butterworths).

HALL, S. (1984) 'The State in Question' in G. McLennan, D. Held and S. Hall (eds), *The Idea of the Modern State* (Milton Keynes: Open University Press).

HARDY, C. (1985) 'Responses to Industrial Closure', *Industrial Relations Journal*, 16, pp. 16–24.

HARRIS, G. and CORBETT, R. (1986) *A Socialist Policy for Europe* (London: Labour Movement in Europe).

HARRISON, J. (1982) 'Thatcherism: is it Working?' *Marxism Today*, pp. 19–25.

HARTMANN, P. (1975) 'Industrial Relations in the News Media', *Industrial Relations Journal*, 6, pp. 4–18.

HAWORTH, N. (1984) 'Posing Problems for Multinationals', in S. Maxwell (ed.), *Scotland, Multinationals and the Third World* (Edinburgh: Mainstream).

HAWORTH, N. and RAMSAY, H. (1984) 'Grasping the Nettle: Problems in the Theory of International Labour Solidarity', in P. Waterman (ed.), *For a New Labour Internationalism* (The Hague: ILERI).

HAWORTH, N. and RAMSAY, H. (1986) 'Workers of the World Untied: International Capital and Some Dilemmas in Industrial Democracy', in R. Southall (ed.), *The International Division of Labour and Third World Unions* (London: Zed Press).

HC 596 (1976) *Public Expenditure on Chrysler UK Ltd*, 8th Report of the Expenditure Committee: Subcommittee on Trade and Industry (London: HMSO).

HC 193 (1986) *Westland PLC: Minutes of Evidence*, Select Committee on Trade and Industry (London: HMSO).

HL 238 (1985) *Report from the Select Committee on Overseas Trade* (London: HMSO).

HOBSBAWM, E. (1968) *Industry and Empire, from 1750 to the Present Day* (Harmondsworth: Pelican).

HOLLAND, S. (1984) 'Out of Crisis – International Economic Recovery', in J. Curran (ed.), *The Future of the Left* (Cambridge: Polity Press/New Socialist).

HOLLAND, S. (ed.) (1985) *Out of Crisis: A Project for European Recovery* (Nottingham: Spokesman).

HOLMES, M. (1982) *Political Pressure and Economic Policy: British Governments 1970–4* (London: Butterworth).

HOLMES, M. (1985) *The First Thatcher Government 1979–83* (Brighton: Wheatsheaf Books).

HOOD, N. and YOUNG, S. (1979) *The Economics of the Multinational Enterprise* (London: Longman).

HOOD, N. and YOUNG, S. (1982) *Multinationals in Retreat: The Scottish Experience* (Edinburgh: Edinburgh University Press).

HORN, R. (1981) *Legal Problems of Codes of Conduct for Multinational Enterprises* (Deventer: Kluwer).

HUNT, J. (1984) 'The Shifting Focus of the Personnel Management Function', *Personnel Management*, February, pp. 14–18.

HYMER, S. (1975) 'The Multinational Corporation and the Law of Uneven Development', in H. Radice (ed.) *International Firms and Modern Imperialism* (Harmondsworth: Pelican).

INCOMES DATA SERVICES (1978) Redundancy Schemes, 175, August.

INCOMES DATA SERVICES (1981) Redundancy Schemes, 250, September.

INCOMES DATA SERVICES (1982) Redundancy Schemes, 280, December.

INCOMES DATA SERVICES (1984) Redundancy Schemes, 327, December.

INCOMES DATA SERVICES (1985) Early Retirement, 327, May.

JACKSON, P. (1983) 'How Perkins Positively Tackled the Recession', *Personnel Management*, November, pp. 24–7.

JEFFREY, K. and HENNESSY, P. (1983) *States of Emergency: British Governments and Strikebreaking* (London: Routledge and Kegan Paul).

JENKINS, R. (1984) 'Divisions over the International Division of Labour', *Capital and Class*, 22, pp. 128–57.

JESSOP, B. (1980) 'The Transformation of the State in Post-War Britain', in R. Scase (ed.), *The State in Western Europe* (London: Croom Helm).

JOINT TRADE UNION RESEARCH GROUP (1978) *Research Paper on the Proposed Takeover of Chrysler Corporation's European Operations by the Peugeot Citroen Company* (London: JTURG).

JURGENS, U.; RUSSIG, H. and DOHSE, K. (1984) *New Production Concepts in West German Car Plants* (Berlin: International Institute for Comparative Social Research).

KEEGAN, W. (1984) *Mrs. Thatcher's Economic Experiment* (Harmondsworth: Penguin).

KILPATRICK, A. and LAWSON, T. (1980) 'On the Nature of Industrial Decline in the UK', *Cambridge Journal of Economics*, 4, pp. 85–102.

KINNIE, N.J. (1983) 'Single Employer Bargaining: Structures and Strategies', *Industrial Relations Journal*, 14, pp. 76–81.

KNIGHTS, D.; WILLMOTT, H. and COLLINSON, D. (1985) *Job Redesign* (London: Gower).

KUJAWA, D. (1980) 'Labour Relations of US Multinationals Abroad', in B. Martin and E. Kassalow (eds), *Labour Relations in Advanced Industrial Societies: Issues and Problems* (New York: Carnegie Endowment for International Peace).

LABOUR PARTY (1973) *Annual Conference Report* (London: Labour Party).

LABOUR PARTY (1976) *Annual Conference Report* (London: Labour Party).

LABOUR'S PROGRAMME (1976) (London: Labour Party).

LABOUR'S PROGRAMME (1982) (London: Labour Party).

LABOUR RESEARCH (1978) *Company Information Service* (London: Labour Research).

LANE, T. (1981) 'Merseyside Under the Hammer', *Marxism Today*, February, pp. 18–21.

LEVINSON, C. (1972) *International Trade Unionism* (London: Allen & Unwin).

LEWYCKA, M. (1986) 'The Way We Were', *New Socialist*, March, pp. 16–18.

LEYS, C. (1983) *Politics in Britain* (London: Heinemann Educational Books).

LEYS, C. (1985) 'Thatcherism and British Manufacturing: A Question of Hegemony', *New Left Review*, 151, pp. 5–25.

LLOYD, J. (1985) *Understanding the Miners' Strike* (London: Fabian Society).

LOCKWOOD, D. (1966) 'Sources of Variation in Working Class Images of Society', *Sociological Review*, 14, pp. 249–67.

LOCKYER, C.; BADDON, L. and OLIVER, T. (1984) *Management, Participation and the Search for Control: A Forty Year Case Study* (Bradford: BSA Conference Paper).

LONGSTRETH, F. (1979) 'The City, Industry and the State', in C. Crouch (ed.), *State and Economy in Contemporary Capitalism* (London: Croom Helm).

LYND, S. (1982) *Fight Against Shutdown* (New York: Singlejack Books).

MARSDEN, D.; MORRIS, T.; WILLMAN, P. and WOOD. S. (1985) *The Car Industry* (London: Tavistock).

MARTIN, R.L. and HODGE, J.S.C. (1983) 'The Reconstruction of British Regional Policy: The Crisis of Conventional Practice', *Environment and Planning C: Government and Policy*, 1, pp. 133–52.

MARXISM TODAY (1980) 'Where Are We Now: A Round Table Discussion', *Marxism Today*, September, pp. 31–6.

MASSEY, D. (1984) *Spatial Divisions of Labour* (London: Macmillan).

MASSEY, D. and MEEGAN, R. (1982) *The Anatomy of Job Loss* (London: Methuen).

MAWSON, J.; BENTLEY, G.; MARSHALL, M.; NAYLOR, D.; ROBERTS, D. and TAYLOR, D. (1983) *Local Initiative Study*, 10 vols, (Birmingham: University of Birmingham, Centre for Urban and Regional Studies).

MERSEYSIDE SOCIALIST GROUP (1980) *Merseyside in Crisis* (Birkenhead: MSG).

MILLER, K. (1982) 'Plessey Co. Ltd. versus Wilson', *Industrial Law Journal*, 11, pp. 115–17.

MORLEY, D. (1976) 'Industrial Conflict and the Mass Media', *Sociological Review*, 24, pp. 245–68.

MORRIS, D.J. and STOUT, D.K. (1985) 'Industrial Policy' in D. Morris (ed.) *The Economic System in the UK*, 3rd edn (Oxford: OUP).

MUSGRAVE, P.W. (1967) *Technical Change, the Labour Force, and Education* (Oxford: Pergamon Press).

NAIRN, T. (1982) *The Break-Up of Britain*, 2nd edn (London: NLB).

OLLE, W. and SCHOELLER, W. (1977) 'World Market Competition and Restrictions upon International Trade Union Policies', *Capital and Class*, 2, pp. 56–75.

PANITCH, L. (1976) *Social Democracy and Industrial Militancy* (London: Cambridge University Press).

PANITCH, L. (1979) 'Social Democracy and the Labour Party: A Reappraisal' in R. Miliband and J. Saville (eds), *The Socialist Register* (London: Merlin).

POLLARD, S. (1983) *The Development of the British Economy*, 3rd edn (London: Edward Arnold).

POLLARD, S. (1984) *The Wasting of the British Economy*, 2nd edn (London: Croom Helm).

PURCELL, J. (1982) 'Macho Managers and the New Industrial Relations', *Employee Relations*, 4, pp. 3–5.

PURCELL, J. (1983) 'The Management of Industrial Relations in the Modern Corporation: Agenda for Research', *British Journal of Industrial Relations*, 21, pp. 1–16.

PURCELL, J. and SISSON, K. (1983) 'Strategies and Practice in the Management of Industrial Relations in Britain', in G. Bain (ed.), *Industrial Relations in Britain* (Oxford: Blackwell).

PURCELL, K. (1979) 'Militancy and Acquiescence Among Women Workers', in S. Burman (ed.), *Fit Work for Women* (London: Croom Helm).

PYKE, F. (1983) *The Redundant Worker* (Durham: Working Paper, University of Durham).

RADICE, H. (1984) 'The National Economy: a Keynesian Myth?', *Capital and Class*, 22, pp. 111–40.

RIDGERS, B. (1979) *Global Reorganisation in the Car Industry* (Rome: Paper presented to the Transnational Information Exchange).

RIGHT APPROACH (1976) *A Statement of Conservative Aims* (London: Conservative Central Office).

ROBINSON, F. and SADLER, D. (1984) *Consett after the Closure* (Durham: University of Durham, Department of Geography Occasional Paper 19).

ROJOT, R. (1985) 'The 1984 Revision of the OECD Guidelines for Multinational Enterprises', *British Journal of Industrial Relations*, 23, pp. 379–97.

ROSS, J. (1982) 'The Plessey Judgement', *Scottish Trade Union Review*, 17, pp. 6–8.

ROWTHORN, B. (1983) 'The Past Strikes Back', in S. Hall and M. Jacques, *The Politics of Thatcherism* (London: Lawrence and Wishart).

RUSTIN, M. (1985) *For a Pluralist Socialism* (London: Verso).

SAMUEL, R. (1985) 'A Plan for Disaster' *New Society*, 7th March, pp. 367–8.

SCOTS LAW TIMES (1983a) 'Plessey Company PLC versus Wilson', *Scots Law Times Reports*, pp. 139–41.

SCOTS LAW TIMES (1983b) 'Phestos Shipping Company versus Kurmiawan', *Scots Law Times Reports*, pp. 388–92.

SEIDLER, E. (1976) *The Autobiography of Ford's Project Bobcat* (New York: Patrick Stevens).

SIMS, D. and WOOD, M. (1984) *Car Manufacturing at Linwood: The Regional Policy Issues* (Paisley: Paisley College of Technology).

SINGH, A. (1977) 'UK Industry and the World Economy: A Case of De-industrialisation?', *Cambridge Journal of Economics*, 2, pp. 113–36.

SMITH, K. (1984) *The British Economic Crisis* (Harmondsworth: Penguin).

SMITH, R. (1981) 'Patterns of Growth in World Capitalism', in S. Aaronovitch and R. Smith, *The Political Economy of British Capitalism* (London: McGraw-Hill).

SPENCE, M. (1985) 'Imperialism and Decline: Britain in the 1980s', *Capital and Class*, 25, pp. 117–39.

STOREY, D. (1982) *Entrepreneurship and New Firms* (London: Croom Helm).

STREEK, W. and HOFF, A. (1984) *Manpower Management and Industrial Relations in the Restructuring of the World Automobile Industry* (Coventry: Conference Paper).

SDA (1985) *Annual Report of the Scottish Development Agency* (Glasgow: SDA).

TALBOT ACTION GROUP (1981) *The Case for the Maintenance of Full Employment and Not Closure: The Workers Answer* (Linwood: TAG).

TEULINGS, A.W.M. (1985) 'The Power of Corporate Management: The Powerlessness of the Manager', *Economic and Industrial Democracy*, 6, pp. 403–34.

THOMAS, D. (1983) 'Should We Still Help the Regions', *New Society*, 1 December, pp. 358–9.

THURLEY, K. and WOOD, S. (1983) *Industrial Relations and Management Strategy* (Cambridge: Cambridge University Press).

TUC (1974) *Report of the Annual Trade Union Congress: General Council Report* (London: TUC).

TURNBULL, G. (1982) 'How I see the Personnel Function', *Personnel Management*, May, pp. 38–40.

TURNER, H.; GARFIELD, C. and ROBERTS, D. (1977) *Management Characteristics and Labour Conflict: A Study of Management Organisation, Attitudes and Industrial Relations* (Cambridge: CUP, Department of Applied Economics Papers in Industrial Relations and Labour, No. 3).

TURU (1982) *Plessey Capacitors Bathgate: A Report on Plant Profitability* (Glasgow: Trade Union Research Unit, Glasgow College of Technology).

TYSON, S. (1985) 'Is this the Very Model of a Modern Personnel Manager?', *Personnel Management*, May, pp. 22–5.

WAINWRIGHT, H. and ELLIOT, D. (1982) *The Lucas Plan* (London: Allison and Busby).

WARWICK, P. (1985) 'Did Britain Change? An Enquiry into the Causes of National Decline', *Journal of Contemporary History*, 20, pp. 99–133.

WATERMAN, P. (1984) 'Wanted: a New Communications Model for Labour', in P. Waterman (ed), *For a New Labour Internationalism* (The Hague: ILERI).

WHIPP, R. and SMITH, C. (1984) *Managerial Strategy and Capital Labour Dynamics. Participation in Context: Cadbury and British Leyland* (Birmingham: ESRC Work Organisation Research Centre, Aston University).

WILLMAN, P. (1984) 'The Reform of Collective Bargaining and Strike Activity in BL Cars 1976–82', *Industrial Relations Journal*, 15, pp. 1–5.

WILLMAN, P. and WINCH, G. (1985) *Innovation and Management Control: Labour Relations at BL Cars* (Cambridge: Cambridge University Press).

WILKS, S. (1983) 'Liberal State and Party Competition: Britain' in K. Dyson and S. Wilks (eds), *Industrial Crisis: A Comparative Study of State and Industry* (Oxford: Martin Robertson).

WILKS, S. (1986) 'Has the State Abandoned British Industry?', *Parliamentary Affairs*, 39, pp. 31–46.

WILKS, S. (1984) *Industrial Policy and the Motor Industry* (Manchester: Manchester University Press).

YOUNG, S. (1974) *Intervention in the Mixed Economy: The Evolution of British Industrial Policy 1964–72* (London: Croom Helm).

Index